Making Place for Muslims in Contemporary India

Making Place for Muslims in Contemporary India

KALYANI DEVAKI MENON

HarperCollins *Publishers* India

First published by Cornell University Press 2022

This edition published in India by HarperCollins *Publishers* 2022
4th Floor, Tower A, Building No. 10, II, DLF Cyber City,
Gurugram, Haryana – 122002
www.harpercollins.co.in

2 4 6 8 10 9 7 5 3 1

P-ISBN: 978-93-5629-409-7
E-ISBN: 978-93-5629-410-3

Printed and bound at
Thomson Press (India) Ltd

For Amma

Sabhi ka khoon shamil hai yahan ki mitti mein
Kisi ke baap ka Hindustan thodi hai.
[Everyone's blood is part of the soil of this place
Hindustan is not anyone's personal property.]

—Rahat Indori, 1950–2020

Contents

Acknowledgments

This book would not have been possible had it not been for the generosity of so many people. I can never repay the kindness of people in Old Delhi who welcomed me into their homes and lives, put up with my intrusions in their worlds, and took the time to share their thoughts and experiences with me. I wish I could name them here, but maintaining their privacy and anonymity is the very least I can do in return for their immense generosity and care. Not a single page of this book could have been written without them, and I remain very much in their debt.

I am grateful to the Wenner-Gren Foundation for Anthropological Research for a post-PhD grant that funded the fieldwork upon which this book is based. I am also grateful to the DePaul University Research Council for multiple grants that funded fieldwork, research, and writing. Several DePaul University Liberal Arts and Social Sciences Research Grants and a Late-Stage Research Grant have also funded research and writing over the many years since I began this project in 2011.

As most anthropologists know, starting a new fieldwork-based project is not easy, and it requires both determination and luck to get things off the ground. I was lucky to meet so many people in Delhi who were enthusiastic about this project, understood its significance straightaway, and trusted me enough to introduce me to others. Of these, I must thank Narayani Gupta for seeing immediately that an ethnography of a place that so many historians have written about was a valuable endeavor. She generously opened many doors for me, even though she barely knew me, and her insightful work has shaped my understandings of place in Old Delhi. I am very grateful to Sohail Hashmi for taking the time to talk to me about Old Delhi, and for very kindly introducing me to people in Old Delhi. There are so many people who were critical to widening my circle of interlocutors, and whose insights very much inflect the contours of this book. Of these I must thank Abdul Sattar, Saleem Hasan Siddiqui, Khalil Ahmed, Shabana Begum, Shahina Begum, and Khairunissa Begum. Several scholars in Delhi made time to talk with me over the many years that I worked on this book. Of these I must thank Hilal Ahmed, Azra Razzak, and Rizwan Qaisar. I am grateful to Mahesh Rangarajan for supporting my work and for his always insightful analysis of Indian politics and history. Zarin Ahmed had finished her fieldwork in Old Delhi just as I was starting mine, and I am thankful to her for always making the time to meet and talk about work.

Several people have shaped this project over the years, providing comments, critiques, and helpful suggestions on different parts of the manuscript. Their interventions have made this a much better book, and I am very grateful to them. That said, any shortcomings that remain are because of my own limitations in internalizing the wisdom they tried to impart. I am particularly grateful to several people who have read and commented on this manuscript, either in its present guise or in the form of the conference papers, talks, or other writings that formed the seed of many parts of this book. In particular I must thank Khaled Keshk, Chris Mount, Gayatri Reddy, Gayatri Menon, Mark Hauser, Keri Olsen, Lisa Knight, Patricia Jeffery, Kaveri Qureshi, Irfan Ahmad, Andrew Willford, and Syeda Asia. Others have shared ideas and engaged in conversations with me over the years that have shaped my own thinking about various elements of this book, including Srirupa Roy, Lalit Vacchani, Patrick Eisenlohr, Razak Khan, Farzana Haniffa, Anand Taneja, Greg Feldman, Ann Grodzins Gold, and Susan Wadley.

I could not have hoped for a better editor than Jim Lance at Cornell University Press. I am so grateful to him for his support of my project from the very beginning, and for patiently shepherding me through the publication process in a year that was so difficult for everyone because of the pandemic. Despite the fact that the pandemic made life even more busy for most people, I was fortunate to have two amazing reviewers who generously gave me their time. I can never thank them enough for engaging so deeply with my manuscript. Their detailed comments and suggestions have made this a much better book.

I am grateful to the many friends who have supported me over the years. Their friendship has sustained me through the ups and downs of book writing, and conversations with them have always been insightful. Yuki Miyamoto, Khaled Keshk, Chris Mount, and Chernoh Sesay have listened to me complain with incredible patience, and conversations with them always make me smarter. Shailja Sharma and Sanjukta Mukherjee have been comrades in work, politics, and TTCs. I do not know where I would be without my old friends. Keri Olsen and Lisa Knight have been friends and sounding boards from the very beginning of this journey. Kwame Harrison, John Karam, Samuel Spiers, Ed Yazijian, and Awanti Seth Rabenhoej have always been there when I have needed them. Chaise LaDousa literally pushed me in the right direction at the Annual Meeting of the American Anthropological Association in Vancouver. I am very grateful for the friendship of Gayatri Reddy, Anna Guevarra, Jorge Coronado, Jana-Maria Hartmann, Shalini Shankar, Shefali Chandra, Francesca Gaiba, Micaela di Leonardo, Rebecca Johnson, and Amor Kohli who make life in Chicago so much nicer.

Although I was far away from family and friends, many people made me feel at home in Delhi. Tuli Brar provided me a home on multiple trips to Delhi, and always made sure there were aloo parathas for me on Sundays. Indira Bhatia also provided me a home when I was working in Old Delhi, and she and Gordon Shannon introduced me to people working on these issues in Delhi. Vidya Rao literally gave me her home, and a cat for company, so I could move to Delhi without worrying about furniture, gas connections, and other things that would have stalled work in annoying ways. Many have helped in other ways. Aliya Latif has helped me translate many words and ideas, consulting others like Alia Latif when she was stumped. Zeanut Ahmad was always a phone call away when I had a question about anything related to various rites and practices in Old Delhi.

I would be nowhere without my family, who love me unconditionally and put up with a lot of moody behavior while I was writing this book. My mother, Ambika Menon, raised me in the cultural commons long before I learned about difference. Perhaps it is because of this that I had to write a book about the commons after writing one about right-wing women. My brother, Hari Menon, and my sister-in-law, Vicki Nicholson, have always provided a home for me where I could work uninterrupted. My sister, Gayatri Menon, has been a constant interlocutor in this book and in pretty much everything else in my life, as well as a cheerleader and confidante through moments of self-doubt. And finally, my husband, Mark Hauser, has read every page of this book and provided critical feedback, even as his love, support, and cooking sustain me every day.

I am grateful to *Etnofoor* for permission to reprint an updated version of my article "'Security,' Home, and Belonging in Contemporary India: Old Delhi as a Muslim Place." I am grateful to *Contemporary South Asia* for permission to reprint an updated version of my article "Communities of Mourning: Negotiating Identity and Difference in Old Delhi." I am grateful to Mark W. Hauser for making the maps and for permission to publish them in this book.

Note on Transliteration

In order to make this book accessible to the widest possible audience, I have chosen to use common spellings of Hindi and Urdu words in the main text. Diacritical markers are available in the glossary. Hindi and Urdu words have been italicized. English words used in Hindi or Urdu quotations have been italicized. While the titles of books have been italicized, I have not italicized the titles of sacred texts. Quotations from sacred texts have been cited by chapter and verse. The first reference includes the translator's name and date of publication. All subsequent citations are from the same translation.

Preface

When I first held a copy of this book in my hands in April 2022, I had already committed to writing a new preface to the South Asian edition, organized around a single current issue illuminating the erosion of the place for Muslims in contemporary India. As I write this preface in July 2022, I am struck by the inadequacies of such an approach in the face of what has been a sustained and multi-vocal assault on Indian democracy and constitutional freedoms in the intervening months. Do I focus on the arrest of Mohammed Zubair, editor of the fact-checking site Alt News, who broke the news that a member of the ruling party had made public statements offending the religious sentiments of Muslims in India and elsewhere? Should I discuss the arrest of Teesta Setalvad, the activist who has worked tirelessly for the last two decades on behalf of Muslims whose lives were destroyed, literally or figuratively, during the Gujarat pogrom of 2002? Ought I write about the multiple petitions working their way through the judicial system claiming that Hindus have a right to pray at the Gyanvapi Mosque in Varanasi, which should have been dismissed because of the 1991 Places of Worship (Special Provisions) Act prohibiting the conversion of a site of religious worship established before 1947 to another religion? Or should I examine attempts to "liberate" world heritage sites like the Qutb Minar in Delhi or the Taj Mahal in Agra for Hindu worship, even though they are protected under the Ancient Monuments and Archaeological Sites and Remains Act of 1958? Each of these issues speaks to the ways in which the institutions of the state have been harnessed in service of establishing a Hindu Rashtra in India by erasing its Muslim past, by intimidating and harassing Muslims and others who have been critical of the current regime, and by silencing those who have fought to support and uphold the principles of the Indian Constitution. Indeed, focusing on a single issue obscures what is in fact an assemblage of actions that threatens the place for Muslims in India—in the present and in the past.

In today's India, where the state literally uses bulldozers to destroy Muslim homes, property, and livelihoods, where Muslim women are told they cannot wear hijabs if they want to attend educational institutions, where Muslims are not allowed the space to gather for Friday prayers, where spurious claims threaten mosques and heritage sites associated with India's Muslim past, where Muslims suspected of eating beef or butchering cows are killed by mobs committed to ensuring the dominance of upper-caste Hindu norms in the country, and where Muslims live with the constant specter of violence in which state actors are often complicit, the place for Muslims is shrinking. This is an India where the Hindu supremacist Bharatiya Janta Party (BJP) has held an absolute majority in Parliament since 2014. The BJP has used its majority to realize its vision of India as a Hindu nation, treating dissent as sedition; sanctioning the arrests of activists, journalists, students, and protesters; and undermining political institutions and the judiciary, which could have provided checks and balances on state power. In the context of increasing authoritarianism and Hindu supremacy, this book looks at the everyday practices through which Muslims in Old Delhi engage with contemporary Indian politics and the revanchist vision of the Hindu Right, and variously make place.

As the country finds itself in the grip of a violent politics of difference and disavowal, religion provides one arena for Old Delhi's Muslims to intervene in the political and situate themselves firmly in place—sometimes through religious acts that assert a visible and distinctive presence, and sometimes through narratives and practices that construct shared religious worlds in which Hindus and Muslims are inextricably intertwined. Their variegated acts challenge any attempt to construct religious traditions as homogenous. Furthermore, by forcing us to reckon with religious worlds in India where the boundaries between traditions can be quite blurred in everyday life, many of these religious practices trouble the use of difference as an analytic to understand culture and religion, and destabilize modern, bounded notions of identity. Paying attention to the varied articulations of Islam and Muslim identity, and to the ways in which they are embedded in place in India, is particularly crucial at a moment when rampant Islamophobia has reinforced stereotypes about Islam as a monolithic, totalizing, and deterministic force, rather than one whose cultural impact has in fact been enabled by its ability to embrace pluralism and multiplicity.

In this book, I look at religion through an anthropologist's lens. I focus on religion as it is lived, practiced, deliberated over, reconfigured, and contested by people living through a very difficult moment in Indian history. It is a moment characterized by increasing intolerance, rising authoritarianism, endemic violence, and an exclusionary and introverted nationalism. I ask how culture and religion are reworked and reimagined as Indian Muslims variously make sense of the world they find themselves in and struggle to make place for themselves in it. As has been the case throughout Islamic history in different times and places, religious narratives and practices are not just about the divine and transcendental, but also very much about living a meaningful life in particular places and historical circumstances. In today's India, the religious narratives and practices of Old Delhi's Muslims are inseparable from their anxieties and aspirations as they live through violence, exclusion, and differential citizenship, and as they struggle to maintain their families, communities, and livelihoods.

Hegemonic discourses of nation and belonging in India configure upper-caste Hindus as the normative national subject and Muslims as backward, suspect, foreign, and potentially dangerous. Such discourses have enabled extreme violence against Muslims in the country, made them targets of the state's security apparatus, and driven Muslim families to relocate to particular neighborhoods where they feel more secure. The landscapes of inequality rendered through these processes manifest the political economy of religious difference and discrimination in India as economic forces capitalize on segregation and systemic inequalities to further profits. In the case of Old Delhi, one sees how businesses capitalize on the political and economic insecurity of Muslims living there, and particularly on the productive and reproductive labor of Muslim women in the informal sector, whose insecurity is exacerbated by the particular intersection of religion, gender, class, and place that configures their everyday lives in neoliberal India.

While powerful forces marginalize Muslims and threaten their place in contemporary India, such forces do not go unchallenged. Imbuing their localities with particular cultural inflections, the religious practices of Old Delhi's Muslims can also be seen as modes of making place that counter the revanchist politics of the Hindu Right. Often debated and contested amongst Old Delhi's diverse communities of Muslims, these variegated religious practices make place in manifold ways. For instance, many participate in transnational communities of belonging forged around particular interpretations of textual traditions. Like earlier Islamic reform movements in colonial and postcolonial India, these too call for a return to the foundational texts of Islam, promote visible acts of piety purportedly prescribed by them, and attempt to delineate, separate, and project a distinct religious identity supposedly unaffected by culture and local influences. While obviously inspired by religious faith, such acts must also be understood in the context of a country, and indeed a world, in which Muslims feel alienated, beleaguered, misunderstood, and rejected. As much as these practices reflect the draw of particular notions of piety, they can also index the desire for support and succor in the face of violent and painful disavowals by others. Attempts to delineate an "authentic" Islam and orient religious practice towards textual prescriptions can also be about connecting to transnational communities of belonging, about finding acceptance and understanding, about asserting identity and presence, and about the politics of representation in a world where Islamophobia is endemic. Through their religious acts and discourses, many drawn to these movements challenge pervasive stereotypes about Muslims and Islam, and engender transnational communities of belonging that connect Indian Muslims to others across the globe. By engaging in very visible acts of piety that assert their presence in India, they make place for these transnational cultures in the country, destabilize insular views of Indian culture, and subvert efforts to make India Hindu.

Other groups of Muslims in Old Delhi engage in religious acts and narratives that variously construct cultural and affective commons across sectarian and religious boundaries, countering the rising tide of Hindu chauvinism and exclusionary understandings of nation and belonging. These practices draw on a long history of religious pluralism within Shii and Sunni traditions of South Asian Islam, and of blurred boundaries in South Asian religious worlds more generally. Through rituals that transcend religious and sectarian differences, narratives that connect their religious practices to articulations of a specifically Indian Islam, and acts that create affective communities that bridge divides, different groups of Shias and Sunnis in Old Delhi variously constitute communities of belonging that contest the politics of difference and exclusionary nationalism. While boundaries and divisions may rear their heads in other contexts, individuals often put aside their differences to forge communities emergent from gendered experiences, class-based struggles, friendship, the desire for sociality, neighborliness, community loyalty, motherhood, secular commitments, and other important configurations that are meaningful in their lives. Practices and narratives associated with these alignments of community have material effects. They connect Muslims to others in India in ways that resist the prevailing politics of disavowal, insisting on a politics and practice that transcends difference. Moreover, they operationalize an India that cannot be construed in exclusive and introverted ways, articulating a past, present, and future in which traditions of Hinduism and Islam are inextricably intertwined.

This book is an ethnography of a place and a people that many historians, political scientists, and scholars of religion have written about. What can anthropology—and specifically ethnography based on long-term fieldwork—add to these important conversations about Old Delhi, Indian Muslims, Indian Islamic traditions, religious pluralism, religious nationalism, communal violence, authoritarianism, citizenship, and political economy? Based on sustained interaction with individuals over many years as they negotiate life's uncertainties and live through the powerful social forces and political events that shape contemporary India, ethnography enables a granular and textured understanding of how such forces and events variously affect people. It allows us to see individuals as complex subjects who are positioned at the intersection of multiple discourses, to understand how they may be pulled in different ways by the competing hegemonies that inform their understandings of self and community, and to recognize how they make sense of and negotiate these forces in diverse ways in their everyday lives. Ethnography troubles any attempt to reduce Indian Muslims to just religious subjects, a reduction that has in fact enabled the Hindu Right's violent politics of disavowal and difference. Instead, ethnography can illuminate how India's Muslims are also, among other things, gendered subjects, class subjects, ethnic subjects, and national subjects. They are friends, neighbors, educators, laborers, mothers, local leaders, politicians, unemployed workers, and entrepreneurs with varying and conflicting aspirations and motivations. They are inspired by piety and politics, love and care, fear and pain, desire and anger, sadness and despair, and the need for community and belonging. And indeed, ethnography shows that what we might understand as the religious is in fact intertwined with all these complexities, as individuals strive to live a meaningful life in the world they find themselves in.

While there is a great deal of valuable and nuanced research that illuminates how these very trying times have affected Indian Muslim communities, ethnography reveals what people experience, say, and do amid the messiness of everyday life. It allows us to see how individuals grapple with the larger forces affecting their cultures and communities, how they are drawn to or reject particular discourses and ways of being for complicated reasons that cannot be reduced to singular subject positions, and how they construct self and belonging in complex and sometimes contradictory ways. In revealing the very messiness that makes us all human, ethnography can trouble the use of difference as an analytic to understand culture and community that has animated so many studies of Indian Muslims and Islam. And importantly, even as an assemblage of actions threatens the place for Muslims in India's past and present, ethnography can reveal traces of another India, one whose emergence is an ever-present possibility.

Kalyani Devaki Menon
Chicago
July 2022

MAKING PLACE FOR MUSLIMS IN CONTEMPORARY INDIA

INTRODUCTION

Aamir Sahib: As far as Old Delhi culture is concerned, our Hindu-Muslim population who lived here before, they shared a Ganga-Jamni culture. This started in Delhi only. . . . Our language was not different, our way of life was not different, our cuisine was similar. Some people . . . were vegetarian. But for the most part people were not vegetarian. But when people came here from Punjab, things began to change.

K: After 1947?

Aamir Sahib: Yes. But even today, those who are from Old Delhi, even if they have left Old Delhi, when you meet them you feel like you are meeting an old relative, you are meeting your brother. It is still like that. If they come here, they always visit. It became necessary for them to leave. When their inheritance became less, they had to move away. But when they come back, they interact with us just as they used to.

On a hot afternoon in June 2013, I interviewed Aamir Sahib in his office in Ballimaran over tea and biscuits.[1] A soft-spoken, erudite, tall, white-haired gentleman, Aamir Sahib was the editor of two Urdu papers in Old Delhi (see figures 0.1 and 0.2). His office was clearly the office of a writer and a reader, as it was crammed with books in English, Hindi, and Urdu. Originally from Bijnor, his family moved to Old Delhi in 1914, initially settling near Turkman Gate, where he was born. In 1947, seeking refuge from the violence that accompanied the partition of India, his family moved to Ballimaran, where they still live. Aamir Sahib was four years

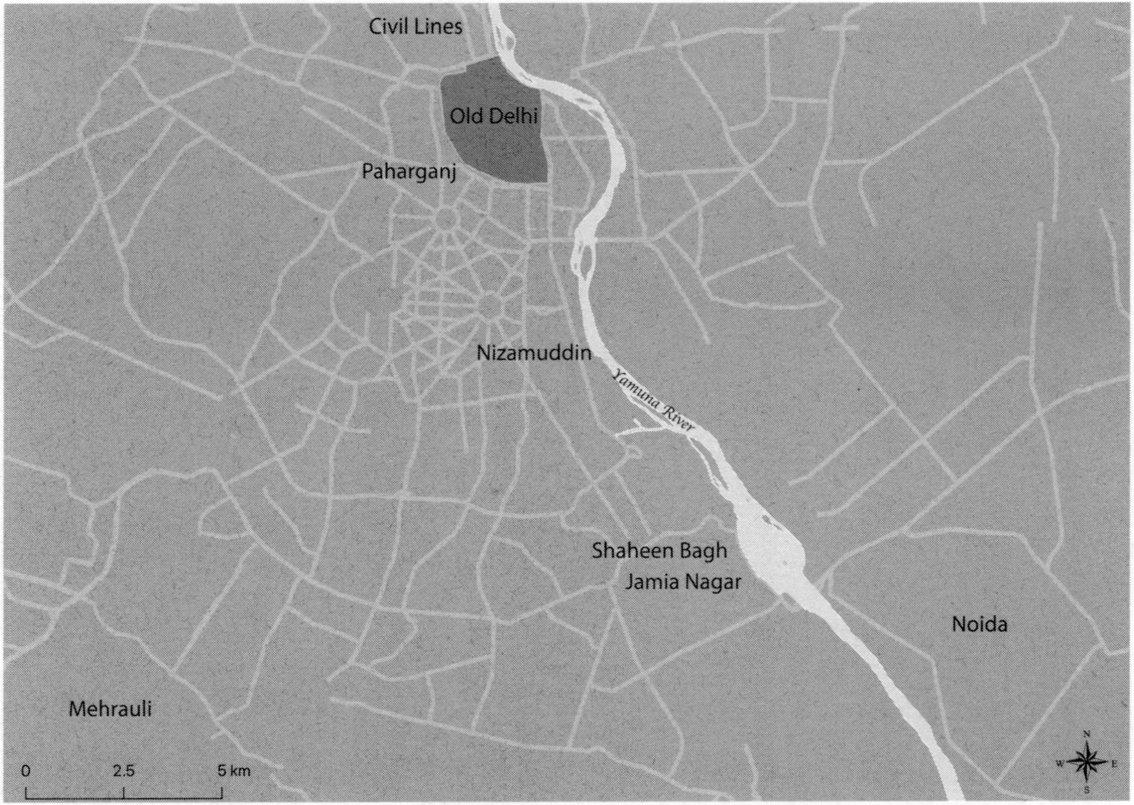

FIGURE 0.1. Old and New Delhi. Illustration by Mark W. Hauser.

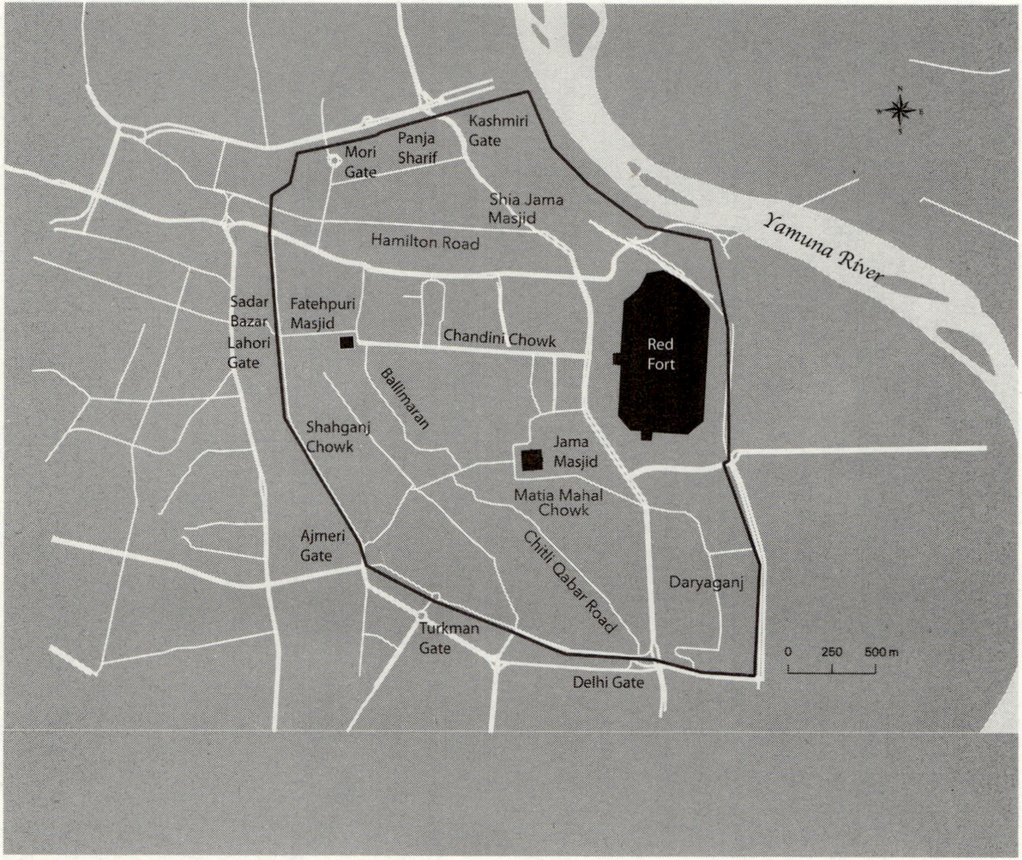

FIGURE 0.2. Old Delhi. Illustration by Mark W. Hauser.

old. He recalls the fear he felt at that time, as those around him were afraid to leave the relative security of Ballimaran. During the partition riots, he said, the Chawri Bazar area was a "slaughterhouse." People in his own family had been killed in their government quarters in Paharganj.

Aamir Sahib's words and experiences resonate with those of many in the city, once called Shahjahanabad. Like many others of his generation, Aamir Sahib spoke of the Ganga-Jamni culture of Shahjahanabad, using the metaphor of the confluence of the two major rivers of North India to reference the shared worlds of Hindus and Muslims, and of Hinduism and Islam, in the city built by the Mughal emperor Shah Jahan in the seventeenth century. Now, older denizens of the city like Aamir Sahib bemoan the loss of this shared culture, precipitated by such events as the violent expulsion of Muslims from the city by the British after the revolt of 1857; the partition of India in 1947, when many of the city's Muslims migrated to Pakistan to be replaced by Hindu and Sikh refugees moving to India; and the increasing hold of a majoritarian right-wing Hindu politics in the country and the city that renders Muslims as "other," as foreign, and as a potential threat to the national fabric.

In this book, I see Aamir Sahib's narrative as more than just nostalgia for an imagined past. I see it as a material force that makes place for Muslims in contemporary India. It is a narrative that situates Old Delhi's Muslims within the cultural fabric of the seventeenth-century city that Emperor Shah Jahan built, a place in which Hindus and Muslims were inextricably intertwined. It is a narrative that makes place for Muslims and makes Muslims part of the place, against the grain of both colonial and nationalist historiography. It is a narrative that roots him in place, distinguishing him from his more recently arrived neighbors of all religions, including other Muslims. And it is a narrative that insists that individuals are not just Muslims and Hindus, but that they can also be *Dilliwale*, those denizens of Delhi who share a commitment to a place, to a people, and to a life that cannot be reduced only to the religious. Living through the violence of partition, the increasing political and economic marginalization of Indian Muslims in postcolonial India, and the Hindu-majoritarian politics and anti-Muslim violence that dominates the sociopolitical landscape of the country today, Aamir Sahib and others like him narrate histories of a city and empire in which religious identity did not determine political belonging, and where cultural traditions and friendships transcended religious boundaries. In so doing, they make place for Muslims by disrupting majoritarian constructions of India as a Hindu place that positions upper-caste Hindus as the normative national subject. Such narratives enable us to question the use of difference as an analytic to understand culture and religion, and to focus instead on how people make place for themselves amid and across difference.[2]

Aamir Sahib is not representative of all Old Delhi Muslims. He is among a small group of Muslims who have lived in Old Delhi from before the partition of India in 1947. Some of these families can trace their lineage to "Mughal times," a vague reference to the period after Shah Jahan began to build his city in 1638 and before it fell into British hands in the nineteenth century. The majority of Old Delhi's Muslims, however, are postpartition migrants to the city. Zulfikar, an artisan whose fine *mukesh* embroidery brings many to his workshop on Kucha Rehman, came in the 1950s from Malihabad in Uttar Pradesh.[3] Initially en route to Pakistan, his family decided to stay in Delhi when they found a place to live. He said, "They thought, why deal with the trouble of going to a new place? We heard there was not much work there anyway. So we stayed." Others such as Zakia and Jafar, Shias from a village in Uttar Pradesh, have come to Delhi very recently. They live in a one-room house with a communal toilet in Shahganj and feel little attachment to the place. Like many small farmers of all religions in contemporary India who have found agricultural work unsustainable, Jafar migrated to the city and now sells fresh orange and sweet lime juice from a handcart in Sadar Bazar, while Zakia only visits during their children's school holidays. Differently positioned in Old Delhi, each of these individuals variously makes place for themselves and their communities in contemporary India, drawing on a variety of narratives and practices—cultural, religious, and historical. It is these multiple, overlapping, and sometimes conflicting placemaking practices that are the subject of this book.

From Shahjahanabad to Delhi 6: Changing Places

Agar Firdaus bar roo-e zameen ast
Hameen ast-o hameen ast-o hameen ast.
[If there is a paradise on earth,
It is this, it is this, it is this.]

—Amir Khusrau

In her important history of Old Delhi, Narayani Gupta poignantly says, "Delhi has died so many deaths" (1981, 55). Each death heralded a cultural and political transformation as Mughal Shahjahanabad became British-controlled Delhi, as Delhi became Old Delhi (*Purani Dilli* in Hindi) when the British shifted their capital to New Delhi, and when Delhi 6 emerged amid the violent transmutations of postcolonial India. Variously known as Shahjahanabad, Old Delhi, *Purani Dilli*, the walled city, or Delhi 6, the city today bears traces of all these transformations, and the narratives of its residents index the many understandings of the place that have marked its past and that continue to inflect its present.

The verse quoted above, written by the famous poet of Delhi Amir Khusrau (1235–1325), and inscribed by the Mughal emperor Shah Jahan (1627–1658) on the walls of his Red Fort, embodies one such inflection. While Khusrau was talking about Kashmir, Shah Jahan was describing Shahjahanabad, the city he built and named after himself. Shah Jahan envisioned his city as a Muslim place, marked by a mosque on every street (Malik 2003, 75). Importantly, Shah Jahan's Muslim place, his "paradise on earth," was a cosmopolitan one that was to be inhabited by people of different religions and occupations whom he invited to live in Shahjahanabad, work in his court, and ensure the smooth functioning of the city. Indeed, challenging Orientalist, nationalist, and Hindu nationalist readings of the past in which Muslims are "foreign invaders" and "oppressors" of Hindus, Barbara Metcalf has argued, that for the Mughal emperors who ruled India from the sixteenth to the nineteenth centuries, loyalty rather than religious identity "held the state together" (2006, 200; see also Pandey 1990). Not only did Hindus serve at all levels of the Mughal administration and share both tastes and style, but also many Hindu pilgrimage centers developed and flourished under the patronage of the Mughal state (Metcalf 2006, 204, 209).

This was certainly true in Shahjahanabad. Historians write about Shahjahanabad as a place with a "composite culture" (Chenoy 1998, 71), where both the Muslim nobility and upper-caste Hindus learned Persian and shared "Urdu culture and etiquette" (N. Gupta 1981, 8, 226), where social gatherings "cut across lines of kinship and religion, but were bound together by an identity of cultural style," and where sharing the sharif culture of the elite, more than personal connections, determined one's access to power and position (Lelyveld 1978, 55, 64). David Lelyveld argues that the sharif culture that developed during Emperor Akbar's reign (1556–1605) and shaped subsequent generations of the Mughal elite, drew on the court culture of Saffavid Iran, was shared by many Hindus, and did not include many Muslims (29). Lelyveld says, "A sharif man was one of dignified temperament, self-confident but not overly aggressive, appreciative of good literature, music, and art, but not flamboyant, familiar with mystical experience, but hardly immersed in it. Sharif social relations involved a pose of deference, but were above all a matter of virtuosity within the highly restricted bounds of etiquette" (30). In addition to the shared cultural worlds of the elite, Shahjahanabad was characterized by a diverse population residing in "mixed urban spaces" that encouraged close relationships and interactions between groups, including Hindus and Muslims, across social classes (see Chenoy 1998, 193).

While much has changed in contemporary India, Narayani Gupta says that the ethos of Shahjahanabad, although fading, still lives on in Old Delhi (1981, 1).[4]

The rapid erosion of this ethos was precipitated by the revolt of 1857, and especially by the British response to it. While the British took control of Delhi in 1803 after defeating the Marathas, Bahadur Shah Zafar, the last Mughal emperor, though entirely dependent on British coffers and political support, was allowed some nominal authority in Delhi until the revolt of 1857. The revolt of 1857 that began in the ranks of the British army but was joined by peasants, aristocrats, religious leaders, and many others of all religions and classes uniting under the symbol of Bahadur Shah Zafar, was ultimately crushed by the British (Bose and Jalal 2004, 75–76). As Gupta illustrates in her fine-grained history of Delhi during this period, the changes the British set in motion after the revolt transformed Shahjahanabad forever (1981).

The most devastating change was the violent siege of Delhi during which many thousands were killed, and those who were lucky enough to escape death were expelled from the city (N. Gupta 1981, 21). Although religious identity does not help us understand either who joined the revolt or who supported the colonial regime, many have noted that the British, schooled in their stereotypes about Muslims, constructed the revolt as a religious war, casting Muslims as the "fanatics" who orchestrated it (Farooqui 2010, 4; Bose and Jalal 2004, 74). Gupta traces how this resulted in the differential treatment of Hindus and Muslims by the British administration after 1857. While Hindus were allowed back into the city by January 1858, it was only in January 1859 that Muslims were permitted back if they had been issued a pass by the authorities. While many properties were seized until the residents could prove their innocence, the majority of these were Muslim homes whose owners were unable to prove their innocence (N. Gupta 1981, 24–25). Consequently, many Muslim families did not return, starting new lives in other parts of Delhi such as Nizamuddin or Mehrauli, or moving to other cities in North India. Death, exile, and migration sealed the fate of Shahjahanabad, whose once-powerful Muslims became an increasingly beleaguered and impoverished minority (231). While other Muslims came to take their place, like the Punjabi merchants who moved in, they did not always share the views of the old Muslim families still living in the city (232). Not only did Shahjahanabad's Muslims become a minority within a minority after 1857 in Delhi, but their cultural worlds were increasingly decentered (Pernau 2013). As Margrit Pernau has shown, after 1857 the Muslim "middle classes" asserted their dominance over the old Mughal elite through the assertion of particular forms of piety influenced by the Islamic reform movements of the nineteenth century, in which religious identities and boundaries became more defined (190, 424; see chapter 3).

There were other major changes that transformed the city and eroded Shahjahanabad after 1857. Many beautiful buildings, including the Akbarabadi Masjid (mosque), were razed after the decision to house the cantonment within the city in the vicinity of the fort and clear the area around the fort to enhance security (N. Gupta 1981, 27). These transformations, which reduced the living area by a third, also meant that the remaining population of the city was crammed into less space (45). A complicated land transaction led to confiscated Muslim properties being auctioned off to rich bankers, who were mostly Hindu and Jain (29–30). These were the people who really benefited from the changes to the city (30). Mahmood Farooqui says that these "financial and industrial barons who rebuilt Delhi after 1857" were among those who "refused to aid Bahadur Shah, but built their fortunes in the aftermath of the capture of Delhi" (2010, xxxi–xxxii). Farooqui continues: "They bought property, invested in factories, controlled trade monopolies and dominated the Delhi municipality in the following years" (xxxii).

While 1857 hastened the transformation of Shahjahanabad to Delhi, which subsequently became Old Delhi when the British shifted their capital to New Delhi in 1912 (N. Gupta 1981, 186), it was 1947 that sealed its fate. The bloody partition of India resulted in Old Delhi losing over two-thirds of its Muslim population. Laurent Gayer says that Delhi's Muslim population shrank from 33.22 percent in 1941 to 5.71 percent in 1951 as many Muslim families migrated to Pakistan (2012, 217). The story of this migration is complex and violent, as revealed in Vazira Fazila-Yacoobali Zamindar's study of what she calls "the long partition" (2007). While others have noted the chaos set in motion by a poorly conceived partition plan and an attenuated timeline (Y. Khan 2007, 2, 11–12), Zamindar shows how it was in the decades after the partition of India that ideas of nationhood and belonging were worked out (2007). Indeed, the context for the migration of Delhi's Muslims to Pakistan was not preformed notions of nation and belonging. Rather, the context in which to understand this mass exodus of Delhi's Muslims is violence—20,000 Muslims were killed in Delhi in partition violence, and 44,000 lost their homes (Zamindar 2007, 21).

While the partition plan had envisioned a transfer of populations in Punjab and Bengal, it had not anticipated or planned for the 323,000 Hindu and Sikh refugees who arrived in Delhi from Pakistan (Zamindar 2007, 28).[5] Amid the chaos that accompanied the arrival of these refugees, there were violent conflagrations all over Delhi in which Muslim families suffered disproportionately. Many Muslims fled their homes, seeking shelter with friends or in camps like the one in Delhi's Purana Qila (Old Fort). While many of these families were simply trying to escape violence, they were labeled "evacuees" by the Indian state; their properties were deemed "evacuee property" and either seized by the state or illegally occupied by the increasingly desperate Hindus and Sikhs from Pakistan (27–33). Zamindar argues that although both sets of populations had been displaced, the newly formed Indian state saw itself as responsible only for Hindus and Sikhs (31, 38–39). As Zamindar powerfully demonstrates, it was not national sentiment as much as violence and dispossession that drove Delhi's Muslims to Pakistan. They had no homes and nowhere else to go to. Many Muslims, and even the Pakistani state, saw their migration as temporary rather than a permanent decision to become Pakistani (7, 42–44).

Many of those I spoke to talked about partition and its enduring legacy for Old Delhi's Muslims. Both Aamir Sahib, mentioned above, and Rafiq Sahib, a wealthy businessman in Old Delhi, discussed the seizure of Muslim homes. Rafiq Sahib told me that homes were declared evacuee property and given to refugees, even when the relatives of those who had left for Pakistan still lived in Old Delhi. Illustrating Zamindar's conception of the "long partition," Aamir Sahib said that most of the older Muslim families in Old Delhi had relatives in Pakistan, and people continued to migrate, mostly in search of jobs, until 1971, when the borders closed. Echoing this narrative, Rafiq Sahib was more explicit. He argued that people considered going to Pakistan because they were met with suspicion when they applied for work in India. "But you are Pakistani," people would say. Still, according to him, many did not go, hearing from relatives there that they were "*pareshan*" (troubled). Many of those who did go returned, unable to deal with the political unrest in Pakistan or the separation from family. The younger generation born after the partition had little interest in going, according to Rafiq Sahib, because they had few connections to the people or the place.

While partition violence eventually abated, Rafiq Sahib's words highlight the enduring legacy of these violent events. Muslims were viewed with suspicion, often passed up for jobs, and increasingly constructed as an "other" (see chapter 1). The plural cultural and social worlds of Shahjahanabad had given way to exclusion, prejudice, and distancing. This change was poignantly captured in the words of Nuzrat Begum, who lived in Chitli Qabar and whose roots in Old Delhi go back to the Mughal era. Born around 1913, she told me that her family kept separate vessels and plates in their homes so that they could entertain their Hindu friends, cook for them, and serve them food using dishes that had never contained meat. Indexing the distance that has grown between Hindus and Muslims in Old Delhi, she said that now there is less need to do so because "the love has been destroyed."

Ameena Baji, a woman who lives in Shahganj and works in Delhi's burgeoning informal sector (see chapter 2), also traces her lineage in Old Delhi to "Mughal times." She told me, "They have excluded Muslims after 1947. If they would allow everyone to work together, India would be very advanced. They have betrayed Hindustan—the BJP and the RSS. The Congress also does it secretly. The BJP does it openly." Another conversation I had with Ameena Baji five months later is even more illustrative of the othering and marginalization that Old Delhi's Muslims have faced since partition, and about who is responsible.

AMEENA BAJI: One day I wanted to pierce my daughter's ears. . . . . He [the ear piercer] said to me, "What are you doing here? Go away from here to Pakistan. When you have been given a place, why don't you go there? What are you doing here?"

K: This was in the nineties?

AMEENA BAJI: This was after 1999—1999 or 2000. . . . Even today . . . they will say this only. That Muslims have no business here. This is not their country. This is not their nation.

K: Do you mean RSS people, or ordinary people?

AMEENA BAJI: Ordinary people.

K: RSS people of course say this.

AMEENA BAJI: Yes, but even ordinary people say this. And I feel that these people who talk like this—I do not mean all Hindus, but those who talk like this—they have no understanding. I believe if people unite and work together, then Hindustan will be much more advanced. But those Muslims who remained behind because of their work or business, those who studied a lot, those who built their own homes here, they did this only from their own effort. Otherwise, there is no place for Muslims in India.

The RSS (Rashtriya Swayamsevak Sangh), referenced in these conversations, is an all-male organization formed in the 1920s. Deeply inspired by and modeling itself on European fascists of the early twentieth century (Bhatt 2001, 124–33), and banned multiple times in postcolonial India, the RSS is the ideological inspiration for a group of right-wing Hindu organizations collectively known as the Sangh Parivar, or Sangh Family. The BJP, or Bharatiya Janata Party, an electoral party that currently dominates Indian politics, is one of these organizations. The organizations associated with the Sangh Parivar espouse Hindu nationalism, a majoritarian movement that views India as a Hindu nation and Muslims and Christians as foreigners (see K. Menon 2010; Hansen 1999; Jaffrelot 1999; Basu 1995).[6] They have been responsible for extreme violence against religious minorities in the country (see Ghassem-Fachandi 2012; Jaffrelot 2007; Appadurai 2006; Sarkar 2002). As I have argued elsewhere, the expansionary power of the Sangh Parivar is enabled in part by its ability to present different faces through its various organizations, some less extreme than others, and to articulate with multiple interests and diverse constituencies in contemporary India (K. Menon 2010). The BJP has risen to dominance not just because of the broad base of the various Sangh Parivar organizations, but also by successfully appealing to the majoritarian sentiments of a larger Hindu right not necessarily affiliated with any of these organizations. What is interesting about my conversations with

Ameena Baji is that she recognizes that the exclusion of Muslims has been done not just by the BJP and the RSS but by centrist parties such as the Congress in their attempts to appeal to Hindus who might otherwise be drawn to the BJP (Hasan 2012, 10–45) and by "ordinary people" compelled by Hindu nationalist sentiments and antipathy to Muslims. What her words suggest is that the marginalization of Indian Muslims cannot be dismissed as simply an artifact of the rise of the right, but rather is more broadly naturalized on the political landscape of the country.

Old Delhi became Delhi 6 on August 15, 1972, when the pin code was introduced to India, and postal addresses in Old Delhi were followed by the postal index number 110006.[7] The major event of that time etched in the memories of Old Delhi's Muslims was the Emergency, declared by Prime Minister Indira Gandhi and her Congress-led government from 1975 to 1977, when constitutional rights were suspended in the name of the national interest. While censorship, arrests of the opposition, and suppression of basic civil rights were rampant during the Emergency, it is remembered most poignantly in Old Delhi for its forced sterilization campaigns, the violent demolitions of property that resulted in the deaths of many Muslims, and the displacement of thousands of Muslim families from their homes. Protests against sterilization and demolitions at Dujana House and Turkman Gate in Old Delhi were met with extreme state violence in which thousands were injured or killed, women were raped, and houses were looted by state authorities (Tarlo 2003, 38–41). Hundreds of thousands were displaced from their homes and relocated to one of forty-seven resettlement locations outside Old Delhi (13). As Emma Tarlo notes, what people lost in the Emergency years was their locality, a loss that she underscores is "different from loss of space" (143). Drawing on Appadurai's definition of locality as "a property of social life, a structure of feeling that is produced by particular forms of intentional activity and that yields particular sorts of material effects" (Appadurai 1996, 182), Tarlo argues, "What these people lost in 1975 was not so much their ancient homes, which they had already lost, but rather their location in the heart of the Muslim community of the Old City. It was a loss of locality" (Tarlo 2003, 143).

Looking back at the history of Old Delhi and its bloody transformations from Shahjahanabad to Delhi, to Old Delhi, and to Delhi 6, it is hard to imagine how any of Shah Jahan's "Muslim place" has survived (see figure 0.3). And yet it is there in the stories people tell about their lives, in the crumbling facades of magnificent buildings trapped in the midst of electricity poles and tangled wires, in the names of streets and neighborhoods, in the regular references to the "walled city" even though most of Shah Jahan's walls were demolished after 1857, in the easily missed *taqs* (alcoves) along the streets where some remember to offer fresh

FIGURE 0.3. Contemporary Old Delhi from a rooftop. Photograph by the author.

flowers to various *jinns* or saints, in the many Muslim spectators who go out to watch the annual Ram Lila procession and performance of the Ramayana at the Ram Lila Maidan, and in the everyday religious practices that still recall shared cultural worlds. Just as Sufi shrines were crucial, as Nile Green has argued, "to the making of Muslim space" or a "space in which Muslims felt they belonged" in India (2012, xiv), in this book I focus on the narratives of people like Aamir Sahib and Nuzrat Begum that recall shared religious and cultural worlds of the past, the practices of piety that visibly assert Muslim identity in the present (chapter 3), and the rituals and religious discourses that root Muslims in place in India (chapters 4 and 5), as ways to make place for Muslims in a country where a resurgent religious right, and an increasingly strident majoritarian politics, threatens the fabric of coexistence that once was and perhaps still might be.

Muslim Place in a "Hindu Nation"

I was leaving Farhana Baji's house in Shahganj when the *magrib azaan* (evening call to prayer) sounded. Covering her head with her *dupatta* (long scarf), as many Muslim women do when they hear the *azaan*, Farhana Baji told me to come back indoors and sit to one side so that I did not block the entrance. I looked confused but did as she told me. After the *azaan*, she explained, "the spirit (*ruh*) of martyrs (*shaheed*) are all over Delhi. They have to go to *namaz* (prayers) too. We should not block their way during the *azaan*." Gesturing to her old home that her husband's family had occupied since at least 1857, she said, "This house does not belong to us. We will die and others will take over. But the *ruh* of these martyrs will stay here forever. This place is actually theirs, not ours. They do not disturb humans, but they are always here." The martyrs were not the only invisible inhabitants of her home; there were also jinn.[8] Since Farhana Baji could not see either of them, she referred to them collectively as "Syed *Sahib*" out of respect. Another time Farhana Baji told me that there is a lot of *ibadat* (worship) done in Old Delhi, and consequently there is *barakat* (blessings) here. Claiming that even earthquakes felt in Old Delhi have not affected most homes, she said, "Look at my own house. It is 250 years old and there are cracks in the ceiling. The kitchen ceiling is being held up by one nail. Last year I felt the earthquake go up and down, but nothing happened. This is because of Allah" (see figure 0.4).

Farhana Baji's words construct Old Delhi as a place filled with the spirits of Muslim martyrs. While its human denizens may come and go, the place belongs

FIGURE 0.4. An old haveli surrounded by modern structures. Photograph by the author.

to those who are not subject to the upheavals caused by changing political regimes or by the indeterminacies of everyday life—indeed, to those whose bodies, on judgment day, will stand as unaffected and indelible witnesses to the manner of their death (N. Khan 2012, 4; Cook 2008). The death of martyrs, the prayers of ordinary Muslims, and the narratives of women like Farhana Baji are acts with "material effects"—they construct "locality" for Muslims in Old Delhi (Appadurai 1996, 182). For Arjun Appadurai, cultural practices such as religious rituals and narratives produce "local subjects" whose everyday acts produce locality. Yet this is precisely why locality is an "inherently fragile social achievement"—because it "must be maintained against various kinds of odds" (178), including the homogenizing drives of the nation-state (190). The odds are decidedly against Old Delhi's Muslims in a country where Muslims have been marginalized by the nation-state since 1947, where Islam has been constructed as "foreign" since the colonial period, where upper-caste Hindus have been configured as the normative national subject, and where the Hindu right has dominated the sociopolitical landscape for decades.

In recent years, scholars, activists, and the media have noted the resurgence of the global right in different parts of the world (Graff, Kapur, and Walters 2019; Durham and Power 2010). While such work is essential, particularly given the rise of hate crimes against religious and racial minorities in places like the United States and the United Kingdom since 2016, it is not enough to focus our attention on the right to understand religious, racial, or ethnic discrimination and violence. In the wake of the 2016 United States elections, and particularly the liberal reaction to it, Jonathan Rosa and Yarimar Bonilla warn against "exceptionalizing the current moment," urging us instead to situate it "within broader historical, political, and economic assemblages" (2017, 202). Indeed, as critical race theorists and feminists have long pointed out, violence against these groups is systemic, the result of social worlds that privilege some groups over others, and in which normative understandings of citizenship and belonging prevail (see Bonilla-Silva 2015; Crenshaw 1991, 2011). In this context it is important to understand how right-wing groups recruit people into their exclusionary and violent nationalisms by drawing on already existing hegemonies—on discourses and structures of power and authority that have been naturalized for decades and that already configure the everyday. In moments of crisis or insecurity, these hegemonies can be effectively transformed into the kind of violent chauvinism we are witnessing the world over—whether among white supremacists in the United States or the Hindu right in India.

That Muslims have been subject to systemic violence in postcolonial India well before the resurgence of the Hindu right has become abundantly clear in recent years (see Islam 2019). The Sachar Committee Report released by the government of India demonstrated that Indian Muslims are the most socioeconomically underprivileged population in the country, with the least representation in government and private sector jobs (Sachar 2006). Indeed, most Muslims in Old Delhi are either self-employed or are part of the burgeoning and very insecure informal sector of neoliberal India (see chapter 2). Their marginal socioeconomic position is enabled and compounded by Islamophobia, stereotypes and prejudice, state surveillance and detention, and violence in everyday life (chapter 1). This precarity, which Judith Butler describes as a "politically induced condition" that makes some groups more vulnerable than others, is not new (2009, 25). It is the result of decades of marginalization of Muslims in postcolonial India. As Christophe Jaffrelot notes, despite being 14.25 percent of the population, Muslims have been significantly underrepresented in major arms of the government since independence, whether one looks at the Indian Administrative Service, the police, or the army (Jaffrelot 2019, 51). While employment discrimination clearly indexes anti-Muslim bias in the Indian government, one can also see how prejudice structures other aspects of life. For example, only 15.8 percent of convicts are Muslim, a figure proportionate to the percentage of Muslims in India, yet they constitute 21 percent of prison inmates awaiting trial (Jaffrelot 2019, 45). Such figures point to the suspicion with which Muslims are viewed in what is increasingly a Hindu-majoritarian state (see Chatterji, Hansen, and Jaffrelot 2019). As Angana Chatterji, Thomas Blom Hansen, and Chris Jaffrelot note, while the BJP has enabled "an unfettered social articulation and acceptability of majoritarianism . . . at the highest level of the state," it is also true that Hindu majoritarianism "has been evolving throughout the twentieth century" and has broad support in postcolonial India (2019, 10).

While economic and political marginalization clearly illustrate the privileging of upper-caste Hindus in India, the ever-present specter of beef-related violence against Muslims reveals the extent to which upper-caste Hinduism has become synonymous with Indian culture and identity. Indeed, beef-related violence, especially lynching by mobs in public spaces, has become the stuff of everyday news since 2014, when the Hindu nationalist BJP formed the national government in India with an absolute majority. Since then, many Muslims and Dalits (oppressed castes) suspected of eating, butchering, or transporting cows have been brutally killed. Of the eighty-six incidents of cow-related violence between 2010 and 2018, 98 percent occurred after the BJP came to power, and 88 percent of those killed were Muslim (Salam 2019, 3–4). These statistics suggest that those responsible for this violence were emboldened by the election of the BJP. This is not surprising, since the current prime minister of India, Narendra Modi, promised to bring an end to the "pink revolution" in his electoral campaign—a reference to the beef industry supposedly enabled and supported by the incumbent party, the Congress.[9] Although Modi stopped talking about the "pink revolution" once he became prime minister, 2014 marked a moment that unleashed extreme violence by self-proclaimed *gau rakshaks*, or cow protectors, against Indian Muslims. What is also disturbing is the way such crimes are viewed by the state. According to a 2019 report published by CSDS and the NGO Common Cause, "35% of police personnel interviewed for the survey think it is natural for a mob to punish the 'culprit' in cases of cow slaughter."[10] Such statistics help us understand why so many perpetrators of cow-related violence have been acquitted of their crimes, as the 2019 acquittal of those who murdered Pehlu Khan for transporting dairy cows has shown.[11]

While orchestrated by right-wing groups, such violence reflects the much broader elision of upper-caste Hindu practices with ideas of nation and belonging in the country that renders Muslims and lower-caste Hindus as "other" and as deserving of violence. The idea that the cow is sacred to Hindus is well entrenched in India and has been used to mobilize Hindus since the colonial period (Addock 2010). But many Indians eat beef, including many Hindus, and not all Hindus consider the cow sacred (K. Menon 2018; Natrajan 2018; Natrajan and Jacob 2018). While beef was eaten in ancient India (Doniger 2009, 112, 149–50; Jha 2009), restrictions on beef eating were introduced by upper-caste Hindus to mark boundaries and to claim status and power (Thapar 2004, 15). Today many Hindus who belong to dominant caste groups, or practice Hindu traditions shaped by them, worship the cow as a goddess (*gau mata*) and do not eat beef, even if it is sourced from other kinds of bovines (bulls or buffalos).[12] But even these Hindus may participate in the beef industry.

To understand this we need to recognize, as Radhika Govindrajan has shown, that not all cows are understood to have ritual power (2018, 79–87), and recent attempts to curtail bovine slaughter have affected the livelihoods of not just Muslims and Dalits in the beef and leather industries, but also those of Hindu farmers who raise cattle for agricultural use and for the dairy industry (64–65, 77). Since the cost of maintaining a bovine is Rs. 30,000 to Rs. 40,000 a year, it is not surprising that Indian farmers, already struggling with debt, are abandoning old and unproductive cattle in government schools and police stations in states like Uttar Pradesh that have sweeping restrictions on bovine slaughter.[13] Unlike in other parts of the world, cattle in India are not raised for beef but are "the byproduct of the farm and dairy sectors" (Z. Ahmad 2018, 94). But beef is a central export in India. Not only has India been vying with Brazil for the position of top beef exporter since 2011–2012, but in 2013–2014 beef was the top agricultural export in India (147). The central irony here has been noted by Meena Khandelwal: "India's increasing beef exports are targeted for political attack by Hindu nationalist politicians as immoral and shameful, but the growing meat industry is . . . a result of the state-led 'white revolution' (the result of the world's largest dairy development program launched by India in 1970) and a source of national pride" (2016, 228). Such inconvenient realities are ignored by cow vigilantes, whose violent actions have been organized by Hindu nationalist groups (Jaffrelot 2017, 56).

Thomas Blom Hansen notes that while violence, especially the public performance of anger, has become routinized in Indian politics, "no other political force has mastered this better than the BJP and its allies. Constantly refreshing the historical archive of anti-Muslim and caste-based stereotypes, the BJP has weaponized civil society by making a faceless Hindu anger an ever-present threat and possibility" (2017; see also Hansen 2018, 1084).[14] Constructing such anger and violence as retaliation for a litany of imagined crimes against Hindus (Ghassem-Fachandi 2012; Jaffrelot 2007), Hindu places (Davis 1996; van der Veer 1988, 1992), Hindu (Brahmanical) traditions (Addock 2016; Doniger 2016; Pennington 2016; and Viswanath 2016), and particularly Hindu women (K. Menon 2010; Bacchetta 2004; Sarkar 2002; Basu 1995) has been a tried and tested strategy of the Sangh Parivar in colonial and postcolonial India.

While the Hindu right may have been particularly adept at using violence, which has indeed become endemic in India, what is particularly troubling from the perspective of my argument here is the widespread tolerance of it, especially when directed at Muslims or Dalits. Junaid Khan, for instance, a teenager returning home from Eid shopping in Old Delhi in 2017, was fatally stabbed on a train after being called a "beef eater."[15] Although Junaid was traveling in a crowded train heading out of Old Delhi during rush hour, was abused, stabbed, thrown out of the train, and then left to bleed to death on a platform, there was apparently not a single eyewitness to the crime, and no arrests have been made to date.[16] Such callous disregard for human life is enabled by a discursive regime, now naturalized on the national landscape, that "others" Muslims and constructs the upper-caste Hindu as the normative national subject.[17] Ghazala Jamil argues, drawing on Giorgio Agamben and Judith Butler, that multiple discourses are woven together to construct Indian Muslims as an "exception," always suspect, not grievable, and therefore subject to violence (Jamil 2017, 95, 120). This "othering" underlies not just the beef-related violence but also the violent denial of belonging and the differential citizenship that Muslims experience in everyday life (Jamil 2017; Sethi 2014; Kirmani 2013). This differential citizenship is both an effect of and an apparatus through which the power of dominant groups in India, namely upper-caste Hindus, is maintained.

Against this violent denial of citizenship and belonging, this indifference to human life, Farhana Baji's narrative about the spirits of the city's martyrs situates Old Delhi's Muslims as people connected to the living and the dead, with ancient claims to the place. Like the *jinns* in Anand Taneja's ethnography of Firoz Shah Kotla (Taneja 2018, 50), the martyred spirits of Delhi illuminate a different history. They are both martyr and witness (*shaheed* and *shahid*) to a past that is no longer remembered, whether because of an "authorized forgetting" by the nation-state (31), or the wide dissemination of nationalist (Irfan Ahmad 2017b, 21) and Hindu nationalist histories (K. Menon 2010) that exclude Muslims and Islam from the nation-space. Against such exclusions, Farhana Baji's narrative imbues Old Delhi with blessings secured by the millions of prayers performed by Muslims over the centuries, a place sacralized and sanctified by the everyday practices of Muslims through history. Indeed, it is through their everyday religious practices that Old Delhi becomes a Muslim place—one where invisible martyrs permanently stand witness to its Muslim past, and where denizens of all religions bask in the *barakat* that permeates it (see figure 0.5).

While religious practices are central to constructing community and subjectivity, in this book I also see them as spatial practices that can forge cultural commons in places like Old Delhi. Scholars have long argued that space becomes place through cultural practices that inscribe it with meaning.[18] Religious practices and narratives, like those described here, are crucial to constructing subjects from whose acts locality is emergent (Appadurai 1996, 198). In her work on Lebanon, Lara Deeb has shown how images of Muslim martyrs and leaders, the call to prayer, and ritual performances in public space are all ways that Lebanese Shias mark al-Dahiya as their place (2006, 52–62). In India, Nile Green has shown how the shrines of Sufi saints and the hagiographies written about them serve not only to create sacred Muslim space in South Asia but also to construct imagined geographies that connect Indian Muslims to other places (2012, 14–19, 27). Indeed, religious practice, narratives of self and community, architectural details, and visual signs not only make place for Muslims in contemporary India, but they also require a transnational approach to studying religious subjects, practices, and places (see chapter 3).

The stories of people like Farhana Baji, Nuzrat Begum, and Aamir Sahib, and the religious practices I examine in this book that reveal the shared cultural worlds that these stories allude to, provide an important corrective not only to Hindu-majoritarian understandings of nation but also to academic constructions of religion and religious boundaries in South Asia. The category of religion, as J. Z. Smith said many years ago, is not a "native category"; it is imposed by others on particular forms of cultural life and "embedded in a history of colonialism" (2004, 269). Talal Asad famously argued that the category itself is the product of a particular history and deeply inflected with post-Reformation understandings of the place of religion in social life (1993). Religion was a central lens through which India and Indians were viewed in the colonial era. Peter

FIGURE 0.5. A street decorated for Ramzan. Photograph by the author.

Gottschalk contends not only that Indians were understood to be fundamentally religious (as opposed to "rational") but also that Indian religions were conceptualized as monolithic and mutually exclusive categories (2011, 24–28). It is precisely this approach to religion that so many South Asianists have questioned in recent years, most notably Jaqueline Hirst and John Zavos (2005), Peter Gottschalk (2000), and Harjot Singh Oberoi (1994).

Scholars such as Anand Taneja (2018), Ann Grodzins Gold (2017), Eliza Kent and Tazim Kassam (2013), Lisa Knight (2011), Sufia Uddin (2011), Carla Bellamy (2011), Karen Ruffle (2011), Anne Bigelow (2010), Joyce Flueckiger (2006), Syed Akbar Hyder (2006), Yoginder Sikand (2004), Jackie Assayag (2004), and Michael Carrithers (2000) have produced nuanced and textured studies of Muslims, Hindus, and Jains that beautifully illustrate how religious boundaries are blurred as people negotiate the complex, interwoven, and fraught landscapes of modern India to live with difference in everyday life (Mayaram 2005, 2008; see also Das 2010). Indeed, there is a long history of blurring boundaries between religious traditions in India, from female Sufi healers in contemporary Hyderabad who incorporate Hindu narratives into their own religious practices (Flueckiger 2006, 196), to the seventeenth-century prince Dara Shikoh, who believed that the Upanishads and the Quran "were part of the same tradition of Prophetic revelation from God" (Taneja 2018, 151). For Dara Shikoh, the very idea of separating Hinduism from Islam in India was equivalent to drawing a line in water (Kent 2013, 3). Anand Taneja sees Dara Shikoh's efforts to use insights from the Upanishads to understand the Quran as indicative of a "translatory mode of thought," still evident in contemporary Delhi, which seeks to fold difference into the self (2018, 151–52). Opposed to the epistemic and ontological modes that prevail under modernity (174–75; Willford 2018, 2), plural selves and fluid boundaries continue to mark India's cultural and religious landscapes. And as Andrew Willford argues, their very existence threatens, and therefore makes more strident, the assertions of exclusionary nationalisms (2018, 3).

Importantly, rather than focus on difference, which has dominated how Islam and Muslims have been viewed, related to, and represented for centuries (Mamdani 2002; Said 1979), all of these works allow us to map what Kamala Visweswaran calls "cultural commons or affinities" (2010, 8) and to use these as an analytic to understand culture, religion, and place. These works are crucial to understanding how I have approached religion, religious practice, and narratives of self and community in Old Delhi. Many of these studies have focused on Sufi traditions or Shii commemorative practices, but in fact, as Muzaffar Alam has argued, Islamic traditions of all hues have always appropriated ideas from the worlds they inhabited (2004, 24). In South Asia, where Muslims have historically been a minority, albeit a powerful one, Muslim ideas have been articulated amid a multiplicity of discourses and have negotiated and grappled with this diversity in different ways. In this context it is particularly important to consider Irfan Ahmad's reformulation of Talal Asad's (1986) pathbreaking conception of Islam as a "discursive tradition" and examine how traditions grapple with not just the foundational texts of Islam but also a plethora of oral and written traditions that have been central to shaping Muslim cultures in South Asia (Ahmad 2011, 110).

My work contributes to this burgeoning literature in its discussion of Muslims in all their diversity: I look at Sunnis and Shias, Sufis and atheists, Barelvis and Deobandis, Ahl-e-Hadis Muslims and others who refuse to identify by *maslak* (path), as they interact and position themselves with and against each other.[19] While individuals may live in and construct shared cultural and religious worlds, this does not mean there is no argument, no disagreement, and no incoherence. Indeed, in making place for themselves, individuals and groups quite often distance themselves from others—whether in terms of class, region, sectarian affiliation, or *maslak*. In the narrative with which I opened this book, Aamir Sahib clearly distanced himself from postpartition residents of Old Delhi by asserting his identity as a *Dilliwala*. Farhana Baji often critiqued "village" attitudes, especially when talking about her friend and neighbor Zehra Baji. Rafiq Sahib was quite disparaging of "lower class" practices, especially when talking about proper etiquette and religious practice. These examples highlight the plural identities (Willford 2018; Pernau 2013) held by people who also happen to be Muslim, and they challenge the tendency to portray Islam, in Irfan Ahmad's words, "as the most religious religion of them all" (2017b, 13), determining every last act, word, and deed of its followers. Analyzing the diverse and often conflicting place-making strategies of Muslims from a variety of traditions in Old Delhi, and showing how these intersect with gender and class among other axes of difference, my focus is on multiplicity, rather than coherence, and on how living with "others" indelibly marks the narratives and practices of Muslims. Examining how Old Delhi's Muslims use narratives and practices to position themselves in various ways amid multiple and conflicting forces, I look at religious practice and narratives of self and community as a form of the political (K. Menon 2013) that intervenes in the fraught landscapes of contemporary India.

Old Delhi's Muslims construct self and community at the interstices of multiple discourses, and religion is not the only framework through which they understand their lives. My interlocutors were men and women of all sects and classes: artisans and scholars, journalists and unskilled laborers, schoolteachers and religious leaders, housewives and government servants. As intersectional subjects (Crenshaw 1991) they were not only shaped by multiple axes of power and positionality, but they also constructed self at the intersection of competing hegemonies

(Ewing 1997, 6). Pulled by complex forces as they negotiated the variegated terrain of everyday life, their identities were certainly not fixed but always in process, constructed in the stories they told about themselves and their lives at particular historical moments (Kirmani 2013, 15). The years after 2012 when I began this research have been marked by many significant moments that undoubtedly shaped the narratives that I discuss in this book. This was a time when many Muslims were deeply scarred by the memories of the Gujarat pogrom of 2002; by the violence and displacement of thousands in Muzaffarnagar in 2013; by the BJP's decisive victory in the 2014 national election; by the installation of Narendra Modi as prime minister, a man many hold responsible for the Gujarat pogrom; by the beef-related lynchings of Muslims and Dalits; by the resounding electoral victory of Modi in the 2019 general elections despite the surge in anti-Muslim violence and communal rhetoric; by the Citizenship Amendment Act (CAA) passed by the Indian Parliament on December 11, 2019, that gave Hindu, Sikh, Buddhist, Zoroastrian, and Christian migrants, but not Muslim ones, a path to Indian citizenship; and by the violence unleashed on Muslims in Delhi in 2020 after a BJP minister threatened to clear CAA protesters from the streets if the police did not. Indeed, this is the context to understand the narratives of Farhana Baji, Nuzrat Begum, Aamir Sahib, and many others, and their efforts to make place for Muslims in a country increasingly under siege by a revanchist Hindu right.

Placing the Anthropologist in Old Delhi

In November 2012, I was talking to Ameena Baji in her *dalan*, a covered area off the courtyard where she spent much of her day, when a friend dropped by to visit her. After sitting down and exchanging pleasantries, the friend looked at me and asked, "Who is this?" After a brief exchange about me and my research, Ameena Baji and her friend, who had moved from Old Delhi to Nangloi recently, caught up with each other. At a natural pause in their conversation, the friend nodded toward me and asked Ameena Baji, "Is she Muslim?" Ameena Baji responded, "No, she is Hindu. But she is not that kind of Hindu." Ameena Baji turned to me and explained, "We all live together, but sometimes Hindus see us as very different." The conversation returned to the two friends and their lives, while Ameena Baji started slicing an apple. When I turned down the slice she offered me, she immediately said, chuckling, "Why aren't you eating? Is it because I am Muslim?" Having eaten at her house before, I knew she was joking, but I felt anxious about her friend's perception. Ameena Baji, perhaps sensing my unease or the possibility of a misunderstanding, clarified by saying to her friend, "She even eats beef."

As the months passed by, several incidents reminded me of this moment, and of Ameena Baji's words. One hot June afternoon, for instance, a Hindu woman claiming to be a representative of the Delhi government came by to collect money for new identity cards. After completing her business, she stayed and chatted for a while, sitting comfortably in the *dalan* and referring to Ameena Baji as "*didi*" (Hindi for "elder sister"). Ameena Baji turned to her daughter, who was rearranging a bookshelf nearby, and said, "Shazia, bring Aunty some water." Quickly, before Shazia could put down the books she was holding, the woman said, "No, no. I do not need water." Shazia then went back to what she was doing, and Ameena Baji and the woman kept up their friendly chatter until she left. No reference was made to this until hours later when Ameena Baji asked me, "Did you notice she refused to drink water?" I said, "Yes, I wondered what you thought of that." She responded as if it was obvious, "She did not drink water because I am a Muslim."

These vignettes powerfully index the multiple slights, distancing, and violence that Muslims experience over their dietary practices at the hands of Hindu neighbors and associates, especially as majoritarian nationalism in postcolonial India transforms older forms of sociality in places like Old Delhi. They reveal the hegemonic positioning of dominant Hindu caste ideologies about food, which renders the eating habits of many problematic, illegal, and/or deserving of violence (Chigateri 2008, 15, 19). In a similar vein, Balmurli Natrajan asserts, "Casteism constructs vegetarian food as a 'casteless universal' to be valorized and consumed by all. In stark opposition, it constructs beef as a 'casted particular,' to be stigmatized and hence consumed only by degraded subjects" (2018, 13). The "casteless universal" of casteism is of course upper caste and Hindu. It is ideologies such as these that underlie why women, like Ameena Baji's Hindu visitor, will not drink water or eat in Muslim homes, or at the homes of lower-caste Hindus and Dalits.

The hegemonic positioning of upper-caste Hindu ideologies about food also creates a problematic landscape for an Indian anthropologist with a Hindu name working among Muslims in Old Delhi. It is not unusual for Hindus from the South Indian state of Kerala to eat beef, and as I have written elsewhere, I come from a family of committed beef eaters from Kerala (K. Menon 2018). Yet many north Indians have little knowledge of the rest of the country, and particularly given the contentious beef politics of the north, my beef eating often provoked surprise among my interlocutors. My initial meetings with Old Delhi's Muslims, who were more used to Hindus like the one who visited Ameena Baji's house, usually included a conversation about whether or not I was vegetarian, before I was inundated with the hospitality that Old Delhi is famous for. This also meant that I could never refuse food or water at someone's house, for it could be read as a stigmatizing act. At the same time, I was very conscious of not being a burden, especially to the many I worked with who did not have a lot but whose hospitality meant that they would always share what they had. As I was told time and again, "The eater's name is written on every grain." This is a tricky place for an anthropologist to be positioned. So I ate and drank, a little, everywhere.

Being a beef eater did open some doors for me among Muslims in Old Delhi because food, at least, was not seen as a point of difference or a potential source of conflict. Dietary practices, after all, are not just about nutrition but are also about community, culture, power, and politics. As Meena Khandelwal says, while the conversation about beef is very different in the United States, "in the politics of meat, place and culture matter" (2016, 223). In a place like Old Delhi, where some Hindus refuse to drink water at Muslim homes, being a beef eater, a person who has no reason to distance others because of dietary practices, matters. It is also largely symbolic, since beef was not actually served in any Muslim home I visited, and mutton (goat) or chicken were preferred by those who could afford to eat and serve meat (see also Z. Ahmad 2018, 133). My being a beef eater, rather than actually eating beef, meant that my interlocutors could safely extend their hospitality (typically water and vegetarian snacks) without the risk of being spurned for their kindness.

While my eating practices may have made it easier for Old Delhi Muslims to relate to me, there were many other points of difference that marked me as an oddity in Old Delhi and have undoubtedly shaped this project in important ways. Indeed, I was viewed with suspicion by many for a variety of reasons. As a researcher with a Hindu name, one of the first questions I was often asked was "Why are you interested in studying Muslims?" While I had a well-considered explanation of how a project on the ways that religious minorities negotiate the exclusionary landscapes created by the Hindu right was a natural extension of my previous work on women in the multiple wings of the Sangh Parivar in New Delhi, such justifications were not convincing to all my interlocutors. This is not surprising given that Indian Muslims have to contend with anti-Muslim prejudice and discrimination in their everyday lives in Hindu-majoritarian India. My Hindu name positioned me within a privileged majority that is not only construed as the normative national subject but is also implicated in the multiple alienations that Indian Muslims experience today. Being a researcher with a Hindu name based in the United States only compounded the issue for some. Given the abiding, and not unwarranted, belief among my interlocutors that the United States does not like Muslims, some wondered whether my presence had a more insidious purpose. Was I a spy? Would I write negative things about Muslims that could create more problems for them? Had it not been for women like Farhana Baji and Zehra Baji, and men like Iqbal Sahib and Raza Sahib, whose generous embrace established me as a trustworthy person among different groups, I might have had a much more difficult time conducting my research.

Being a woman in Old Delhi also shaped my experience and this project in particular ways. Many of my female interlocutors did not socialize with men who were not natal kin. Some kept very strict *purdah* (veiling), donning burqas and hijabs outside the home and maintaining various degrees of physical distancing and/or seclusion. Others did not veil in any obvious sense but often maintained forms of distancing and regulation that, as Patricia Jeffery notes, is common to women of all religions in many parts of North India (2000, 6). In this context, being a female researcher meant that women were able to bring me to their homes and share their lives and worlds with me in ways that would have been difficult, and in many cases impossible, had I been a male researcher. But it also meant that my relationships with men were more formal and circumscribed. While I could meet women in their homes, I generally met men in their places of work or, less frequently and usually in the company of others, the male domains of the home. While I could have more casual interactions with the brothers and sons of women I met in their homes, I had very formal interactions with their husbands, and with men I met outside the familial context. I could "hang out" with women more easily, accompanying them as they went about their daily lives at home, in the market, at religious events, and as they visited each other. This enabled a more familiar relationship with them. I could not have such a familiar relationship with men, or "hang out" with them in the same way without violating etiquette in Old Delhi. This is reflected in this book in the fact that I call a lot more women *baji* (sister) than I call men *bhai* (brother), using instead the more distancing, and deferential, *sahib* (sir). However, despite the more circumscribed nature of my interactions, I did develop close relationships with some men, such as Raza Sahib and Iqbal Sahib, who were older and forged a paternal relationship with me.

While being a woman affected my interactions and relationships with people, being a female researcher meant that I violated many gender norms in Old Delhi. I lived alone without a husband or parental figure, I traveled all over Delhi on my own, and I talked with men and women without the usual inhibitions. Reflecting gender expectations across religious groups in India, even more odd was the fact that I had no children despite having been married for well over a decade. This triggered several embarrassing (for me) and hilarious (for them) conversations among women, replete with graphic hand gestures, about how to have intercourse to ensure conception. That childlessness could be a choice was inconceivable to many, except for Zehra Baji, who once rescued me from an inquisitive male relative by telling him off curtly, "What will she do with children? She has her work to do. If she had a child it would do *potty* and *susu* [urine] in the middle of the interview and then how could she work? She will have to run after the child." She paused and added, "I've told her to have a child and give it to me. That way she can work and I will raise the child." A woman with no formal schooling and who could not read or write (apart from Arabic to read, but not understand, the Quran), Zehra Baji eloquently summarized not just the gendered struggles of the female academic everywhere but also the informal labor of others, often differently positioned in terms of race, class, caste, religion, gender, and age, that enables their work.

Although I may have cut an odd figure in Old Delhi, and some kept their distance, most Muslims I worked with in Old Delhi welcomed me into their homes, showered me with hospitality, and tolerantly allowed me to impose on their everyday lives. They did not expect me to be like them, but at the same time, women especially schooled me patiently on norms they expected me to follow. For instance, I was gently told how to conduct myself at various religious events, or less gently told how to dress for weddings when they found my attire sadly lacking. As an anthropologist learning about everyday life in Old Delhi, I found these conversations very productive. Other things made me uncomfortable but were still ethnographically interesting—such as offers to straighten my very curly hair or comments that equated beauty with fairness—revealing prejudices shared by people of all religions in India, where standards of beauty are inflected with racial hegemonies.

Yet, and perhaps this is the essential point in a book that seeks to take Visweswaran's "cultural commons" seriously, my difference was never a point of exclusion or a source of discrimination or danger. People looked out for me, cared for me, and respected me in ways I had not expected, including those people I did not know and who did not know me. Even strangers who first met me alone at night on the ninth of Muharram at Panja Sharif Dargah near Kashmiri Gate looked out for me, insisting that I sit with their family during the overnight commemorations and dropping me home after *fajr namaz* (morning prayers) that day and the next (Ashura).[20] Indeed, having conducted fieldwork since 1999 in different parts of the National Capital Region (Old Delhi, New Delhi, and parts of Uttar Pradesh, Haryana, and Rajasthan) infamous for sexual harassment and gendered violence, I felt safer walking the lanes and by-lanes of Old Delhi at all hours, especially in the Muslim areas that bustle with activity till late into the night, than anywhere else in this very unsafe city.

I experienced such cultures of care from individuals belonging to all the diverse groups of Muslims I worked with in Old Delhi, who generously agreed to participate in semi-structured interviews and conversations, gave me permission to tape our interactions or quickly jot down phrases and responses in my notebook, and allowed me to be a participant observer in homes, schools, mosques, shrines, and at public functions and religious events. I worked with a hundred individuals (fifty men and fifty women) and informally encountered many more, from all classes, sects, *maslaks*, regions, and positions since I began this research in 2012. Some traced their lineage to "Mughal times," while others were recent migrants from villages and small towns across North India. Some belonged to well-established and well-off families in Old Delhi, while others were part of its burgeoning informal sector. Some were highly educated, while others had no formal schooling and did not read or write. They belonged to different sects (Shias and Sunnis) and religious *maslaks* (Deobandi, Barelvi, Ahl-e-Hadis) and, consequently, had very different, and often conflicting, understandings and practices of Islam (see, for instance, I. Ahmad 1981; Jeffery 1981, 2000). They belonged to different *biradaris* (occupational groups) that, as many have noted, have distinctive cultural practices and religious preferences (see, for instance, Z. Ahmad 2018; Murphy 1986; Goodfriend 1983; Ahmad 1978; Ansari 1960). I have tried to capture some of this diversity through the place-making practices I discuss in the chapters that follow.

Kamala Visweswaran warns anthropologists against culturalisms, which treat culture as an "insurmountable difference" and "insist on culture as the residuum or limit point for understanding communities, rather than as a site of multiple determinations working to produce the 'effects' of culture or community" (2010, 7, 10). This approach to thinking about culture guides us to consider the material effects of the stories about praying martyrs and shared blessings, narratives of self and community that transcend religious boundaries, gestures of care and hospitality such as those I experienced from so many, forms of affect encoded in speech and conduct, visible acts of piety that assert presence, and religious practices that operationalize shared religious histories. As I argue in this book, such words and deeds construct particular kinds of subjects in a particular kind of place, amid a fraught cultural landscape where other constructions of subjectivity and place are already hegemonic. The words of Aamir Sahib and Farhana Baji are not just nostalgic memories of an imagined people and place in the distant past. Retold and reenacted today in the presence of an anthropologist writing a book about Muslims in Old Delhi, they intervene in the hegemonic renderings of the present and become a presence for a future reckoning. They are forms of place making that disrupt, however momentarily and marginally, the exclusionary nationalism that dominates the sociopolitical landscape of the country.

Part 1
LANDSCAPES OF INEQUALITY

1

A PLACE FOR MUSLIMS

> REHANA: This is the image they have of Muslims. That they are terrorists. That they are combative [*jhagadaalu*]. They are all like this. But if you saw their daily life you would know that they are struggling, they are stressed, they are not like this. . . . There are Hindu terrorists too. But no one thinks all Hindus are terrorists. But they think all Muslims are terrorists. Some people are going in a wrong direction. All this is not in Islam. Even then they are doing this. They are individuals and will handle things in their individual way. Even when they go up [die]. Because Islam does not allow all this.
>
> K: What does Islam say about this?
>
> REHANA: Islam will never allow you to kill an ordinary person. It is not allowed. If these people are doing this then they are not one of us. They are not Muslims.

Rehana does not like Old Delhi very much. Although she was born in Old Delhi, her natal family now lives in Okhla, a neighborhood in South Delhi with a substantial Muslim presence that she likes better. But she and her husband, whom she met as a student at Zakir Husain College, live in the flat her husband inherited in Old Delhi. When I asked her what specifically she disliked about Old Delhi, Rehana said that she hates the way everyone knows everything about each other. If someone visits, everyone knows the details of who visited, what they were fed, and what gifts were exchanged. She feels that men are always hanging around on the streets and staring at her as she walks by. To avoid gossip, when she wears trousers to work, she will often wear a big skirt over her trousers as she is leaving Old Delhi. She said that even if she and her husband have a fight, he always drops her off and picks her up from the metro station on his motorcycle. "This is our routine. No matter what," she said. Given my own experiences as a female researcher in a region that is notoriously inhospitable to women, I asked Rehana whether this was because she felt unsafe as a woman in Old Delhi, specifically raising the issue of sexual assault. She immediately insisted that this was not an issue, saying, "If I scream, everyone will come running." In fact, she and her husband do not lock their front door. The very aspects of Old Delhi that she dislikes are in fact what make her feel safe there.

Rehana works as a salesperson at a high-end clothing shop in one of New Delhi's posh marketplaces and encounters prejudiced views on a daily basis. While there are many things that irritate her about Old Delhi, anti-Muslim prejudice is not part of her everyday life there. In New Delhi, customers at her shop often air their prejudices and stereotypes about Muslims in her presence, not realizing that she is Muslim. For instance, a woman at her store once told Rehana she was scared of Muslims. Rehana responded, "I am a Muslim. Are you scared of me?" The woman apparently said unabashedly that she was not scared of Rehana but was scared of other Muslims. Rehana feels that the loyalty of Muslims is always questioned in India. She says that people accuse Muslims of being Pakistani or supporters of Pakistan. "I have never even been to Pakistan," she said, "so how can I be Pakistani?" While Rehana can wear what she wants in New Delhi and has the anonymity she longs for, she has to grapple with hurtful stereotypes that make her feel out of place there.

Rehana is not alone in feeling out of place in parts of New Delhi. Others like her who spend a lot of time outside Old Delhi express similar views. Nazia, a young woman who works in an NGO focusing on gender and sexuality in New Delhi, said that when people do not realize she is Muslim, they say things that reveal their prejudices. She asked, laughing, "What does it mean to be Muslim? Do I have horns on my head?" Rehana and Nazia do not hide their Muslim identity. But as Muslims who do not display visible markers of religious identity, they are not always identified as Muslim. Others working in New Delhi, particularly those who are more economically insecure, do actually hide their religious identity. Several Muslim men who worked as health attendants for the infirm in the wealthy South Delhi neighborhood of Defence Colony adopted Hindu names or used religiously neutral nicknames, concerned that they would not get these positions if they identified as Muslim. This is also true of several male and female domestic workers I met in posh homes in South Delhi. Such acts are engendered by the deepening insecurity of being Muslim in a country that has witnessed the rise to dominance of the Hindu right, extreme violence against Muslims and Christians enabled by exclusionary visions of nation and belonging, and—greatly facilitated by this politics of difference—the increasing suspicion, surveillance, and targeting of Muslims by the Indian state.

In urban India, where the securitization of the state impacts everyday life in the form of metal detectors, security cameras, checkpoints, identity verification, and armed personnel policing public space, notions of security are inflected by majoritarian understandings of nation and citizenship that position Hindus as the normative subject, while relegating religious minorities to the murky margins of the national imaginary. As the Hindu right has prevailed in recent years, this normative construction of Indians as Hindu has become increasingly entrenched, while Indian Muslims, as illustrated in my conversation with Rehana, have been simultaneously cast as marginal, suspicious, and, in this era of global Islamophobia, dangerous subjects. National discourses and practices of securitization articulate with global discourses about Islam and Muslims, and indeed global priorities and interests, to reiterate these normative constructions, so that formal citizenship does not guarantee security. Building on the work of scholars who have examined how different subjects are extended different kinds of citizenship (Jamil 2017, 27; Grewal 2014, 4, 305; Maira 2009, 82; Ong 1999, 20), I show how varying experiences of security reflect differential citizenship. This is because, as Anna Yeatman (2010) has shown, a self/other dichotomy that ensures the protection of some at the expense of others structures much security discourse and practice in the world today. This is certainly true of notions of security in India. Ultimately, this logic of securitization both reflects and enables a powerful politics of belonging that creates boundaries which include some and not others (Yuval-Davis 2011, 18), and places Muslims differentially on the national landscape.

This construction of Muslim subjectivity, and the politics of nation and belonging that it indexes, is what makes Muslim domestic workers and health attendants insecure, prompting them to eschew markers of religious identity, to pass for the norm at their workplaces in New Delhi. Such acts enable Muslims to inhabit places that may otherwise be hostile to them. How do Indian Muslims make place for themselves in a country in which they are routinely cast as security threats—as potential militants who threaten public order, as ambiguous subjects with questionable national allegiance, or as a community driven by religious impulses that keeps India from realizing its global aspirations? Here I examine how Old Delhi's Muslims negotiate insecurity in everyday life to make home and construct belonging in modern India. I suggest that those I worked with increasingly perceived Old Delhi as a Muslim place, as a refuge in insecure times.

I begin with a discussion of some of the prejudices and inequalities that Muslims negotiate in everyday life and that make them insecure in contemporary

India. I then discuss how the targeting of Muslims by the Indian security state has compounded these feelings of insecurity. I argue that these feelings of insecurity are engendered by a powerful politics of belonging that excludes Muslims from the national imaginary, compelling those I worked with to challenge their displacement by crafting a place for themselves in Old Delhi. Ultimately, I suggest that even as Muslims contest their erasure from the national imaginary and assert their presence on the national landscape by making place for themselves in neighborhoods in Old Delhi, they simultaneously acquiesce to a national cartography that enables their continued marginalization in contemporary India. Indeed, they are both "secure" and "secured" in Old Delhi, since their actions are ineluctably linked to discourses of nation and security that render some places inhospitable to Muslims while "securing" them in others.

Negotiating Landscapes of Prejudice

The stereotypes that make Rehana insecure are enabled by deeply problematic views about Muslims and Islam. As several scholars have noted, not only has Islam been portrayed as a religion with violent proclivities, but also ahistorical and monolithic understandings of Islam have been used to construct the religion as a totalizing system that determines the behavior, beliefs, sentiments, and politics of Muslims in the contemporary world (Mamdani 2002; Asad 1986; Said 1979). Such culturalisms are not only inaccurate, but they also assume that individuals are mere automatons of powerful cultural discourses and that their acts are produced by culture rather than history and politics (Mamdani 2002, 767). Arguing against scholars who use Islamic texts and culture to explain Muslim politics and violence (see Cook 2005; Lewis 2003; Juergensmeyer 2000), what he calls "theological-cultural theories," Irfan Ahmad says, "It is not the seamless culture or sacred text of Islam that fosters radicalism but, on the contrary, it is the dynamics of politics, particularly the role of the state in the (mis) treatment of its citizens that sets the discourse of jihad in motion" (2009, 166). However, rather than recognizing the compulsion of politics and social injustice, culturalisms insist that it is the text, or culture, that compels.

Such culturalisms also efface plural identities, what Andrew Willford calls the "cosmopolitan pasts" that threaten the "monocultural fantasies of the nation" (Willford 2018, 2) and ignore how in places like Old Delhi, religion is not the only factor shaping people's behavior and interactions. Indeed, as I have already suggested, in the case of nineteenth-century Old Delhi, *sharif* identity could be more important than religious identity in certain milieus (Pernau 2013;

Lelyveld 1978), and even today, at least for someone like Aamir Sahib, being a *Dilliwala* could be as important as being Hindu or Muslim. Yet as Rehana's words suggest, while Old Delhi's Muslims may have plural identities, culturalisms about Islam have a tremendous impact on their lives. Whether religious or not, their structural position as Muslims situates them in the unequal topographies of Hindu-majoritarian India, and they must negotiate landscapes of prejudice in their everyday lives even as their experiences are variegated because of other factors like gender, class, and educational background.

Old Delhi's Muslims are from diverse backgrounds in terms of class, caste, sect, occupation, region, education, and language. Some are daily wage laborers, moving heavy carts through narrow streets, working in small factories scattered throughout the old city, or selling produce on street corners. Some ply cycle rickshaws and auto rickshaws, and many are college students, teachers, professors, scholars, or housewives (see figure 1.1). Some are journalists and social workers, while others are businessmen, builders, traders, shop owners, and artisans. Some work with local politicians, though very few have government jobs, while others do piece-rate work on clothes, shoes, and jewelry in their homes. Some are unemployed, others are the moneylenders the unemployed live off, and a few work in Old Delhi's infamous red-light district. This diversity leads to inevitable tensions—over class and education, over sectarian practices and understandings of Islam, and over cultural modalities and constructions of self. However, underlying all these ways of being Muslim in Old Delhi, and despite the tensions that such differences engender, one can sometimes detect a sense of common fate, of uncertainty, of insecurity in contemporary India. And as I soon discovered, such feelings of insecurity are deeply etched into the landscape.

Places are made. As Arjun Appadurai has argued, locality is "emergent" from the actions of subjects in everyday life (1996, 198). Indeed, Old Delhi emerges as a Muslim place in everyday life through the words and deeds of people who live there, but also from the ways that people elsewhere talk about it or relate to it. For my interlocuters, Old Delhi was not just a Muslim place because of its history and its demography, but also because it was a place where they felt secure to be Muslims. That many Muslims felt out of place in New Delhi was eloquently illustrated one morning when I took the metro from the Chawri Bazar Metro Station in Old Delhi with Ameena Baji. As the train pulled out of the station toward New Delhi, she pulled off her burqa in the lady's compartment, folded it, and placed it in her handbag. I asked her why she was doing this when our destination was a hospital near the Rajiv Chowk Station only two quick stops away. Ameena Baji said she did not like to wear a burqa when visiting a doctor. They treat you differently she said, "as if you are dirty." They are very brusque with you, she claimed, and "so, if

FIGURE 1.1. A scholar at home. Photograph by the author.

I am going to the doctor, I never wear a burqa. I want to make sure I get the best treatment if I go all the way to the doctor." I pointed out that she had worn a burqa when we had gone to consult an Old Delhi physician in her neighborhood for the same ailment a couple of days before. "Yes," she said, "but he is a Muslim doctor." I was particularly surprised because, unlike some of her neighbors, Ameena Baji never stepped out of her home without a burqa in Old Delhi, and I had never seen her remove it in a public area. And here she was wearing a short-sleeved, stylish black *kurta* (tunic) over matching leggings. Naively I asked, "What if someone from Old Delhi sees you?" She replied dismissively, "They'd probably think I am going to the doctor." She only put her burqa back on when we returned to the Chawri Bazar Metro Station after consulting the doctor, doing a battery of tests, and then wandering around Connaught Place snacking and window-shopping until it was time to pick up the results.

A few weeks later, in a conversation about prejudice against Muslims in India, Ameena Baji said, "Today there is more prejudice. Before Hindus and Muslims stayed together. Today when I wear a burqa, I realize how much prejudice there is because I see people look at me differently—as if I am illiterate, backward, a thief." It soon became clear to me that Ameena Baji was not the only woman I met who chose not to veil, an obvious marker of Muslim identity, when outside Old Delhi. Indeed, the desire to avoid prejudice prompts many women to remove their burqas in New Delhi even though they may view it as a necessary part of their religious practice. For many Muslim women veiling is an expression of piety, and not, as stereotypes about Islam suggest, an expression of gender oppression or coercion.[1] Yet as Ameena Baji's actions and words illustrate, she lives in a world where she must negotiate the stereotypes about Muslims attached to the burqa and the consequences such meanings might have on her life. Her burqa signifies competing narratives not just about her as a woman but about her as a Muslim, powerfully exemplifying the extent to which these categories of difference are mutually constituted in her world (see Puar 2012; Yuval-Davis 2011, 7; see also Agnes 2012, 51). As Nira Yuval-Davis argues, "Social locations, . . . even in their most stable format, are virtually never constructed along one power vector of difference" (2011, 13). Eschewing the burqa in New Delhi, Ameena Baji attempts to minimize the effects of her religious identity in a locality where she feels out of place as a Muslim. Her act of donning her burqa upon her return marks Old Delhi as a place where she is secure, where she belongs, where she is "at home" (10).

However, my conversations with women and men in Old Delhi also revealed that while many of them feel out of place in New Delhi, it is not as if they do not encounter prejudiced views in parts of Old Delhi. When Zafar, a young man in his twenties who lives in Shahganj, went to talk to a Hindu man who runs a coaching center in Old Delhi about employment as a tutor there, he decided to change out of the white *kurta-pajama* (tunic and pants) and *topi* (cap) he had worn to attend Friday prayers at the mosque, saying, "These are too Muslim." The jeans and shirt he donned instead revealed that men too are concerned about facing prejudice because of their clothing choices. While his name might have revealed his religious affiliation, Zafar tried to inhabit a different subject position through his sartorial choices—that of an educated youth whose identity was not overdetermined by religion.

Additionally, particular neighborhoods in Old Delhi are understood to be less accepting of Muslims than others. This was evident in a conversation I had with Zafar about heightened police presence around his Muslim neighborhood on Choti Eid (Small Eid), the last Friday before Eid during Ramzan.[2] Zafar said that on Choti Eid they always send more police to areas around his neighborhood that are lined with Hindu shops, because they expect tension. Indeed, I had noticed many armed police on the streets on my way to his house that day. Zafar told me of a time when his father had gone to do some repairs on Choti Eid at the home of a wealthy Hindu merchant in Sitaram Bazar. As he was leaving after completing his work someone stopped him on the street and said, "What are you doing here? What work do you have here?" Refusing to accept that Zafar's father had legitimate business there, he and others gathering around started getting aggressive. It was only when Zafar's father called the person he worked for that he was allowed to leave. Zafar said, "The Hindu Lala told the group that Papa had been working for him for years and to leave him alone. So in the end he was fine. But they do not like Muslims in these areas." His mother, who was sitting with us interjected, "They won't rent houses to Muslims in those areas. They want them to only have Hindus." Indeed, while most of my interlocutors constructed Old Delhi as a refuge from prejudice, using general terms like "walled city" or "*Purani Dilli*," it was also clear that such constructions were relative. Not only was security attached to particular places within Old Delhi, but ideas of security were refracted through the lens of the particular relationships involved.

Ameena Baji's and Zafar's actions reflect their particular negotiations of the landscapes of prejudice that they experience in everyday life. Many of these prejudices reveal not only the extent to which Muslims are stereotyped, but also the lack of understanding of the issues facing Muslim communities. For instance, one of my interlocutors, referring to a conversation I had witnessed a few days before between her and her Hindu sewing teacher in which the teacher had invoked a common stereotype about Muslim neighborhoods being dirty, said,

> You heard the sewing teacher that day. She is always talking about how dirty it is here. But she does not understand why. The sweeper who comes here wants money from each household to take the trash. The government says we should not pay her because she already gets a salary of 30,000 a month from them. But if we do not pay her then she will not take our trash. Most families here are like mine. They cannot always afford to pay her every month. So she does not pick up the trash that often, and people just end up throwing the trash on the streets. Even that they do not sweep up that often. . . . [Hindu areas] are very clean because they can all afford to pay the sweepers what they want.

Indeed, many like the Hindu sewing teacher do not stop to consider the political economy of clean places. And importantly, while street litter is found in many urban neighborhoods, it is litter in Muslim neighborhoods that is singled out to "other" and to bolster existing prejudices. Such deep-seated prejudices engender feelings of insecurity among Old Delhi's Muslims. Sometimes these insecurities result in changes to sartorial choices as noted above. At other times, as I suggest below, they have resulted in assertions of Muslim identity in particular neighborhoods that speak to the everyday struggles of Muslims to hold on to their place in a country overrun by the Hindu right.

Religious Identity and Differential Citizenship

While prejudice and stereotypes make Muslims insecure, so does their precarious socioeconomic and political position in India. According to the Sachar Committee Report commissioned by the Government of India in 2006, Indian Muslims are the most economically and politically marginalized group in the country, even in comparison to other historically underprivileged groups (Sachar 2006). In his discussion of the report, Thomas Blom Hansen notes the lack of government support for education in Muslim-dominated areas, the high dropout rate among Muslims in educational institutions, and the tendency toward self-employment or work in the informal sector because of their inability to find private or public sector jobs (2007, 51). Hansen says, "The feeling of being outside the state and the mainstream economy means that very few young Muslims appear in the qualifying exams for the civil service and even fewer actually apply for government jobs" (51). What the Sachar Committee Report illuminates most profoundly is that systemic violence ensures that legal citizenship does not guarantee the same rights and privileges to all Indians. Indeed, resonating with the work of scholars who have argued that citizenship is mediated by difference (Jamil 2017; Maira 2009; Ong 1999), the Sachar Committee Report reveals how religious difference affects access to the rights and privileges of citizenship in India. The differential citizenship experienced by Indian Muslims is clearly reflected in the human security indicators that the report measures.

An awareness of systemic violence and differential citizenship was clearly articulated by my interlocutors in conversations about the report. Rafiq Sahib said, "Whatever Muslims are, they have become by their own efforts." Echoing what has been articulated in many recent publications (Islam 2019, Rahman 2019), Aamir Sahib said that little had been done to address the concerns raised by the report in the years since it was published. According to him, this illuminated the lack of political will to do anything for Muslims. He told me that while government schemes designed for the uplift of Indian minorities do exist, it is often difficult for Muslims to access the benefits associated with these schemes. For one, he said, Muslims must compete with other groups such as Jains and Sikhs for the benefits available through these schemes. These groups are relatively privileged in comparison to Muslims—politically, economically, and socially—and therefore better positioned to access the benefits. Further, poor representation in government positions has created more disparities. Since applications for these positions require the endorsement of a gazetted officer, Aamir Sahib said that the lack of Muslim officers holding such positions—a result of some of the issues raised in the Sachar Committee Report—also puts Muslims at a severe disadvantage relative to these other groups.[3] He said, "Muslims do not know who to get to sign these forms. The result is that they cannot take as much advantage of these schemes as they should."

Muslim insecurity is not just about the paucity of governmental initiatives in Muslim areas, or their inability to access them. These insecurities have been exacerbated by the prevailing attitude toward Indian Muslims reflected in the actions of individuals and institutions in the private sector. In a long conversation in his office in Old Delhi's Ballimaran neighborhood, Aamir Sahib traced how the interplay of multiple axes of inequality and discrimination—from stereotypes, suspicion, and neglect to structural disparities and violence—has contributed to the increasing marginalization of Muslims in India today. Telling me that he was going to reveal a "bitter reality," he explained how the changing demographics of Old Delhi have adversely affected Muslims. As Hindus have left Old Delhi, good schools that catered to them have angled to move too. Aamir Sahib said,

> The Hindus of the walled city, they are slowly, slowly shifting. . . . Their feeder schools that are here, like Ramjas School, Anglo Sanskrit School, and Commercial School, these are good schools. . . . The Hindu population here is finished. So Muslim children are going there. Because Muslims have also become interested in studying. So they [the schools] want to close now. . . . It is their right to close or not. They do not want Muslims to benefit from them. . . . No school has opened here since 1947.

Highlighting the precarious place of Muslims on the national landscape, Aamir Sahib argued that these trends particularly affect Muslims because while "Hindus can live anywhere," Muslims will only live in places where they feel "safe" and "secure." He said these are areas "where there is a Muslim block, where Muslims live." In a country where Muslims have had to negotiate Hindu chauvinism and violence for decades (K. Menon 2010), and where a disturbing number of Muslims have been lynched in cow-related violence since the BJP came to power in 2014 (Salam 2019), it is not surprising that Muslims would seek safety in numbers. This violence and exclusion are part of a powerful politics of belonging that entails both the creation "of boundaries but also the inclusion or exclusion of particular people, social categories and groupings within these boundaries by those who have the power to do this" (Yuval-Davis 2011, 18). Such boundaries, "sometimes physically, but always symbolically, separate the world population into 'us' and 'them'" (20).

It is an awareness of these boundaries that drives Muslims to live in Muslim neighborhoods at times of heightened tension, as Juliette Galonnier illustrates in her work on the North Indian city of Aligarh (2014, 18), and Ghazala Jamil

(2017), Nida Kirmani (2013), and Laurent Gayer (2012) have shown in their work on different parts of the National Capital Region. However, while Muslims might feel safer residing in Muslim areas, Aamir Sahib notes that schools and other institutions that ensure the continuing development of these communities are moving away because of their own priorities and prejudices. Consequently, these patterns of residence in neighborhoods like Old Delhi have enabled the further marginalization of Muslims in these places. While such topographies of marginalization are clearly linked to the existing hegemonies and prejudices I have discussed above that endow Muslims with differential citizenship, they must also be understood beyond the frame of the nation because, as I discuss in more depth in the next chapter, they are fundamentally connected to global processes of capital accumulation in the neoliberal era (see Jamil 2017; Ong 2006).

While many Muslims complained about the overcrowded streets, dilapidated buildings, and poor living conditions in Old Delhi, they did not necessarily view moving out of Old Delhi as an option. Exclusionary understandings of nation and belonging have ensured that it is difficult to find housing to rent or buy outside Old Delhi and other Muslim enclaves if you are Muslim. Tariq Sahib, an older man from a prominent Old Delhi family, spoke of his struggle to purchase a home in New Delhi despite being a well-known public intellectual, columnist, and advocate for secularism and pluralism in India. Not keen to live in Jamia Nagar, the enclave outside Old Delhi to which many Muslims have moved (see Gayer 2012), Tariq Sahib took a long time to find his home in South Delhi. Having struggled against prejudice and stereotypes in his search for housing, Tariq Sahib is not surprised that most Muslims either continue to live in Old Delhi despite the conditions, or move to places like Jamia Nagar. The attractions of the relatively affluent enclave of Jamia Nagar, and the comforts and anonymity available to those living in South Delhi notwithstanding, Tariq Sahib said that many Muslims, including members of his own extended family, are moving back to Old Delhi. Some have never left Old Delhi, or rarely venture beyond its now mostly metaphorical walls. One woman told me that some she knew "have never been outside to see what life is like out there. You know these walls of Old Delhi? They stay within them." An elderly lady, Huma Khala, who was sitting with us chimed in, "I do not leave. Everything has changed outside."

Even as the places they occupy become increasingly marginal, other forms of marginalization and erasure work to compound the feelings of insecurity that many Muslims expressed. Aamir Sahib highlighted the tendency to sideline and forget Muslim contributions to India. "What about all those Muslims who were part of the independence movement," he asked, those who said, 'No sir, we do not want Pakistan; we want to stay in Hindustan [India]'? Today those Muslims are being beaten. Those Muslims are being killed." Highlighting the erasure of

Muslims from common struggles of the past, Aamir Sahib spoke of the active forgetting of Muslim contributions to India's freedom movement in nationalist histories promoted in educational institutions in independent India:

> In the history you are teaching, you should include the contributions of everyone. Muslims started the movement, made sacrifices. They should also be mentioned. This is not in our history. I am not saying that what they are saying about the people mentioned is wrong. It is correct. I am saying they should also talk about these people [Muslims] so that their children can see what Muslims have sacrificed. . . . It is the government's duty to come up with a syllabus that recognizes Muslim contributions to history.

With these words Aamir Sahib echoes the sentiments of the eminent historian Mushirul Hasan, who lamented the "woefully inadequate" literature on Indian Muslims, a dearth that has not only effaced the contributions of Muslims in India but also enabled the tendency in academia to focus on the Arab world in discussions of Islamic traditions, culture, and politics (2008, 1, 14). Indeed, key intellectuals who ushered in Islamic modernity in India, especially those who fit uncomfortably into the grand narrative of Indian nationalism, are marginalized in nationalist histories. Sir Sayyid Ahmad Khan, founder of the Aligarh Movement that sought to modernize Muslim society and of Aligarh Muslim University (Muhammadan Anglo-Oriental College), which he founded because he anticipated the need for European learning for Muslims (Lelyveld 1978, 2013), "is portrayed as wicked and threatening because of his aversion to the Congress" (Hasan 2008, 43).[4] While many an Indian might be able to sing "*Sare jahan se accha Hindustan hamara* (Our Hindustan is the best place in the world)," not many know that this ode to Indian pluralism was penned by Muhammad Iqbal some years before rising communalism and Hindu majoritarianism led him to conclude that Indian pluralism could only be protected by the creation of "autonomous states" within the Indian polity (Hasan 2008, 87–88).

Many would understand Muhammad Ali Jinnah as the chief antagonist in the national drama of independence in which Jawaharlal Nehru and Mohandas Karamchand Gandhi are imaged as the benevolent protagonists struggling for a secular and undivided India. But not as many recognize how the insecurities created by the Indian National Congress's (INC) susceptibility to Hindu majoritarianism, the dominance of Hindu symbols and imagery in nationalist narratives, and, eventually, Nehru's refusal to accept a federation that would grant some autonomy to Muslim majority regions in an independent India, led Jinnah to embrace the two-nation theory that became the rallying cry of the Pakistan movement. It is these circumstances that led Jinnah, the person Sarojini

Naidu once called "the ambassador of Hindu-Muslim unity," to declare in 1944, "We are a nation of a hundred million, and what is more, we are a nation with our own distinctive culture, civilization, language and literature. . . . We have our own distinctive outlook on life and of life. By all canons of international law we are a nation" (Toor 2011, 9). Figures like Maulana Maududi, founder of the Jamaat-e-Islami and an influential voice in Islamic political philosophy, moved away from the INC because he believed its nationalism privileged Hindus at the expense of Muslims and their culture (Irfan Ahmad 2017b, 95). As Irfan Ahmad argues, Maududi "was driven to theodemocracy" because he was confronted by another "theodemocracy"—namely, "the majoritarian, assimilationist democracy of the Congress," which Maududi feared would not only dominate minorities but erase their particularity (96, 97).

Even Muslims who were leading figures in the Indian National Congress have been marginalized in nationalist histories produced in postcolonial India. While the contributions of Gandhi and Nehru are celebrated, less acknowledged are the contributions of Maulana Abul Kalam Azad, who said, "Our shared life of a thousand years has forged a common nationality. . . . Whether we like it or not, we have now become a nation, united and indivisible" (Noorani 2003, 32–33, cited in Irfan Ahmad 2009, 20). Maulana Azad, along with religious leaders from the Jamiatul Ulema-e-Hind, used Islam to make a case for Hindu-Muslim unity (Irfan Ahmad 2017b, 15; 2009, 19–20). While many I knew in Old Delhi were well aware of these figures, and in fact Iqbal Sahib was busy conducting research to write an article in Urdu about Muhammad Iqbal when I visited him in 2016, these key players in India's colonial history rarely figure in textbooks on Indian history. Indeed, Aamir Sahib's assertion that the contributions of Indian Muslims have been left out of the curriculum of Indian schools illuminates the biases implicit in the nationalist rendering of India's past.

What Aamir Sahib and the others mentioned here reveal are the intersecting issues that create differential citizenship and thereby contribute to Muslim insecurity in contemporary India. Lack of access to education, housing discrimination, employment discrimination, lack of government jobs and political connections, employment in the precarious and poorly paid informal sector, suspicion and stereotypes, communal violence against Muslims, and the systematic erasure of Muslim contributions to Indian culture and politics have intersected to intensify feelings of marginalization and insecurity among those I worked with.

In this context, Old Delhi has become a refuge to many, and it is increasingly produced as a Muslim place in everyday life. It is a Muslim place in the sense that the crumbling edifices of Mughal architecture are a constant reminder of a bygone era when Delhi was the seat of Mughal India—of Mughal culture, politics, speech, architectural style, food, and patterns of interreligious engagement.

It is a Muslim place in the sense that while religiously diverse, it is home to a significant Muslim population, concentrated in particular neighborhoods in the Old City.[5] It is a Muslim place in the sense that it is produced as a Muslim locality in the everyday actions of individuals, such as Zafar's cousin, who writes a new hadith on the blackboard at the entrance to his street after *fajr namaz* (morning prayer) every day (see figure 1.2). And it is a Muslim place in the sense that the sounds (the *azaan* five times a day or the daily siren signaling the end of the fast during Ramzan), the sights (men and women in clothing that signals religious identity, or goats, and the occasional sheep, tied to shops and street edges chomping on leaves and being fattened for Eid sacrifice), and the smells (*nehari* and *korma* bubbling in large pots, or *naan* and *bakharwadi* being freshly baked in underground ovens) of everyday life are the modalities through which Muslims make Old Delhi a Muslim place (see figure 1.3).[6]

Calling the *azaan*, cooking and baking, donning a burqa to walk through crowded streets and marketplaces, and writing hadiths on public blackboards are not just ends in themselves, but as routine, visible, everyday practices of Muslim life, they can also be understood as forms of place making.[7] They are an integral part of what Arjun Appadurai calls the "relational and contextual" dimensions of locality (1996, 178). Appadurai understands locality as "a property

FIGURE 1.2. Hadith board. Photograph by the author.

FIGURE 1.3. Sheep with henna before Bakra Eid. Photograph by the author.

of social life" (182), one that is "emergent from the practices of local subjects in specific neighborhoods" and inextricably linked to the pressures of the nation-state and global flows (198). Locality is inherently "fragile" because its existence depends on human actions that, inevitably, must contend with and respond to local, national, and global forces (179, 185). As Muslims are increasingly marginalized in the national imaginary, and as an exclusionary politics seeks to make India a Hindu nation, everyday practices of Muslim life, variegated narratives of identity and belonging, and articulations of forgotten histories that index not just a Muslim past but one that is deeply embedded in the cultural commons (Visweswaran 2010, 8) can all be seen as practices through which Muslims make place for themselves in contemporary India. Indeed, drawing on Raymond Williams, Jean Comaroff and John Comaroff remind us that "hegemony is never total" and can always be challenged because it is "intrinsically unstable, always vulnerable" (1991, 25, 27; also see Williams 1977). Constructions of Old Delhi as a Muslim place, however tentative and partial that place might be, certainly rupture and potentially weaken the hegemonic constructions of India as Hindu. And it is precisely for this reason that there have been such concerted efforts on the part of the state and others in postcolonial India to erase all reminders of India as a place for Muslims (Taneja 2018, 60, 170).

According to Tariq Sahib, since 1947 when India gained independence, deepening insecurity has led to more ritualism and public displays of identity in Muslim communities. Growing up in Old Delhi, he remembers people attending Eid prayers, and perhaps, "if they had nothing else to do" on Fridays, *Juma* prayers.[8] Now, he said, there is an increasing emphasis on *namaz* (daily prayer), religious processions, and projecting particular kinds of identity that are more global. These, said Tariq Sahib, "are all signs of being beleaguered. It comes from a desire to belong." As Tariq Sahib makes clear, such displays of religious identity are not simply an effect of culture and religion but are inextricably linked to the anxieties and politics of the contemporary world.[9] Some might disagree with Tariq Sahib's views here. That said, the perception that there has been an increasing assertion of religious identity, whether real or imagined, has indeed driven some Muslims away from Old Delhi (and Jamia Nagar) to places where they do not feel the weight of community expectations. Yet for others, as Tariq Sahib's words suggest, it is through ritualism and public displays of identity that locality is produced a la Appadurai (1996), and Old Delhi becomes a place where one can safely be Muslim in contemporary India. It was a place where women like Ameena Baji could wear a burqa without being deemed suspicious, or stereotyped as "illiterate" or "backward." Indeed, religious acts are one way to produce Old Delhi as a Muslim place, to assert belonging in the face of exclusion and differential experiences of citizenship (Maira 2009, 82), and to imagine an alternative "moral geography" (Grewal 2014, 6) where Muslims unquestionably have a place in contemporary India.

Importantly, such place making was not framed in exclusionary terms by Old Delhi's Muslims. When speaking of the discrimination they faced, most I spoke to were quick to add that not all Hindus discriminated against Muslims. For instance, Raza Sahib, who often reminisced about growing up in Old Delhi at a time when friendships crossed religious boundaries, insisted that most Hindus he knew were not divisive or communal. He asserted that there are people of all religions who are divisive, and equally people of all religions who are not communal and who see each other as human beings first rather than as people belonging to particular religious traditions. Such people do not get caught up in this kind of politics, he said. However, clearly, those who do so make Muslims insecure. Rising religious tensions and violence, increasing Islamophobia and suspicion of Muslims, experiences of exclusion, systemic violence, differential citizenship, and, as I discuss below, the deep entrenchment and enactment of discourses of security have led many Muslims to seek shelter in Old Delhi in recent years, especially in neighborhoods with a large Muslim presence. They increasingly imagine such places as refuges, move there or refuse to leave, and construct them as Muslim places through everyday practices and narratives. At the same time, as I will suggest, in the context of an exclusionary nationalism that produces boundaries which construct Muslims as the "other," such actions and narratives also facilitate the containment of Muslims in place, and enable surveillance and control by the security state.

Terror in the Security State

Nobody actually wants to live in Old Delhi, according to Tariq Sahib. They only live there, he said, because they feel safer in Old Delhi than the rest of the city. Many Old Delhi Muslims who consider Old Delhi home and cannot countenance living anywhere else would disagree with Tariq Sahib. Nevertheless, his statement would certainly resonate with many I worked with. Why do so many Muslims feel safer in Old Delhi? Below I examine some of the ways in which Old Delhi is imagined as a safe place, sometimes as a refuge from the crime associated with the rest of the city, and at other times as a sanctuary from the discourses and practices of securitization that target Muslims and ensure that they experience security, and indeed citizenship, differently in everyday life.

Many of my interlocutors claimed that there was relatively little crime in Old Delhi compared to the rest of the National Capital Region. Some noted instances of petty theft (pilfering of gas cylinders or metal parts, pickpocketing), attributing this to the increasing numbers of drug addicts in the walled city, but they claimed that larger crimes were not common. Indeed, most of those I visited did not lock their front doors during the day. While some left their doors ajar, many simply hung a curtain across so that women practicing *purdah* (veiling) inside would be hidden from public gaze. This was in stark contrast to parts of New Delhi where front doors (including my own) were generally fitted with multiple locks and dead bolts. In the months after the violent rape and murder of a young female college student in New Delhi on December 16, 2012—the "Nirbhaya" case—many concerned women insisted that I call or text them when I got back to my apartment in New Delhi after fieldwork every night. Like Rehana, many women asserted that such crimes are rare in Old Delhi. While these claims do not mean that there is no sexual assault and violence in Old Delhi, they suggest that these incidents are rarely attributed to strangers walking into homes and engaging in violent acts.

I learned very quickly that people generally know the comings and goings of their neighbors in Old Delhi. Children running in and out of homes belonging to friends and relatives, and shopkeepers chatting with customers, often exchanged details about who was visiting whom. This of course included the latest updates on the visiting anthropologist too! Such security, however, does come at a price. Many women, like Rehana, complained about the lack of privacy in Old Delhi. One changed her burqa multiple times so that shopkeepers and young men hanging out on the streets in deference to *purdah* requirements would not be able to keep tabs (and pass judgment) on how often she left home.[10] These irritants aside, women remarked on how safe they felt, noting that if any stranger entered their home, those outside would keep a watchful eye and enter at the slightest sign of trouble.

However, a perceived lack of major crime is not the only reason why Muslims feel relatively safe in Old Delhi. Many expressed their fears of being Muslim in a country where heightened security concerns have resulted in increased surveillance of Muslims; unwarranted detentions, torture, and arrests; and the extrajudicial killings of Muslim youth in apparent "encounters" with the police. The justification for such acts comes from a notion of security that is globally prevalent, in which "the security of one or some is bought at the expense of the security of others" (Yeatman 2010, 14). This understanding of security protects particular interests at the expense of those who are considered at best unworthy of such protection, or at worst as threats to these interests.

In this polarizing discourse, those deemed suspicious have a very different experience of security and of the security state, as scholars working on these issues in the United States after 9/11 have shown (Cainkar 2009; Maira 2009). The specter of the enemy who secretly lurks among "us," who, according to the former United States attorney general John Ashcroft, "live in our communities—plotting, planning, and wanting to kill," has been used to legitimize the curtailments of many rights and freedoms in the name of security (cited in Cainkar 2009, 110). Sunaina Maira views the security measures in the United States taken against South Asian Muslim Americans after 9/11 as "dramatic enactments of exclusion from cultural citizenship . . . despite legal citizenship" (Maira 2009, 82). In fact, different experiences of security provide a good way to track how citizenship is mediated by axes of difference whether of religion, race, class, gender, or ethnicity (Maira 2009; Ong 1999).

For Indian Muslims, feelings of insecurity engendered by the security state index their exclusion, their contested access to cultural citizenship in a nation that increasingly casts Hindus as the normative subject, and their growing erasure from the national imaginary. This nationalist imaginary is premised upon the rejection of a cultural landscape in which Hindus and Muslims are inextricably intertwined, and it recasts Muslims as dangerous subjects—as "terrorists" and as "*jhagadaalu*," in Rehana's words. The deep historical interconnections between Hindus and Muslims, and the obvious presence of Muslims who defy these categorizations, generate uncertainty, highlight "the impossibility of identity" (Hansen 2001, 7–8), and reveal the tenuousness of this nationalist imaginary (see Willford 2018; Appadurai 2006; Hansen 2001; Hansen 1999). While these uncertainties can enable the extreme violence that we see in India today

(Appadurai 2006; Hansen 2001), it can also enable alternative forms of identification that contest these exclusionary imaginings (Willford 2018, 161).

Arguably, such security measures do not make the world a safer place, especially since they are based on the profiling of entire communities as security threats. Indeed, they are better understood as providing the means to increase the reach of the state not just in the public arena but also into the intimate spaces of everyday life. For instance, in his work on South Asian Muslim immigrants in post-9/11 America, Junaid Rana asserts that the logic of "panic" and "peril" enables greater and more effective state regulation and control (2011, 54). Nicholas de Genova argues, "The 'terrorist' menace is the state's . . . most perfect and ideal enemy, whose banal anonymity and phantasmagorical ubiquity prefigure and summon forth the irradiation of the everyday by the security state as our savior and redeemer" (2011, 144). The "spectacle of terror is inseparable from a spectacle of security," according to de Genova, precisely because the security state thrives on feelings of insecurity:

> The spectacle of security, conjured by all the ideological apparatuses and governmental techniques of the antiterrorist security state, must produce—above all else—the state's most precious and necessary political resource, and must advance what may likewise be its most politically valuable end; namely, heightened *insecurity*. Thus, unprecedented securitization and the more general militarization of everyday life on an ever more expansive scale and intensity conjures the permanent spectacle of its own purported insufficiency, preemptively supplying the justificatory rationale for still more state power. (2011, 144)

In India, daily reports of "encounters" with militants, detentions and arrests with or without convictions, and potential violence ensure heightened insecurity that must apparently be rectified by increasing the insecurity of some for the hypothetical security of privileged others (see Yeatman 2010). Many Muslims in contemporary India are conscious of their increasing insecurity in an India that prioritizes the security of Hindus over Muslims. In this context, Old Delhi is understood to be a safer place, a place where Muslims are less likely to be terrorized by the security apparatus of the Indian state.

The imaging of Muslims as threats to the state is not new in India. Indeed, as Aamir Sahib alluded to earlier, Indian Muslims who chose to remain in India at partition have had to negotiate suspicion, exclusion, and violence since 1947. After independence, Nehru insisted on a secular state, precisely to counter the majoritarian tendencies of India's political leadership and their suspicion of Muslim loyalty (see Irfan Ahmad 2009, 17–18). Nehru argued that only a secular state would ensure minority rights and inclusion in this context (18). In the decades since independence, the Hindu right, particularly the Sangh Parivar, has actively worked to keep anti-Muslim sentiments alive, using the specter of Muslim disloyalty to mobilize support to make India Hindu (see K. Menon 2010; Jaffrelot 1999, 2007; Hansen 1999). Blurring the lines between "Muslim" and "Pakistani," the Sangh Parivar has not only configured Muslim subjectivity as outside the nation but has also, drawing on its constructions of Pakistan as an "enemy state," cast all Muslims as potential threats to India. Disseminated at political, religious, and cultural events, and taught at *shakhas* for children, youth, and adults all over India (K. Menon 2010; Bacchetta 2004; Bhatt 2001; Hansen 1999; Jaffrelot 1999; Basu 1995), such discourses have become entrenched in India, have shaped the views of many far beyond the Sangh Parivar's membership, and have become part of the lived reality that Indian Muslims must negotiate in their everyday lives.

That this blurring of boundaries and questioning of national allegiance is not limited to Hindu right organizations but has influenced people belonging to the "secular" institutions of the Indian state became abundantly clear in an interview with Rafiq Sahib in which he discussed his aspirations to become a fighter pilot for the Indian Air Force. Rafiq Sahib told me that as a young college student in the mid-seventies, he and two Muslim friends from Old Delhi participated in the National Cadet Corps Air Wing Program in New Delhi. The National Cadet Corps is a voluntary organization associated with the Indian military that recruits school and college students to give them basic military training and create a potential reserve.[11] After completing three years of training, Rafiq Sahib and his friends went for an interview to enroll in the corps' gliding program, saying that they wanted to become fighter pilots. The *fauji* (soldier) doing the initial screenings told them, "You can see the Pakistani Embassy from here. Why have you come here?" Rafiq Sahib said, "They broke our resolve right there."

For Rafiq Sahib and others, Muslim insecurity in contemporary India is linked to a long history of suspicion, systematic discrimination, and violence against Muslims. It is the result of a "loss of place" arising from "a shift in economic, social, and political security while remaining in place" (Feldman, Menon, and Geisler 2011, 11). Most agreed that this insecurity was deepening in contemporary India, where profiling, targeting, and detention of young Muslims at the hands of the security apparatus of the Indian state has become increasingly frequent. Speaking of the daily terrors that Muslims face as a result of their religious identity, Rafiq Sahib said,

> Catch one, then unnecessarily use the label of terrorist to detain them. Now every man is scared to send his children anywhere. They will be caught. . . . The fear settles inside them. . . . If you catch a Muslim in a place where something has happened—a blast has happened, something

> has happened—if the name is Muslim, then the police have solved their problem. They have caught him. Enough. Whether he was or not, he has been caught. Enough. Then he gets let off in the court.

I interjected, "Sometimes after ten years." Rafiq Sahib continued:

> Yes, sometimes after twenty years. Their life has been destroyed—theirs and their family's. There are many cases like this. They are all being acquitted now. Has anyone been convicted? Only Ajmal Kasab was hung for this. He was convicted. Another is Afzal Guru. Who knows what is happening with him? The case is ongoing. But so many have been caught. Terrorist? Who is a terrorist? One who is caught? . . . Those who are in an encounter? They have been called terrorists and killed.[12]

The fears that Rafiq Sahib expressed here are deep and came up repeatedly in our conversations. In one of our earliest conversations, he told me that he lives in fear of what will happen to his sons. When either of his sons is required to travel outside Old Delhi for work, he is scared to let them go and tries to stop them unless it is absolutely necessary. He is concerned that they will be arrested on trumped-up charges, be labeled terrorists by the police simply because they are Muslim. Rafiq Sahib wants his sons to work for him in the family business in Old Delhi rather than seek employment elsewhere and risk their safety. He said, "They are safe here. They are not safe anywhere else." Several months later, he echoed those fears again in an animated conversation about the insecurities of being Muslim in contemporary India with three young men, all educated professionals, who were born and raised in Old Delhi—Aslam, Mustafa, and Atiq. The insecurity they expressed powerfully illuminates how different national subjects experience security differently and how citizenship is mediated by difference, in this case religious difference.

Aslam, who works for All India Radio, said that when he worked on the 2011 census in Old Delhi, people kept telling him they felt safe in the "walled city." Responding to Aslam, Mustafa asserted that while it was true that Muslims felt safe in Old Delhi, staying there was detrimental to them. This comment provoked a strong reaction from Aslam and Rafiq Sahib:

> RAFIQ SAHIB: There are real reasons why people are fearful. They are worried that they will be accused of being terrorists.
>
> ASLAM: Unity is a big issue. People do not want to live in places where there are only a few Muslims and they live isolated lives—in flats. Here everyone lives together. Everyone knows what is going on with others on the street. Nobody is isolated. As minorities, people want to live together.

Aslam said that if people have to leave Old Delhi, they move to areas with many Muslims, such as Seelampur and Lakshmi Nagar. Then, he added, Hindus in those areas move out because they are suspicious of Muslims. Aslam said that earlier he would say "*Salam*" to everyone, and Hindus might respond with a "*Ram Ram.*" But today they just stare at him because "people are suspicious." Rafiq Sahib added, "Look at what happened to Ishrat Jahan. They killed her in an encounter after accusing her of being a terrorist. People are concerned that if they leave the walled city they will be caught and killed like her and any number of other Muslims." Ishrat Jahan, a nineteen-year-old college student from Mumbai, was killed with her three male companions in an apparent "encounter" with the Gujarat police on June 15, 2004. The police claimed that Ishrat and her companions were members of the militant group Lashkar-e-Taiba and were attempting to assassinate Narendra Modi, then chief minister of Gujarat.[13] According to the Central Bureau of Investigation (CBI), the "encounter" was fake, since the four had already been in police custody.[14] Aslam continued:

> It is one thing if these people who were caught were terrorists. The problem is when three years after they have been detained the person turns out to be nothing but a *chaiwala* (tea seller). This is what happened in Batla House, no? The other problem is the media. When someone is caught, then it is all over the papers and the TV. But when he is let go, then no one reports it. This presents a skewed picture that increases suspicion and fear. Non-Muslims only hear of Muslims being detained for terrorism, not when they are released for not being terrorists. This is the big reason why people want to live in Old Delhi. If you are staying in some flat in New Delhi and the police come and take you away, no one knows you and no one will come to your defense. Here, if the police come and pick me up, a thousand people will show up at the police station tomorrow and confirm that I am not a terrorist, that they have known me since the day I was born. The catchers [*pakadnewale*] also know this—that there is unity here. So they do not hassle us the way they hassle people in other parts of Delhi.[15]

The concerns expressed by Rafiq Sahib and Aslam cannot simply be dismissed as paranoia. The percentage of Muslims in prison awaiting trial exceeds the percentage of Muslims convicted of crimes, and illustrates the suspicion with which Muslims are viewed in Hindu-majoritarian India (Jaffrelot 2019, 45). The fear of extrajudicial killings among those I worked with was also not unfounded. The CBI probe into the extrajudicial killing of Ishrat Jahan and her companions in the 2004 fake encounter was ongoing at the time of this conversation, and a reminder that several young Muslims had been killed in fake encounters with the police. Indeed, more recently, Rana Ayyub's disturbing expose of the cover up, *Gujarat Files: Anatomy of a Cover Up* (2016)—self-published because no publisher was willing to take the risk of publishing it—shows that such fears are well grounded.

Especially between 2012 and 2013, extrajudicial killings consistently crept into everyday conversations with Muslims in Old Delhi, signaling the anxieties that inflected daily life for those I worked with. For several months preceding this conversation, the subject of young Muslim men who spent years in jail on trumped-up charges only to be cleared of all charges and released had been headline news thanks to a report released by the Jamia Teachers Solidarity Association (JTSA) on the fourth anniversary of the Batla House encounter in September 2012. The report discussed sixteen cases in which Muslim men had been arrested on terrorism charges, only to be cleared of all charges and acquitted several years later (JTSA 2012). Maqbool Shah, a Kashmiri man arrested in connection with a blast in Lajpat Nagar in New Delhi who spent fourteen years in jail until he was acquitted of all charges in April 2010, attended the launch of the report.[16] Muhammad Amir, whose case is discussed in some detail in the JTSA report, also attended the event. Amir was acquitted of all charges in the seventeen cases filed against him. In one instance, the court notes, "the evidence on record reveals that there is absolutely no incriminating evidence against the accused" and that the "complainant and the injured persons have not stated anything against him" or even "identified the accused" (JTSA 2012, 41). In another case, charges were filed against an individual who was a police informer, who claimed in a letter to the prime minister published in the JTSA report to have been set up by the police (179–85). In many of these instances, the report shows how the media did not question police versions of events (2012, 118–19).

To be clear, those I worked with never claimed that individuals responsible for violent attacks should go unpunished. In fact, although the case against Afzal Guru was highly contested, a few days after the news broke that he had been hung for his alleged role in the 2001 attack on the Indian Parliament, Zehra Baji told me as we sat in her one-room home in Old Delhi, "Anyone who plots against Hindustan should be hung. Look at what he did. He attacked the parliament. This is a very bad act. He deserved to be hung."[17] Many in Old Delhi and beyond may have challenged Zehra Baji's interpretation of events and her pronouncement of Guru's guilt, especially given the shaky evidence against him. Importantly, apart from Zehra Baji, most Old Delhi Muslims avoided being drawn into a discussion with me about Guru's case. Such reluctance is a sign of insecurity, particularly given the speed with which individuals who speak out on such issues are slapped with sedition charges on flimsy grounds in India today. The cases against Umar Khalid, Kanhaiya Kumar, and others who spoke at the anniversary of Afzal Guru's hanging in 2016 are a case in point.[18] More recently, the detention of students, activists, and scholars in 2020 who voiced their opposition to the discriminatory Citizenship Amendment Act of 2019—which creates a path to citizenship for people from Afghanistan, Pakistan, and Bangladesh as long as they are not Muslim—illustrates the swift reprisals for those who challenge India's increasingly authoritarian state. However, while Zehra Baji's statement is not representative of the views of Old Delhi Muslims, her insistence that those who act against the Indian state must be punished is an important reminder that Muslim insecurity in contemporary India is not about protecting the guilty but rather about being mistaken for criminals simply because they happen to be Muslim. The fear expressed was about *innocent* Muslims being picked up, detained, or tortured by the police, of the anti-Muslim sentiments that made Muslims suspicious in the eyes of both state and nonstate actors, of "encounters" where innocent people might be killed with no possibility of a defense, and of the disrepute that accompanies such charges, however false they may be. As Iftikar Sahib, an elderly advocate from a well-known Old Delhi family, said, the majority of Muslims "caught under the garb of being terrorists . . . are being released. . . . But *badnami* [dishonor] has happened."

Such insecurities have led many Muslims to see Old Delhi as a refuge. For many like Rafiq Sahib and Aslam, Old Delhi is clearly a place where they can safely be Muslim in contemporary India. In their narratives, those I worked with were clearly making place for Muslims in the fraught landscapes of contemporary India against the tide of both a resurgent right and nationalist hegemonies that engender insecurity and differential citizenship. Nevertheless, in some sense, Mustafa is not wrong when he says that while Muslims may feel safer in Old Delhi and make place for themselves in its by-lanes and *mohallas* (neighborhoods), living there might be detrimental to them. Living in Old Delhi means living in overcrowded and often unsanitary conditions, in crumbling buildings with poor wiring, on streets where fire engines and ambulances cannot pass. It means working in makeshift factories with little to no safety requirements, uncertain wages, and no job security. For many, it means sleeping on street corners and cycle rickshaws even when temperatures are perilously high or low, and sharing space with drug addicts huddled on street corners chasing a high. And it means living in a zone that can be closed off from the rest of the city at the slightest sign of trouble.

Arjun Appadurai (1996, 189) argues that while in many cases the nation-state might view locality as a threat to the national community it is trying to fabricate, in some instances it might also encourage the creation of places for better surveillance and control. This is powerfully evident when one encounters the tall metal gates across narrow alleys in Old Delhi that may be closed by police order—supposedly to protect its residents, but in effect also containing them and regulating their movements. The hostility that Muslims face in other parts of the city, the security they feel in Old Delhi, the gates that symbolize boundaries, distinction, and a potential for containment—all operationalize ideas of where Muslims belong and where they do not. As Muslims construct Old Delhi as a Muslim place through everyday practice, they also reinforce a national cartography that marginalizes Muslims on the national landscape and "secures" them in particular places.

Ultimately, as Muslims seek shelter in Old Delhi, they also inadvertently acquiesce to a particular form of government, what Michel Foucault describes as "the way in which the conduct of individuals or of groups might be directed" (Foucault 1982, 790), the conduct of conduct (789). Such government enables the reproduction of particular hierarchies of privilege, spatial dynamics, patterns of residence, and relations of inequality, and it facilitates particular forms of surveillance, regulation, and control through the everyday acts described here. However, Mustafa's cautionary words and Tariq Sahib's struggle to live in New Delhi are important reminders that there are other ways of place making that might disrupt the logics of nation and belonging, and security and securitization. And indeed, as I argue in this book, through religious practices and narratives that defy exclusionary visions of nation and community, historical accounts that blur such boundaries, and constructions of identity and accounts of friendship that privilege alternative understandings of self and belonging, Old Delhi's Muslims build cultural commons within Old Delhi, disrupting existing hegemonies that operationalize hierarchies of self and "other" and position Hindus as the normative national subject.

Conclusion

I still remember how wounded I felt when I learned through the grapevine that one of my interlocutors had expressed concerns to others in Old Delhi that I might be a "U.S. agent." I had expected people to be suspicious of me given my Hindu name. What I had not anticipated was being associated with the very global security apparatus whose Indian incarnation I have discussed, and critiqued, here. Upon further reflection, and some self-indulgent wound licking, it dawned on me that my bruised ego was a manifestation of my own privilege. As an educated, upper-middle-class, urban Indian with a Hindu surname residing in the United States, I experienced the security state differently in my life, especially in India. Why should I have expected Muslims in Old Delhi, subject as they are to all kinds of national and global surveillance, undercover operations, and other forms of policing, not to be suspicious of my motives? What might have struck me as an unwarranted suspicion may not have seemed strange to a Muslim from Old Delhi whose subject position marks him or her as a target of the security state. In India at least, my Hindu name gives me a privileged position—I am a person whose security is to be protected, the normative subject with full cultural citizenship who is understood to have "the right to self-preservation," often at the expense of "others" (Yeatman 2010, 10). Indeed, there are many kinds of privilege that anthropologists have to come to terms with while conducting fieldwork, and this was an important lesson to me about the gulf that separated me from Old Delhi's Muslims. The need to be ever vigilant, suspicious, and concerned about the motives of others is an expression of insecurity. The encompassing nature of the security apparatus ensures that this is the case. Never knowing who might be part of this apparatus, watching you and reporting to others, is an integral part of this insecurity, driving some to limit their movements to Old Delhi, others to reduce their interactions with outsiders, non-Muslims, and strangers, and a few to question the motives of those privileged enough to insert themselves into their lives, into their place.

For those I worked with, Old Delhi was a place where they were not only relatively safe from the prying eye and violent reach of the security state, but also where they were less burdened by the stereotypes about Islam and Muslims that they had to negotiate in other parts of the city. Especially in the Muslim *mohallas* they reside in, they are protected from the kind of everyday provocations that Rehana described when discussing her interactions with non-Muslim customers in the New Delhi shop where she is employed. In her neighborhood, Rehana has no need to explain that Islam does not sanction violence and that not all Muslims are terrorists, or to declare her national allegiance. In fact, in her neighborhood she is not reduced to her Muslim identity at all, and she can articulate all kinds of desires, concerns, and frustrations as a woman, as an employee, or as a resident of a neighborhood that sometimes gets on her nerves. Elsewhere, many feel reduced to their Muslim identity and attempt to overcome this by relinquishing obvious markers of religious identity, such as names, clothing, or expressions of piety. This is an eloquent reminder that while people might embody plural identities, they still have to struggle against the force of culturalisms that circumscribe their lives and worlds.

By removing her burqa in the metro, Ameena Baji sought to claim a position where she was not reduced to majoritarian constructions of Muslim subjectivity. The burqa is an obvious and visible marker of religious identity that clearly made her feel insecure outside Old Delhi. The New Delhi doctor would probably have guessed her religious identity from the name on her patient information form. However, Ameena Baji's anxiety about her meeting with the doctor is that the name in conjunction with the burqa might mark her as a stereotype—

one that operationalizes problematic assumptions about gender and character associated with her subject position. Her act of removing her burqa reveals her anxiety regarding the stereotypes about Muslim women and her attempt to disrupt or challenge their effect on her life. For her, Old Delhi is a place where she can be Muslim—one who is in fact more comfortable in a burqa for reasons of piety, privacy, and cultural politics. In New Delhi, she feels compelled to eschew her personal preferences to pass, to have a place, to have the same privileges of citizenship that Hindus and others command, to have security, and to belong. By donning her burqa on her return, she enacts a spatial logic that constructs Muslims as out of place in New Delhi and, at the same time, marks Old Delhi as a Muslim place.

While her acts are prompted by her insecurity about being Muslim in a nation increasingly dominated by the Hindu right, they also reiterate a particular understanding of Muslim subjectivity and Muslim belonging in India that reinforces existing hierarchies, logics of containment, religious privileges, and understandings of nation. If power works most effectively through the "conduct of conduct," Ameena Baji's acts reveal how existing hegemonies have infiltrated the most intimate realms of her being. Her acts, the movement of Tariq Sahib's relatives back to Old Delhi, the narratives of Rafiq Sahib, Aslam, and others about the relative safety they experience in Old Delhi, and the sights, sounds, and smells of Muslim life and religious practice encountered as one walks down the narrow streets of the walled city, are all part of the production of Old Delhi as a Muslim locality in the face of anti-Muslim sentiment and exclusionary nationalism. This production of locality is, of course, not unique to Old Delhi but, as I have noted, can also be seen in other areas where Muslims feel secure. However, as Muslims move to places like Old Delhi in search of security, they reduce the visibility and presence of Muslims elsewhere. Even as their acts contest their erasure from the national imaginary, and their narratives and practices articulate alternative visions of community and belonging in which Hindus and Muslims are inextricably intertwined, they can simultaneously enable their containment in place, on the very margins of the national landscape. And yet margins do not always remain so. This was clearly manifest in the hundred-day protest against the Citizenship Amendment Act of 2019 lead by Muslim women at Shaheen Bagh in South Delhi, and at "Shaheen Baghs" all over the National Capital Region and across the nation. Joined by thousands of people of all religions, castes, classes, genders, and sexualities, these stunning enactments of citizenship made Shaheen Bagh the epicenter of resistance to an increasingly authoritarian state, illuminated an alternative polity that can still be mobilized despite violent erasures and silencing, and reflected the pluralism that still lingers amid Hindu majoritarianism.

2

GENDER AND PRECARITY

Saadia Baji lives in a lovely old haveli off Kucha Pandit. I walked through the entrance, across which a curtain was drawn in deference to *purdah* requirements, and stepped into a large courtyard. Rooms with tall doors and beautiful transom windows embellished with colored glass led off the courtyard. In need of repair, the house hinted at a past in which it had been home to wealthy denizens. One of these rooms was the home that Saadia Baji shared with her husband and four children and in which she had created a small space to sell bangles. Saadia Baji's "shop" was on a mezzanine high above the living area, where boxes of bangles had been arranged on shelves running along the walls. Referred to as the *churiwali*, or bangle seller, by her neighbors, Saadia Baji did not come from a family of bangle sellers. Although she has lived in Old Delhi since she moved there from Okhla when she got married in the late eighties, Saadia Baji only became a bangle seller after her husband became too sick to work in the early 2000s. They needed the money, she told me, and so she started to do this work.

One cold February day as I sat with her in her tiny shop surrounded by shelves of bangles and plastic bags with garments in them, I got a glimpse of how Saadia Baji makes her living. It was wedding season, and she was very busy. As she told me about her work, she pulled garments out of plastic bags and made up sets of bangles that matched the colors in them. For a black chiffon *dupatta* with bright pink flowers embroidered on it she had combined black, pink, and silver bangles—some glass, some metal, and some plastic embellished with paste ornamentation, which she called "fancy." Several women dropped by, either dropping off or describing outfits they had chosen for particular events for her to match, or picking up the sets she had made for them, changing things around if they did not like particular combinations. While some paid her as they left, others told her they would send the money later, or pay in installments. Saadia Baji was clearly more than a bangle seller. She designed sets to go with particular outfits, thus saving women whom she knew were too busy to scour the market for their own needs and desires both the bother of going to the market and the uncertainty of finding the right set of bangles to match their garments. A female entrepreneur who used her knowledge of Old Delhi to support her family, she knew where to buy goods at low prices and, wary of revealing her sources or markup, dealt with the wholesalers herself. She used this knowledge, her own understanding of local consumption habits, and her expertise in design to make life a little less insecure for herself and her family.

Saadia Baji was one of many women I met in Old Delhi who labored to help their families make ends meet. Many were schoolteachers, some lucky enough to work in relatively well-paying government schools, while others, who lacked the required certification, worked in private schools for much less money. Several women worked as tutors, opening up their homes to schoolchildren who needed help with their daily homework. But many women, especially those from less-privileged backgrounds, lacked the education, proficiency, or space necessary for such work. These women often engaged in different forms of home-based labor that connected them to intricate local and global commodity chains, receiving low wages in a system designed to reap profits elsewhere (see figure 2.1). Some engaged in dangerous and insecure work, trying to make ends meet in a country where unemployment reached a forty-five-year high in 2019. Indeed, life for many in Old Delhi is economically insecure, even as Indian businessmen continue to claim their position among the world's richest year after year.

Judith Butler argues that precariousness is a condition of all life, because "there is no life without the need for shelter and food, no life without dependency on wider networks of sociality and labor, no life that transcends injurability and mortality" (2009, 24–25). She distinguishes this from precarity, which she defines as a "politically induced condition" that is not distributed equally, and in which "certain populations suffer from failing social and economic networks of support and become differentially exposed to injury, violence, and death" (25). In India today, precarity affects many populations—from small farmers unable to live because of drought, debt, and probusiness government policies, to Adivasis (indigenous groups) struggling against a state that covets their lands for resource extraction, to Dalits and Muslims experiencing the violence of the Hindu right. All of these groups contend with structural violence in their everyday lives, enabled by a system that benefits some and both tolerates and normalizes the suffering of others (Gupta 2012, 21). Here I examine how

FIGURE 2.1. A woman doing home-based work while teaching the Quran. Photograph by the author.

diverse groups of economically underprivileged Muslims in Old Delhi negotiate precarity in contemporary India. While both men and women have to negotiate precarity, I focus on the everyday labor of Muslim women from such families as they struggle to make ends meet and support their families in neoliberal India.

According to Butler, precarity is inextricably linked to how particular populations are perceived, to "representational regimes" or "frames" that have tangible material effects (2009, 29). That Indian Muslims are the most politically and socioeconomically marginalized group in the country, as the Sachar Committee Report (2006) noted, is directly connected to hegemonic understandings of India that render upper-caste Hindus as the normative national subject while relegating Muslims to the very fringes of the national imaginary. Pervasive Islamophobia, the suspicion with which Muslims are viewed by the state, and the violent chauvinism of the Hindu right have all ensured the continuing marginalization of Muslims in postcolonial India. These factors, as I have argued, have instigated many Muslim families to move to Muslim neighborhoods, where they feel more secure, but this has also compounded their precarity.[1] While I have already suggested that variegated religious landscapes can enable practices of differential citizenship, here I contend that in neoliberal India they also create the conditions for market forces to "differently regulate populations for optimal productivity . . . through spatial practices" (Ong 2006, 6; see also Jamil 2017).

Muslims in Old Delhi have been significantly impacted by what Gayatri Menon and Aparna Sundar identify as the "neoliberal context of jobless growth, increasingly unregulated and precarious forms of employment, and market-based forms of service provision" (2019, 2). Maidul Islam has argued that an overwhelming proportion of Indian Muslims work in the unregulated and insecure informal economy, are vulnerable because they lack the rights and benefits of organized labor, and are among the groups whose conditions have worsened with neoliberal reforms (2012, 64–65, 76; 2019).[2] This is certainly the case with Muslims in Old Delhi, and especially Muslim women. Muslim women in Old Delhi are among the 94 percent of Indian women who work in the informal economy, a statistic that reflects a trend seen in many parts of the world where women dominate the informal economy (Dunaway 2014, 1).[3] Preferring to reside in Muslim neighborhoods in Old Delhi where they feel more secure, and tied to their homes because of a gendered division of labor that affects women across religions and castes in India, many Muslim women engage in home-based work that is poorly remunerated. Precarity associated with their religion, gender, and class has drawn capital and commodity chains to Muslim women, as businesses exploit the cultural politics of religion, gender, and class in India to maximize profits (Ramamurthy 2004, 754).

As Muslims face increasing economic insecurity in neoliberal India, women's labor has become crucial to meeting the everyday needs of families. Defying gendered stereotypes that configure women, especially Muslim women, as housewives rather than breadwinners and as helpless victims of oppressive and deterministic cultural systems, the Muslim women I worked with labored to ensure the survival of their families and communities in the face of deepening economic insecurity.[4] Doing embroidery and handicraft work, making slippers and shoeboxes, cutting areca nuts imported to India, selling bangles and clothes to their neighbors, or working as beauticians, these women labored to pay school fees, buy food and medicine, and make sure their families stayed afloat in insecure times.

Even as increasing numbers of Muslim women have joined the informal economy, working long hours for little remuneration or engaging in work that endangers their health or status, for many, money remains tight. Moreover, their unpaid domestic and caregiving work, so essential for social reproduction, has also increased in neoliberal India, where social welfare spending has proved to be inadequate (Mondal et al. 2018; Naidu 2016). The challenging conditions of their lives often lead women to turn to other resources to take care of themselves and their families. Sometimes they lean on religious resources, petitioning God and engaging in various rituals to change their fortunes. At other times they draw on various sources of credit, some more risky than others. They use their creativity and skill, engaging in different forms of work and using the limited resources available to them to ensure that they can provision themselves despite economic uncertainty. Their productive and reproductive labor is not only central to negotiating economic insecurity in Old Delhi, but it also enables the wheels of the economy to keep turning even as everyday life becomes more difficult for so many in contemporary India.

Tales of Precarity

Women engage in many forms of labor to support their families in Old Delhi. Although I worked with Muslim men and women from different classes, *biradaris* (occupational groups), educational levels, and neighborhoods in Old Delhi, here I focus on the stories of Shia and Sunni women from underprivileged backgrounds, whose precarity was exploited by local and global businesses or by local entrepreneurs struggling for a foothold amid the changing conditions of neoliberal India. In all of these cases, women's labor had become crucial to their family's well-being. Some of these women joined the informal economy because they no longer had the support of their husband's income because of sickness or death. For other women, decreasing wages, employment discrimination against Muslims, and rising unemployment in neoliberal India had affected the economic circumstances of their fathers, husbands, sons, and brothers and necessitated their participation in the informal economy.

While women's remunerative labor in the informal economy has become essential for many Muslim families negotiating economic insecurity in contemporary Delhi, it is important to recognize that this is not the only work that women do. Women's unpaid domestic and caregiving responsibilities, which are common across religions and castes in India because of the gendered division of labor, are crucial for the reproduction of both the family and the labor force, as scholars studying gender and social reproduction have long argued (Dunaway 2014; Lamphere 1986; Beneria 1979). Women's reproductive labor has only increased under neoliberalism, as the state has increasingly withdrawn from social provisioning (Bakker 2007; Katz 2001). This is certainly the case in India, where women's unpaid work has increased because of what Sirisha Naidu calls the "crisis of reproduction" triggered by neoliberalism (Naidu 2016; see also Mondal et al. 2018).

While my focus in this chapter is on Muslim women's paid work in the informal economy, it is important to situate these activities amid this "crisis of reproduction." For some women with ailing family members, this has meant not just more caregiving but also traveling long distances to get free or subsidized medication and healthcare, or to purchase food grains for less at wholesale markets to stretch household income further. Other domestic responsibilities such as childcare, cooking, and cleaning have kept women tied to the home. In this context, women often prefer to engage in home-based paid work that can be fitted in between tasks, forgoing employment and educational opportunities that might improve their economic and social position but that require time and money they cannot spare. In this chapter I examine women's work in neoliberal India and the ways in which businesses exploit, reproduce, and constitute local hierarchies of gender and class, and indeed the marginality of particular places and communities, to maximize profits in contemporary India.

Zardozi Artisans

Saiba Baji is a zardozi artisan who resides in Shahganj along with other members of her extended family. Although she was born here, her paternal grandfather's (*dada*) family moved to Shahganj in 1947 to escape violence in Paharganj outside the walled city. They left Paharganj with what they could carry, as the homes where they had lived for centuries were taken over by refugees pouring in from Punjab. Like many women in her extended family, Saiba Baji has done zardozi since childhood. Zardozi is a form of intricate embroidery done with silver or gold thread, sometimes embellished with precious and semi-precious stones, and often used in wedding finery (see figure 2.2). Many have noted that zardozi flourished in Mughal India because of patronage from the Mughal court—especially during the reign of Emperor Akbar.[5] Gupta and Channa note that during the Mughal period, zardozi was done by male artisans, mostly Sunni, who worked in *karkhanas* (workshops) that were part of the imperial court and transmitted this highly skilled and high-status work to their sons (1996, 105–6, 109). Indeed, as the authors argue, the transmission of the skill from father to son made sense given the time and effort needed to teach and learn the craft. Many of the zardoz of Old Delhi moved to the city when the seat of Mughal power shifted from Agra to Delhi (106). In the British period, the demand for such work continued; however, the centers of production shifted to private *karkhanas*, some commercial and specializing in the production of large and heavily embroidered items, and some domestic and specializing in smaller pieces. This opened the door to women's involvement in zardozi within the context of household production (107–8).

Today, larger workshops are struggling in Old Delhi because male artisans find it more lucrative to work outside the insecure handicrafts sector. Additionally, small businesses such as these in Old Delhi have been adversely affected by

FIGURE 2.2. A woman doing zardozi. Photograph by the author.

the new taxation system brought in by the Goods and Services Tax regime (GST) implemented in 2017 that not only requires a GST number, which few have, but also employs a complicated tax structure best understood by trained accountants that few can afford. As a result of such changes, many workshops have closed or moved elsewhere. However, work is abundant for women like Saiba Baji as long as they are willing to do home-based work for long hours and low remuneration. Independent male brokers bring orders to them from the largely Hindu-owned shops in Old Delhi's Kinari Bazar and Nai Sadak. While earlier most of those engaged in zardozi belonged to the endogamous Ansari Zardoz *biradari* with its own organizational structure and system to distribute work and resolve disputes (Gupta and Channa 1996, 111; see also Goodfriend 1983, 135–36), this is not the case today. Like many other Muslims residing in the Shahganj neighborhood, Saiba Baji identifies herself as Sheikh Ansari (weavers), rather than as part of the Ansari Zardoz subgroup. Consequently, unlike the Old Delhi zardoz who are the focus of Gupta and Channa's study (1996), the work that Saiba Baji and her neighbors engage in is not organized through a *biradari* network, and lacks the few protections the *biradari* system might offer.

Saiba Baji's life and work reveal the gendered burdens on women in everyday life. When I first met her, Saiba Baji and four of her daughters were busy working on a zardozi order at home, embroidering "Om" in Hindi and Punjabi on headpieces for Hindu bridegrooms. Her daughters had never been to school because they worked with her. Saiba Baji's husband used to be a tailor but was sick and unable to work. Her two sons did not earn enough to support the family. Like many I encountered in Old Delhi, the family relies on women's work to survive. We sat around the wooden frame that stretched the fabric (*palla*) on which Saiba Baji and her daughters were embroidering "Om" in their rented one-room home with a corrugated-metal sheet for a roof and the constant hum of five fans. That they were embroidering a symbol sacred to Hindus revealed the extent to which craft production and economic networks transcend the religious boundaries that may assert their centrality in other aspects of everyday life. Indeed, it is interesting that North Indian weddings, even as they reproduce religious difference and caste particularity in their ritual performances, also reveal their reliance on economic networks that cross caste and religious lines in their demand for things like zardozi. Rapidly embroidering the headpieces for grooms, Saiba Baji and her daughters did not stop working as they spoke to me. To do so would mean losing money. They worked twelve hours a day, seven days a week, to finish a *palla* together in two weeks. There is no shortage of work, but to make ends meet they must work constantly.

In 2012, Saiba Baji and her neighbors received Rs. 800 to Rs. 1,000 per *palla* of forty headpieces, although each headpiece sold for Rs. 1,000 in shops in Kinari Bazaar or Nai Sadak. When I met her again in 2019, Saiba Baji told me that after demonetization in 2016, when the Modi government caused a crisis by suddenly taking all higher denomination currency notes (Rs. 500 and Rs. 1,000) out of circulation, and with the implementation of GST in 2017, she began getting less money for her work (see Reddy 2019). Where earlier she would have gotten Rs. 20 per item embroidered, now she was getting Rs. 15. In fact, only one daughter was working with her now. The others, and many of her neighbors, stopped doing zardozi because they could not subsist on what they earned from it (*guzara nahi hota*). Now in her late forties, Saiba Baji did not know how much longer she could work. Her eyesight was getting weaker as she labored daily under the single tube light in her windowless home, and her back hurt at the end of long days. As another woman who does piece-rate work at home in the same neighborhood said, "*Maximum* people here do *labor work*. The problem with *labor work* is that after sixty you are not able to do it. They *suffer* so much in life. And their families *suffer*, especially the elderly."[6] It is hard work for little pay. In another conversation she said, "I told you earlier, Kalyani, there is an advantage in a government job. If I work till sixty years, I will get a pension. In these kinds of jobs, when your hands and legs do not work anymore, you do not have anything." She continued: "This is why this craft is dying, because workers do not get paid enough to do the work. We would not want our kids to learn this. We see the difficulties that people have experienced. Whichever side they fall asleep, they wake up that side. They do not turn because they are so tired."

Several of Saiba Baji's female neighbors, most of whom are related to her, were also zardozi artisans who told me similar stories of how their work kept their families afloat as their husbands fell on hard times. For instance, Saiba Baji's neighbor and relative, Faiza Khatun, told me that her husband, who is in the printing business, earns Rs. 4,000 a month now instead of the Rs. 8,000 he earned before. She said, "Costs are going up, but earnings are not." Although he gave her money to run the house, everything else has come from zardozi. She bought gold jewelry for her daughters' weddings with the money she earned. She also gave money to the indigent because, as another woman sitting with us explained, "if we do not give to the poor, then we become strangers to God." Faiza Khatun gestured toward her mother, who was sitting with us, and said, "Ammi did zardozi work and brought up her whole family on what she earned." She said that although the price per item embroidered was and remains low, "within that she married her daughters, built her home, and bought gold jewelry."

Doing the fine embroidery required in zardozi takes a toll on women. The work is not only tough on the eyes and the back, especially in the cramped and dimly lit spaces of their homes, but it is also difficult to complete orders in the time given. Faiza Khatun said that when an order comes in, sometimes they have to drop everything to complete it: "If it comes at night, then we have to give it in the morning. So we have to work at night." If they do not do so, they may not get the order the next time. Today neither her mother nor she can work because their eyesight has become too weak, she told me. Hearing this, her twenty-year-old daughter Usra said, "You brought us up. Now we will take care of you," referring to her elder sister and herself. Usra and her sister have not followed their mother and grandmother into zardozi. While her sister works outside the home, Usra does home-based work making metal closures for necklaces. While this work is perhaps less backbreaking and skilled than her mother's, it is also more insecure; Usra informed me that she had not received any orders for three days. Thus, while we see some diversification in terms of the work that these women are doing, the point that is important here is how families increasingly rely on women's work, as the earning capacity of men shrinks due to illness, the economy, employment discrimination, and other factors.

Wedding finery embellished with zardozi can be found in stores from Old Delhi to Chicago. As the stories of Saiba Baji and Faiza Khatoon suggest, the Muslim women in places like Old Delhi who labor over it unequally bear the costs of production as it ruins their eyes, causes pain, and leads them to forgo education to do the fine metal embroidery that is valued by so many and at which they are very skilled. Yet as sources of income in the formal economy shrink in neoliberal India, the burden on women, who make up much of the informal economy, increases. Their work is important for the survival of their families and the social reproduction of their communities even if, as with Saiba Baji's daughters, it means they must forgo education and the possibilities that may be opened by it to negotiate the difficult conditions of their lives. When orders arrive, the work is distributed among many different women, often members of an extended family network. Understanding that the domestic unit located within the home is central to such production explains why networks remain within the family.[7] As Gupta and Channa suggest in their analysis of how the craft was transmitted through the patrilineal line from father to son in the Mughal era (1996, 105–6), today, too, the transfer of such a skill set requires time and commitment. As women who practice *purdah* and as home-based workers who have little contact with people outside the home, women like Saiba Baji are most likely to recruit family members into the craft, especially daughters who live with them and whose labor is important to family survival.

Keeping the family afloat is a central problem in Old Delhi, especially given the "jobless growth" that characterizes neoliberal India (Menon and Sundar 2019, 2; see also A. Gupta 2012). When I asked Khalil Siddiqui, the principal of a well-known Urdu medium school in Old Delhi, about the problems faced by religious minorities in Old Delhi, he said,

> In every family, the problem starts with bread: *how to feed himself and his family.* So the first problem for every family is they cannot earn enough to think beyond their daily earnings. At night, when they come home from work, they are worried that the next day will I get work or not. Tomorrow will I get money or not. Tomorrow will we cook food or not [*chulha jalega ki nahin*]. So they do not talk to their children about the future. They do not think about the future.

Siddiqui argued that rather than prioritize their children's education, many parents want their children to start earning money: "How should they earn it? This is not their problem. How ever they earn, whatever job they get, they should make money." Saying that most Muslims in Old Delhi do what he called "petty jobs" as "semi-skilled or unskilled workers," he insists that parents need to "understand the value of education."

Many might agree with Siddiqui's analysis here, reflecting as it does the developmentalist axiom that more education leads to better development outcomes. However, the Sachar Committee Report (2006) is an important reminder that education in neoliberal India does not necessarily guarantee a job or reduce precarity, especially for Muslims who face high levels of employment discrimination.

Additionally, gender regimes can make it difficult for women to work outside the home, especially as sexual violence against women in India, and particularly Muslim women at the hands of the Hindu right, is an ever-present threat. And finally, amid the precarity that Indian Muslims face in the everyday, women's labor in the informal economy becomes increasingly important to everyday survival. If Saiba Baji's daughters went to school, how indeed would the family make ends meet? While the productive and reproductive labor of these women ensures that the wheels of the global economy keep turning, it does so precisely because it reproduces, structures, and indeed constitutes the gender, religious, class, and spatial inequalities that keep costs low and profits high.

Global Commodity Chains in a Shii *Mohalla*

Fatima Baji's two daughters Kulsum and Nazima, unmarried and in their early twenties, were also always at work. When Kulsum and Nazima were not cooking, doing other household chores, or taking care of their sick parents, they cut *supari* (areca nuts) in the one-room home they shared with their parents and younger brother. They paid Rs. 2,500 a month for their home and an additional Rs. 5,000 for the small workshop below their home where their brothers cut foam for the soles of shoes with a machine that they had installed there. Their elder brother, with whom they shared a terrace and toilet, lived with his young wife and baby daughter in the room he rented next to theirs. Theirs is the only home with its own toilet in their small *mohalla*. Most of their neighbors, who are part of their extended Shii family from the same village in Uttar Pradesh, use the communal toilet below, with one preferring to bathe and urinate on her terrace under a large beach umbrella to minimize her need for the small, dark, dank, and dirty toilet below. This small group of Shias residing in a neighborhood just a street away from Old Delhi's infamous red-light area, negotiate precarity and struggle to make ends meet in their daily lives. They are absolutely dependent on the productive and reproductive labor of each member of the family. Many are beholden to money lenders who charge exorbitant interest rates. In fact, one woman's relative committed suicide while I was conducting fieldwork because he could not repay his debt. Such is *rozmarra zindagi*, or everyday life, for this community.

Although too close to the red-light area for their comfort, this Shii family can afford the rents in their neighborhood. But to do so they must work. They are part of local and global commodity chains, doing home-based work for little remuneration but generating high profits for others situated in other places. Their lives and livelihoods make manifest Jane Collins's argument that "wherever a global commodity chain touches down, it intersects with local social relations"

(2014, 32). Indeed, the global commodity chains that this extended family of Shias participates in capitalize on their intersecting vulnerabilities to maximize profits: as minorities in a nation that privileges Hindus, as Muslims subject to the violence of both the Hindu right and the security state, as Shias who are a minority within a minority, as denizens of a neighborhood in Old Delhi that is marginal, as economically underprivileged migrants to the city who found themselves unable to sustain themselves on agricultural work in rural India, and as members of the informal economy too dependent on daily incomes to prioritize education in contemporary India. While ensuring profits for businesses in India and abroad, this community continues to negotiate precarity, reproducing and reinforcing the very inequalities that make them vulnerable. Indeed, their precarity is not just exploited by global forces but is reconstituted by these forces in everyday life.

Kulsum and Nazima were part of a global commodity chain connecting Delhi to Calcutta and Indonesia. Fatima Baji used to help them but then became too sick to work. Her husband used to sell fruit from a handcart near the Chawri Bazar metro station, but he also became too sick to do this anymore. Both had tuberculosis, a disease that is quite common among those I worked with in Old Delhi, and relied on their children's labor to make ends meet. When Fatima Baji's husband succumbed to his illness while I was doing fieldwork, he left gambling debts that the children suddenly found themselves having to repay, in addition to the costs of the funeral and the various ritual observances in the months after he passed away. It was abundantly clear that the family would have a difficult time making ends meet without the labor that Nazima and Kulsum do. Kulsum and Nazima received Rs. 2 for every kilo of *supari* they cut—Rs. 150 per seventy-five-kilogram sack. It usually took them eight days to get through a sack of *supari*, amounting to Rs. 450 to Rs. 600 a month depending on how much they got done. The *supari* came from either Indonesia (used to make *ghutka*—a combination of tobacco, powdered areca nuts, and other substances) or Calcutta (used to prepare *paan*, or betel leaves). They provided their own *sarota*, or cutter, which they balanced between their hands and toes as they cut the *supari*. Rarely glancing down as she chatted with me and rapidly cut the *supari*, Kulsum told me that although they cut themselves occasionally, the real toll was the pain caused by bending over the *sarota*.

The particular social world they belonged to impacted their lives and position in the commodity chain in interesting ways. Like her mother, Nazima had never been to school and could not read or write. Kulsum had attended school but was made to leave after the fifth standard because her maternal grandfather (*nana*) felt she was not safe. A vivacious young woman, Kulsum told me that she loved studying and would have been inclined to continue with her education had it not been for her grandfather's insistence that she stop. In fact, Fatima Baji told me few women in her community were educated, and most parents did not want their girls to work outside the home. Now both Kulsum and Nazima are engaged to their *phuphi*'s (father's sister) sons in Seelampur and hope to continue to live close to each other after they get married. Belonging to a conservative family, neither daughter leaves the house much, unless it is to attend religious events like the *majalis* (mourning assemblies) during Muharram. On the rare occasions that they go to the market, it is usually in the company of other women in the family. While their Shii neighbor's daughter wanders around Old Delhi on her own commuting to school, attending tuitions, and visiting friends in the neighborhood, as someone who believes that young women should stay at home as much as possible, Fatima Baji takes great pride in the fact that her daughters do not wander around on their own. While both must work, given these priorities, it is important that they find work they can do at home, even if it pays less. Consequently, businesses, ever on the lookout for cheap labor, are able to capitalize on these social conditions, paying very little for backbreaking work.

Most of Fatima Baji's relatives are also involved in various commodity chains. Her young daughter-in-law, who has completed school and can read Hindi, Urdu, and Arabic, also does piece-rate work at home assembling shoeboxes. She gets thirty-five paisa a box for every one hundred she assembles. Yasmeen, who is married to Fatima Baji's brother and lives next door, sewed soles onto slippers that someone else had made, earning Rs. 1 a sole for slippers that sell for Rs. 55 in the market. When Yasmeen found it difficult to meet a deadline, her teenage daughter helped her after school. While both men and women work in these families, it is clear that women get the lower-paid jobs. Any machine work, such as cutting foam for shoes, earns more money and is typically assigned to men. Selling fruit or juice from a handcart, which many of the men in these families do, is also more lucrative, although it is seasonal. Moreover, women sometimes have to contend with gendered vulnerabilities that render them unable to rely on male financial support. For instance, Yasmeen's husband left her when the youngest of her three children, her son, was six months old. At that time she made a promise to perform a *niyaz* every month to the Sixth Imam if her husband returned. As Diane D'Souza notes, the term *niyaz* refers to a "petition, supplication, [or] prayer" in which an offering is made, usually by Shii women, "in the name of a powerful figure like the Prophet or his family, the Imams, or other revered martyrs" (2012, 357). Since her husband's return, Yasmeen offers a *kunde* (clay pot) of *kheer* (rice pudding) and another of sweet *puris* (deep fried dough) every month and, as per the tradition, invites all the Shii women in the neighborhood to share it and make their own requests to the Sixth Imam (see figure 2.3). Living alone with three children was clearly difficult for her, and she would have

FIGURE 2.3. Yasmeen's *niyaz*. Photograph by the author.

had a difficult time making ends meet if she did not have the money from sewing soles onto slippers.

As for Fatima Baji's daughters, like many women in her extended family, working outside the home was simply not an option. Gender regimes can make it difficult for women to attend school or work outside the home, especially as sexual violence against women in India, and particularly Muslim women at the hands of the Hindu right, is an ever-present threat. Speaking about similarly positioned Muslim women in Mumbai, Sameera Khan argues that they too are urged toward home-based work (2007, 1530). While Khan notes that women of all religious communities face restrictions on "their mobility and access to public spaces," she argues that communal violence, especially sexual violence against women at the hands of the Hindu right, has "made Muslim women's claim to public space even more restricted and fraught with anxiety" (1531). While such difficulties faced by Muslim women are often blamed on "tradition," as Patricia Jeffery and Roger Jeffery note, it is important to understand the ways in which these inequalities are enabled by communalism and upper-caste Hindu hegemony (2006, 118). As Muslims increasingly face the specter of right-wing violence or the long reach of the security state, and as they move to particular neighborhoods in Old Delhi where they feel safer and less insecure, they also have to contend with the limited economic opportunities available to them. This is particularly so for women who, in these circumstances, are even less likely to venture beyond the old city's metaphorical walls. Located in marginal and marginalizing spaces, they make a living doing work they can get in these areas, often for very little remuneration.

Priti Ramamurthy has argued that we must pay attention to how economic forces capitalize on local cultural politics—of caste, religion, gender, and so on (2004, 754). This is certainly true in Old Delhi, where shopkeepers in Kinari Bazaar profited off the labor of Muslim women from underprivileged backgrounds who, due to economic necessity (like Saiba Baji's family) or family pressure (like Kulsum and Nazima), were unable or unwilling to get better-paid jobs outside the home. Businesses also capitalize on landscapes of prejudice, discrimination, and unequal citizenship—the "representational regimes" or "frames" (Butler 2009, 29)—that create precarity for Muslim families in neoliberal India. Whether we look at zardozi artisans or women in Fatima Baji's extended family, we see how social relationships informed by *biradari*, class, gender, and increasingly divisive religious identities intersect with commodity chains (see Collins 2014, 32).

Not only do communal violence, discrimination, and differential citizenship in India result in the concentration of Muslims in certain neighborhoods as I have suggested, but Ghazala Jamil convincingly argues that this spatial segregation along religious lines is related to capital accumulation. Jamil demonstrates how such processes restrict labor mobility and maintain labor market segmentation, ultimately ensuring capital accumulation for some at the expense of others (2017, 66–67). Indeed, as I have shown here, economic forces clearly capitalize on difference in Old Delhi to ensure that commodities are produced for less in some places and can be sold for high profits elsewhere. Moreover, as Priti Ramamurthy notes, "Production generates more than commodities," also constituting "individual and collective identities" (2014, 45). Even as businesses capitalize on gender, class, caste, and religious hierarchies, they reconstitute and reproduce those very hierarchies. Saiba Baji's and Fatima Baji's daughters do not go to school and, like their mothers, do home-based work for little remuneration. Their vulnerability is both constituted by and constitutive of the commodity chains that they are mired in, as their work reaps profits for others located elsewhere. While Hindu shopkeepers in Kinari Bazaar and Chicago, or the global networks of areca nut production, capitalize off restrictions on labor mobility and labor market segmentation related to gender, religion, and class, another generation of young Muslim women live insecure lives as India's most politically and socioeconomically depressed group.

Jane Collins urges us to open the "closed boxes of the commodity chain" so that we can "recover some of what neoclassical economics makes us forget: living, breathing, gendered, and raced bodies working under social relations that exploit them; bodies living in households with persons who depend on them and on whom they depend; and bodies who enter into the work of making a living with liveliness, creativity, and skill" (2014, 27). In Old Delhi, the closed boxes of the commodity chains I have described here open to reveal individuals caught within intersecting axes of difference—gender, religion, class, *biradari*, sect, and educational background—that position them in particular relationships within the global economy. Moving beyond an "anthropology of abjectness" (A. Gupta 2012, 25), it is important to recognize how, while caught in circumstances they cannot control, women use their creativity and skills to make ends meet, to take care of their families, and to construct home and belonging in their neighborhoods. Kulsum's vivacious personality and constant chatter as she cuts *supari* or cooks food for her family, Yasmeen's *niyaz* to improve the circumstances of her life and her invitation to others to partake in it, and Usra's resolution to take care of her mother who sacrificed so much to raise her children illuminate how people live, love, and engage in relations of care that build community even in the midst of precarity.

Stigmatized Labor

The women I have discussed in this chapter negotiated the insecure circumstances of their lives through their contributions to the burgeoning informal economies of neoliberal India. While invisible and unregulated, much of the work in the informal economy does not carry a stigma. However, a handful of women in Old Delhi who engaged in sex work to make ends meet elicited moralizing, derision, or pity from their neighbors. Their work exacerbated their precarity because of the stigma attached to women who engage in sex work in Old Delhi. Tahira Begum was one of these women. Now a widow in her sixties, Tahira Begum was married to an addict. She used to organize women to do embroidery, but when the handicrafts industry declined, there was no work. When her husband's business failed and she could not make enough in the handicrafts sector, she began to organize sex work to support her family and her husband's habits. Unlike the *kothas* (brothels) of Delhi's infamous G. B. Road a couple of streets away, Tahira Begum's work was discreet. She arranged liaisons between male clients and young women willing to engage in clandestine sex work. When her husband died, she stopped doing this work. But today she struggles to make ends meet, often borrowing money from neighbors that she is unable to return. Commenting on Tahira Begum's monetary struggles, her neighbor told me that when you make money in this profession, it does not stay with you. When I asked why this was so, she replied, "It is not pure [*pak*]."

Engaged in piece-rate work for the garment industry, Tahira Begum's neighbor believed that some young women in the neighborhood were drawn to sex work because they earned a lot more money than she did. She said, "You consider this. You work hard from morning to night to earn Rs. 50 to Rs. 100. They go and bring back Rs. 500 or Rs. 600—in one or two hours." Indeed, although many sex workers in Old Delhi's red-light district are the victims of trafficking, this statement is an important reminder to be wary of viewing sex work solely through the framework of trafficking and victimhood. Doing so can obscure the complex motivations of those who participate in the kind of work Tahira Begum organized and who do not operate in brothels, which account for only 5 to 9 percent of sex work in India (Kotiswaran 2011, 12). It can also conceal the efforts of many sex-worker movements in India to mobilize support for categorizing their labor as "work" (Vijayakumar 2018; Azim 2012; Ghose 2012; Kotiswaran 2011).

Whether viewing them as victims of economic necessity or as willing participants in work that was lucrative even if morally suspect, most women I worked with disapproved of those who engaged in sex work. One woman said, "I won't call them bad. They are not bad. But they should understand that good and bad times come and go. This they should understand. I won't call them good either. They are not good either." Speaking of how she has managed her own financial difficulties through work that has enabled her to maintain her social standing, she asked, "Are they respected in society? Can they sit in society?" She did not draw too sharp a distinction between those who exchanged sex for money and those who engaged in sexual liaisons in exchange for other kinds of favors. "*Prostitution* is everywhere," she said, claiming that perks and promotions come to those who succumb to such pressures. While her statement reveals the gendered precarity that working women everywhere often have to negotiate, it simultaneously elides any discussion of the inequalities, insecurities, pressures, or violence that might accompany their decisions.

Those who engage in sex work usually do so to support their families. Twenty-four-year-old Humera, for instance, supports her parents. Others have husbands who live off their income. One woman told me, "There are people like this, who have no work. They think, this is good, we have found someone who can earn a living." Ehsan is one such man, a heroin addict whose wife supports his habits through sex work. Unlike Ehsan's wife, who I was told was a "*professional prostitute*," Hamida engages in sex work only when she cannot find other work. Hamida's husband, who was described by his neighbors as a wastrel, does nothing. When I met Hamida, she was assisting families get their children into good private schools through the EWS scheme by helping them process their paperwork through a "fixer" for a small fee. The EWS scheme is a government scheme that requires expensive private schools like Rabiya, Mater Dei, Presentation, and

Convent of Jesus and Mary to reserve 10 percent of their seats for "Economically Weaker Sections," who pay lower fees. While Hamida is in great demand during admission time, such work is seasonal, and she sometimes has to rely on sex work in leaner times.

Hamida's story is important in connecting sex work, which is in fact not counted as work by the government (Mondal et al. 2018), to the other forms of work I have discussed here that are part of the informal economy of Old Delhi. While almost all the women I worked with would not be willing to engage in sex work under any circumstances, what Hamida's story illustrates is that sex work is one among a number of strategies through which *some* women negotiate economic insecurity in neoliberal India, where the lack of jobs in the formal economy and an agrarian crisis that has driven many to urban areas (G. Menon 2018) have drawn more and more people into the informal economy. In her insightful ethnography of day-wage labor in Mumbai, Svati Shah convincingly argues that although the scholarship on prostitution and on informal economies often sees sex work and day-wage labor as mutually exclusive categories, in fact "legitimized and stigmatized, and legal and criminal, income-generating strategies may be deployed sequentially, or simultaneously, by migrants working in Mumbai's informal sectors" (2014, 4). Since the number of day laborers exceeds the jobs available on any given day, "the need to fill income gaps in a field of relatively limited options for survival within the lowest rungs of the Indian economy" results in day-labor points becoming "sites of regular, intermittent, and irregular solicitation for sexual commerce" (4). While Hamida is not a day-wage laborer, what is clear from her story is that sex work is simply one of many strategies she uses to make ends meet in contemporary Old Delhi. As Shah asserts, "Sexual commerce is not a totalizing context for everyone who sells sexual services; for many, it is one of numerous livelihood strategies that people engage concurrently, or over the course of their working lives" (8; see also Vijayakumar 2018, 348–49). In Old Delhi, for a few women unable to make ends meet through other means, sex work is one, usually occasional, strategy to provide for their families.

Faith and Fortune in Insecure Times

While many of my interlocutors found a way to make ends meet, sometimes money was hard to come by. At these moments, the women I worked with relied on a number of strategies to tide them over during lean periods, from religious practices that petitioned God to intervene, to participating in local chit fund schemes, to borrowing from unscrupulous moneylenders who thrived on their misfortune by charging exorbitant interest rates. Moneylenders were usually a last resort, approached when none of their other strategies worked. While such strategies revealed their vulnerabilities, they also illustrated the tremendous resourcefulness of women negotiating precarity, many of whom could not rely on their husbands for financial support.

Women often told me that ritual vows made in exchange for divine assistance, practices of piety such as daily prayers, and simply striving to be good Muslims helped them negotiate the challenges in their everyday lives, because God would intervene on their behalf. Indeed, many believed that God was a powerful force in their lives, and their acts of piety were seen as interventions made to negotiate their precarity. A Sunni Muslim woman told me that whenever she has been in need, "Allah Pak takes care of me." Sometimes it has been through work coming her way or friends and relatives lending her money. Occasionally, it was because her cousin's husband gave her some of his *zakat* money. *Zakat* is one of the five forms of *ibadat* (worship) expected of Muslims that also include the confession of faith (*kalma*), the daily prayer (*namaz*), the pilgrimage to Mecca (*Haj*), and the monthlong fast during Ramzan. All Muslims who can afford to do so are expected to give 2.5 percent of their income as *zakat* to those in need, as a way to purify their wealth. The woman told me that since God had no need for human assistance, it was important for Muslims to engage in *huquq ul ibad*, worshipping God by fulfilling the claims that other humans have on one. To emphasize her point, she quoted a *shairi* (poem) in which God says, "For my needs, the angels are more than enough. I have made human beings for human beings." She said that to ignore a needy person in order to read the Quran defeats the purpose of *ibadat*. It is not what God wants, she insisted. While her cousin often extracts free labor from her in exchange, she believes her cousin's husband is a good man who, unaware of these exploitative demands, gives with the right intention. She views his charity as a gift from God that materializes when she needs it most and asks for God's intervention.

She firmly believes a person must have faith in God. She told me a story about two men, a *namazi*, or devout man, who said his prayers regularly, and a *sharabi*, or alcoholic. The devout man saved all his money, saying that a person must always have money for emergencies. The alcoholic spent it all on alcohol. When people asked, "How will you buy food?" the alcoholic would say, "That is all in God's hands." When they died, the alcoholic went to heaven and the devout man went to hell. The devout man asked, "God, why did you send me to hell when I said all my prayers?" God responded, "You said your prayers but you had no faith in me." The alcoholic had faith that God would take care of him, so he went to heaven. The woman delivered this story with a smile on her face. The point of the story is not to reward alcoholism or laziness; the story is intended to be ironic, to show through a humorous example with an unexpected twist that it was not enough to perform rituals of worship to attain God's favor; humans must understand that everything is in God's hands and they must have faith. Without faith, without understanding God's expectations of human beings, without the right intention, rituals of piety were meaningless.

Faith that God would help them negotiate economic insecurity guided many women. Zehra Baji, who is part of the same Shii community that Fatima Baji belongs to, hid a roll of bank notes amounting to a couple of thousand rupees in her sewing machine, which she called *Maula mushkil hataane ki paisa*, or money offered to the *Maula* to remove difficulties. *Maula* is a term used to refer to the Prophet or any of the Shii Imams. This was money that she secretly saved from the amount her husband gave her to run the house. It was not to be spent on household expenses but saved to give to the poor in God's name or to distribute *nazr*, an offering made when a petition to God is fulfilled.[8] For instance, Zehra Baji drew on this money after her daughter passed her exams, having vowed to distribute *nazr* if this happened. Zehra Baji told me that sometimes she was forced to borrow from her *Maula* money, especially when she fought with her husband, who was violently abusive and withheld money for household expenses or school fees. But she always returned the amount, usually at the beginning of the month when her tenants who lived in the small house she had built in Seelampur, paid her the Rs. 2,000 they owed her. Since her husband thought the rent was Rs. 1,500, she was able to use the extra Rs. 500 to replenish her *Maula* fund or to save for a rainy day.

Petitions to God do not always work quickly enough. Consequently, women also resorted to other means to make ends meet. Schemes called *lotteries* or *committees* were popular among many women in Old Delhi across religions and castes. These are essentially informal chit fund schemes in which participants make monthly contributions of a set amount, and one member gets to take the monthly collection. For most of these committees there is no formal structure, since every month one participant gets the whole pot. This works as a savings scheme for women and is found in different parts of the world. Writing about such schemes, also called rotating savings and credit associations (ROSCAs), Shirley Ardener argues, "An advantage of traditional ROSCAs is that they do not need a banker because when dues are collected they are immediately given to one of the members, until all have taken turns. Importantly, the rota can be quickly adjusted to help a member in need" (2014, 3). As Ardener notes, trust is central to these schemes, and participants are careful in their selection of new members (3–4). Ameena Baji participated in one of these schemes, putting Rs. 2,000 in a lottery every month with twenty other women. Once, when her name was picked, Ameena Baji paid to get her kitchen tiled. Another time, she put in a water connection to the toilet she shares with her neighbors upstairs. Knowing her neighbors would never contribute to the expense, Ameena Baji paid to improve both their lives and homes through her lottery money.

Zehra Baji wanted to join a more formal committee in her locality, which allowed participants to borrow money and was run by members of the Muslim Ghosi *biradari* that raises buffalos to meet local dairy needs. She needed money from the committee to pay back a money lender from whom she had borrowed two lakhs (Rs. 200,000) to build a second level to her one-room Seelampur house. Her indebtedness to the moneylender illuminated her precarity as an unemployed Muslim woman who could not read or write and who had no access to a bank loan because she was understood to have few marketable skills and no assets deemed worthwhile. The debt only deepened her precarity by making her vulnerable to extortion. Such debts must be paid back quickly, Zehra Baji told me, because for every Rs. 50,000 you borrow, they charge Rs. 10,000, and then you pay interest on top of that. She wanted to put money into the committee to pay off her debt before the interest became overwhelming. She explained to me that if the goal of the committee is that each person puts in a lakh of rupees (Rs. 100,000) over a specific period of time, then if she waits until all the money is in, she will get her full amount back. In this case, it works like a savings scheme. If, as she plans to do, she asks for her money back in the fourth or fifth installment of the committee, then she will get Rs. 15,000 to Rs. 20,000 less at the end. She would rather pay this penalty than the exorbitant interest that would compound on the debt she had taken from the moneylender. However, in the end, Zehra Baji was unable to put together the money to participate in this committee. Indeed, the level of contribution required of each member protects wealthier Muslim families, like those in the Ghosi *biradari*, from incurring the debts and risks of those who are more economically insecure, like Zehra Baji, thereby constituting and reinforcing the class differences that separate Muslims in Old Delhi. Sometimes, try as they might, women like Zehra Baji are reminded not just of their economic insecurity but also of their political precarity as Muslims in a city where they, their husbands, and their children cannot find jobs that pay decent wages, and where they do not have access to cheap credit because of decades of structural violence, continued religious discrimination, and the conditions of "jobless growth" in neoliberal India.

When faith and loans did not work, women engaged in other interesting strategies to make sure they had what they needed. For instance, Zehra Baji engaged in a barter system with a member of the Muslim Ghosi community. The young man would come by weekly with a bag of small onions and exchange this for the day-old bread, *basi roti*, that Zehra Baji kept for him because she no longer considered it edible. No cash was exchanged, but he fed his milk-producing buffalos for free in exchange for small onions that he grew, an essential ingredient in much Old Delhi cuisine that many like Zehra Baji struggle to afford. The exchange reveals the everyday interdependencies between those who experience deep economic insecurity and those who are less economically insecure. It also shows how women like Zehra Baji creatively find ways to surmount the difficulties they face in everyday life. They petition for divine intervention and struggle to be good Muslims who they believe would be worthy of God's favor. They participate in various schemes to boost their chances and those of their children, to improve their homes and lives, and to pay for their children's education. And they engage in barter systems with their neighbors, creating a community that supports each other's needs. Sometimes they are forced into debt, but they work hard to pay back their debts.

In some cases their husbands do not help. Zehra Baji's husband spent much of his money gambling and purchasing *ghutka* laced with tobacco for his own consumption. Fatima Baji's husband drank excessively and spent much of the money he earned selling fruit on gambling, leaving her to feed and clothe the family with the money she, or her daughters, earned from cutting *supari*. He also left huge gambling debts for his children to repay when he died of complications related to tuberculosis. Fatima Baji said he never gave her anything, and she has nothing today because she has had to struggle to make ends meet all her life. While these are problems faced by women across religions and castes, their precarity makes it particularly difficult for Muslim women like Fatima Baji and Zehra Baji to surmount them. Left with the burdens of home and family, women like Fatima Baji do what they can to make a life, to take care of their families, and to support their communities in Old Delhi. As so many men and women in Old Delhi have told me over the years, it is women who bear the brunt of the costs of social reproduction in their communities. Thus, while many Muslims have to negotiate precarity, the gendered landscapes of this precarity shape *rozmarra zindagi*, everyday life, in particular ways for women.

Conclusion

For many of the families I worked with in Old Delhi, life was becoming increasingly challenging. Not only were the numerous beef-related lynchings since the election of the BJP in 2014 a constant reminder of the ever-present specter of right-wing violence (98 percent of beef-related lynchings have occurred since 2014), *notebandi* (demonetization) in 2016 also hit many families badly. For instance, Tahira Begum said she received her wages on November 7 in five-hundred- and one-thousand-rupee notes. For many like her in Old Delhi, this created a huge problem on November 8 when Modi declared these denominations void. Tahira Begum said that many stood in lines at banks all day to get the notes changed to smaller denominations, only to be told the banks had run out of cash. Tahira Begum recalled how people could not get food and other necessities because vendors, like the vegetable seller, refused to give change for Rs. 500–notes. He wanted people to purchase Rs. 500 worth of vegetables, which they could not afford to do. While wealthier Muslims in Old Delhi did not face these issues, they were affected in other ways. Many of them ran businesses that were badly affected. Old Delhi's is a cash economy, where wages are paid in cash, often to day laborers who do not necessarily have or use bank accounts. The sudden ban on higher-currency notes, and the resulting shortage of all notes of smaller denominations, meant that the lives of many who lived from hand to mouth, and others who needed cash to purchase raw materials or to pay wages, were severely compromised. Modi's demonetization experiment not only wreaked havoc on many in India whose lives were already insecure, but it also did not do what it was supposed to—namely, get rid of black money, or untaxed money, and corruption in India. Of the notes taken out of circulation, 99.3 percent were returned to the Reserve Bank of India, showing that black money held in these notes was negligible.[9]

The introduction of the Goods and Services Tax (GST) the following year, in 2017, further compounded the economic crisis that demonetization and the subsequent liquidity shock had triggered in the lives and livelihoods of many I worked with. Indeed, all over the country the complexities of the new taxation structure and its many requirements brought many small businesses to a standstill. In an article in *The Wire* in 2018, Manoj Kumar noted, "A survey by the All India Trade Union Congress (AITUC) in July found that a fifth of India's 63 million small businesses—contributing 32% to the economy and employing 111 million people—faced a 20% fall in profits since the GST rollout, and had to sack hundreds of thousands of workers."[10] This has led to a sharp rise in unemployment, undoubtedly contributing to the fact that the rate of unemployment in India in 2019 was at a forty-five-year high. The sectors most affected by GST were those that specialized in the kind of work that most Muslims in Delhi are involved in—small manufacturing units that specialized in tools and machinery, handicrafts, and the garment industry. Indeed, most Muslims in Old Delhi are self-employed, and many run small factories and businesses or are employed by them. As I have noted, increasing prejudice against Muslims, and the inability to get jobs in the private or public sector, has only driven more Muslims toward self-employment in recent years. Rafiq Sahib, whose experiences with prejudice led him to run his own small business with his sons in Old Delhi, told me that business had been tough since the introduction of GST and that work at his factory making small machine parts had slowed. As life gets more insecure, especially for families who are less privileged than Rafiq Sahib's, they start relying more on women's labor. This was true for Saiba Baji's neighbor, whose husband's income halved in recent times. As the zardozi artisans noted, there was no shortage of work for women, as long as they were willing to put in the long hours for little pay.

If, as Butler insists, precarity is a "politically induced condition" that affects some more than others, how people negotiate this precarity does not always makes their lives any less insecure. Yet even as businesses and moneylenders capitalized off the landscapes of precarity that women negotiated every day, sometimes making their lives even more insecure, the stories I have narrated also show how women used their ingenuity and employed multiple skills, resources, and strategies to help their families negotiate mounting economic insecurity in neoliberal India. In so doing they not only helped themselves and their families, but they also created networks and exchanges through which they supported their communities through difficult times. Their contributions were central not just to production but also to the reproduction of their families and communities, their neighborhoods and places, making them indispensable to local, national, and global systems and economies. Most importantly, the lives of these women cannot be understood solely through the lens of religion, or be reduced to their "Muslimness." We have to examine how their religious identity intersects with their other identities—as women, as laborers, as artisans, as migrants, as friends, as neighbors, as creditors, as debtors, as patients, as graduates, as daughters, and as wives—all of which affect their positioning in different ways and shape how they will traverse the social, economic, and political forces operating in contemporary India.

Part 2
MAKING PLACE

3

PERFECTING THE SELF

There was a steady drizzle as I followed some women across the *maidan* (open space) at Mori Gate. They were heading to a colorful tent, with pastel pink and blue panels, set off to one side of the *maidan*. Directly in front, men in crisp white kurtas and pajamas were already lining up for Eid prayers. I was glad to be among the women, sheltered from the persistent drizzle. As I entered the tent, women were taking off their burqas and lining up for prayer in their Eid finery. I met up with Abida and other members of her group, what I call the Muslim Club. As I stood at the back with women who were not offering prayers that day, others positioned themselves in neat rows and offered Eid prayers in congregation, following the imam who was standing in the rain outside with all the men (see figure 3.1). After Eid prayers, several women began to leave, but Abida and other members of the Muslim Club stayed till the end of the Eid sermon.

To attend Eid prayers with other women praying in congregation and following the imam along with the men is an unusual phenomenon in Old Delhi and elsewhere in South Asia, though not in other parts of the world.[1] Indeed, when I told others in Old Delhi that I had attended Eid prayers with women at Mori Gate, they expressed surprise. Jamal, a Sunni Muslim in Old Delhi said, "Oh, they must have been Shia." In fact, no Shii women I knew in Old Delhi attended Eid prayers in congregation. When I explained that they were Sunni women, he said, "They must be Ahl-e-Hadis or Tablighi Jamaat," referring to different *maslaks,* or paths, in Sunni Islam, or more specifically, the "normative orientations" associated with different schools of Islamic reform in South Asia (Tareen 2020).

FIGURE 3.1. Women's Eid prayers. Photograph by the author.

Most members of the Muslim Club do not identify with a *maslak*, regard their practices as "authentic" Islam, and are extremely critical of both Shii Muslims and other Sunni Muslims in Old Delhi who follow Deobandi or Barelvi teachings. As members of the Muslim Club, they organize regular monthly gatherings, inviting women of various class backgrounds to these meetings. They also spread their ideas in more informal conversations with groups of women at a variety of venues and contexts. They urge women to adopt religious practices that they believe are prescribed in the foundational texts. They are particularly critical of Muslim practices that they claim are steeped in Indian "culture" and "tradition," and they teach women to follow "authentic" Islam, what they believe is prescribed in the Quran and is modeled in the words and deeds of the Prophet Muhammad in the seventh century. In this they are similar to other Islamic reform movements that attempt to orient religious beliefs and practice toward "what are held to be the core foundations of Islam, by avoiding and purging out innovation, accretion and the intrusion of 'local custom'" (Osella and Osella 2013, xi). However, while they may urge Muslims to "return" to a "pure" scriptural Islam, these variegated movements are shaped by, and grapple with, the social and political circumstances of their worlds.

Here I examine constructions of Muslim subjectivity articulated by Abida and other women in the Muslim Club, who engage in *dawa* (religious outreach) and teach others in their communities about Islam and its place in the modern world. I analyze how they draw on movements and conversations among Muslims all over the world to articulate their vision of what it means to be a good Muslim in contemporary India. Illuminating an ongoing dialogue with the challenges and politics that shape their lives, I show how these women question global and local Islamophobia and culturalisms about Muslims, to make place for themselves in India and the world. Insisting on visibility, and marking their distinction against the tide of Hindu majoritarianism and disavowals of Muslims and Islam in the country, members of the Muslim Club assert their presence in contemporary India and embed transnational Islamic cultures in places such as Old Delhi. I argue that their efforts, although contested by many other Muslims in Old Delhi, not only make place for Muslims in India today but also require us to understand Muslim subjectivity, and indeed religious cultures in India, through a transnational framework.

Discourses on Muslims in Contemporary India

The Muslim Club of Old Delhi was a small group of women committed to teaching other Muslims, particularly women, how to be good Muslims in contemporary India. In 2013 the Muslim Club had thirty members from a range of economic backgrounds. Some, like Abida, were schoolteachers with high levels of education who engaged in the club's activities after work or on weekends. Others, like Tanveer, had less formal education and were not employed outside their homes. Wealthier members, such as Rabiya Baji, often hosted gatherings at their homes, which were spacious enough to accommodate large groups. Most members would identify as middle class, constituting what Raka Ray calls the "middle classes" to include groups who "claim ownership over the term" even if they fall outside its traditional scope, in recognition of its "increasingly blurred" boundaries (2019, 217). By 2016, the Muslim Club itself had ceased functioning because its founder, Abida, had moved to Mumbai. However, since former members like Tanveer and Rabiya Baji continued to organize events and engage in religious outreach, I refer to them as members of the club in this chapter. Members of the Muslim Club understand their work as *dawa*, propagating Islam in their communities. To this end they organize gatherings on the second Saturday of every month when schools in Delhi are closed, inviting women of various class backgrounds to these meetings. At these gatherings, often held in the homes of wealthier members who have the space for large groups, members of the Muslim Club lecture on a variety of topics.

In this chapter, I view the activities of the Muslim Club as attempts to intervene in an ongoing conversation among Muslims in Old Delhi about what it means to be a good Muslim in India and the world today. Such conversations are not just limited to groups of Muslims within India, but require a transnational framework that allows us to see how Muslims in India are in dialogue with Muslims and non-Muslims in South Asia and beyond. Numerous scholarly works have examined the problematic construction of Muslim subjectivity as "backward," "communal," "violent," and "antinational" in colonial (C. Gupta 2002; Pandey 1990) and nationalist (Sethi 2014; K. Menon 2010) narratives in India, and elsewhere (Gottschalk and Greenberg 2018). Muslim articulations of self in India are inflected by an awareness of these constructions, even as they are immersed in debates among Islamic scholars within and beyond the country. In her book on the Pakistani middle class, Ammara Maqsood argues that it is important for scholars to understand not just debates among Muslims about Islam but also "the impact of discussions, or imagined dialogues, on Islam by non-Muslims" (2017, 12). As she notes, Pakistani Muslims she worked with were only too aware of how people across the globe view Islam and Muslims in the world today (35). Consequently, she argues, their representations of self are "a kind of theater that involves a set of actors who speak on behalf of a community, an audience that watches them, and a stage. In other words, self-representations bring a set of insiders (actors) and outsiders (audience) together within a particular frame of reference" (35).[2]

Like the Pakistani Muslims Maqsood worked with, members of the Muslim Club in Old Delhi are also deeply aware of Islamophobic constructions of Muslim subjectivity in the world and challenge them in their lectures, conversations, and articulations of self. And indeed, as a non-Muslim anthropologist residing in the United States and conducting research for a book on Muslims in Old Delhi, I was often both the audience and a conduit to a much larger audience. As such, members of the Muslim Club often contested stereotypes about Muslims and Islamophobia in their conversations with me. The following conversation was fairly typical of my interactions with members:

> ABIDA: Who do we call Muslims? Those who follow commandment of Allah. Allah says, if any human being . . . whether he is a Jew, a Christian, a Muslim, to respect them is our duty. Allah Tala [God the exalted] says, whoever saves one human being, whether a Hindu, a Jew, a Muslim, they have saved all of humanity. . . . And whoever has killed one person, whether a Hindu or a Muslim . . . they have killed all humanity. It is such a big sin to kill one person. So those who kill people in the name of jihad . . . they do not know what a big sin they are committing. . . .

K: And they believe they are being religious?

Abida: They believe they are religious. The reason is they have not read the Quran. They have not read the Quran and are following their culture.

K: Ordinary Muslims are facing many problems because of this.

Abida: People have given such a wrong impression that Muslims are viewed as uncivilized [*jahil*]. . . . Every community has its *black sheeps*. Among Muslims there are some *black sheeps* who are ruining the community. But there are also very good people.

The above exchange reveals how Abida, the founder of the Muslim Club, contests the increasingly dominant association of Islam and Muslims with violence by non-Muslims the world over. Contesting this view by drawing on the Quran (5:32)—and adding a reference to "Hindus" in recognition of her positioning as an Indian Muslim who negotiates these stereotypes on a daily basis, and, perhaps, as one speaking to an anthropologist with a Hindu name—Abida insists that a good Muslim, one who has read and understood the Quran, would not be violent.

By suggesting that violent individuals are following their "culture," Abida also subtly references a larger conversation with other Muslims about how to be a good Muslim. The above exchange had me, and those who might read my book, as the audience. As such, Abida makes the point that the Quran explicitly condemns violence, a view few Muslims in Old Delhi would disagree with or even need to be told. In this context, the reference to "culture" suggests that the violent acts of "those who kill people in the name of jihad" have nothing to do with Islam, and are part of the local cultural milieus such individuals and groups belong to. But also coded in the reference to culture is a much longer conversation with other Muslims as the audience. This is a conversation that suggests that the influence of "culture" on religious practice must be strictly curtailed because it is dangerous, both from the perspective of salvation and from the perspective of reputation. For members of the Muslim Club, any practice that is not in the foundational texts is deemed "un-Islamic," a cultural accretion that must be rejected. For them, Islam is not a "human and historical phenomenon" (S. Ahmed 2016, 72), or a set of practices that reference a "discursive tradition" associated with the foundational texts (Asad 1986), or other oral and written texts that are central to everyday life among Muslims (Irfan Ahmad 2011, 110). For women like Abida, Islamic practice is limited to those practices that are literally found in the foundational texts. Everything else is considered a dangerous cultural accretion.

In their discussions with women in Old Delhi, Abida and other members of her Muslim Club express views that are very much in keeping with Islamic revivalism, variegated efforts seen across the world and characterized by the endeavor to return to the prescriptions of the foundational texts, engage in practices of piety, and inhabit religious norms (see Maqsood 2017; S. Ahmad 2009; S. Mahmood 2005). While piety movements have been the subject of much scholarly attention in the anthropology of Islam, recent work has shifted the focus to "everyday Islam" (Fadil and Fernando 2015). Commenting on this shift, Nadia Fadil and Mayanthi Fernando warn against conceiving of the "everyday" as a site of "moments of disruption, of *not conforming* to religious norms" (2015, 69; emphasis in original). They argue that opposing "piety and the everyday" not only implies that piety is somehow outside the domain of the everyday but also reinforces a "normative frame that enables the restoration of a conceptualization of agency primarily understood as creative resistance to (religious) norms" (65). This view would understand the efforts of women in the Muslim Club to inhabit the norm rather than question it as "exceptional," instead of as one of the many ways people choose to live their lives in the everyday (61). It could also imply that the actions of those in piety movements are determined solely by their religious identity, conflating aspiration with practice and effacing the plural identities such individuals also have—of class, of gender, and of nation. Fadil and Fernando urge us to look instead at the "various ways in which religious—as well as other—constraints and commitments inform and structure human conduct, and how these are continuously negotiated" by all individuals (80). These insights are important to understanding the narratives of women in Old Delhi's Muslim Club.

The subject is constituted at the interstices of "competing hegemonies" (Ewing 1997, 35). The Islamophobic stereotypes that dominate the representations of Islam and Muslims in India and the world today, the Muslim Club's interpretations of religion, the various traditions of Islam they are in conversation with, and discourses of class, gender, nation, and modernity that pull individuals toward different commitments are among the many systems of representation struggling for hegemony amid which women in the Muslim Club articulate understandings of self and identity. It is crucial therefore to locate the self-understandings of members of the Muslim Club not just in relation to religious ideas and debates among Islamic movements and scholars in India and across the globe, but also in terms of other discourses that are central to their lives and worlds—including those of modernity, gender, class, and nation. Paying attention to how members of the Muslim Club situate themselves amid these competing discourses enables a richer understanding of how some Muslims make place for themselves in contemporary India.

Lessons from Old Delhi's Muslim Club

In some ways, members of the Muslim Club are unlike other Muslims I met in Old Delhi. In their attempts to model their behavior on the Quran and the words and deeds of the Prophet and his companions in seventh-century Arabia, they seek to eschew practices that they understand to be local accretions. They also engage in practices that are not widely followed by other Muslims in Old Delhi. For instance, Abida told me that she cleans her teeth with a miswak twig because the Prophet and his companions did this. When I spoke to Rafiq Sahib, a prosperous Deobandi Muslim who does not follow the Islam prescribed by the Muslim Club about this, he laughed and said, "Well, they did that in the Prophet's time because they did not have toothbrushes!" But for members of the Muslim Club, such activities are what Saba Mahmood calls the "affective and embodied practices through which a subject comes to relate to a particular sign . . . through attachment and cohabitation" (2009, 70). Mahmood eloquently argues that the Prophet's words and deeds provide a way to "acquire a devoted and pious disposition," and "inhabitation of the model . . . is the result of a labor of love in which one is bound to the authorial figure through a sense of intimacy and desire" (78). While the particular practice might not be widely followed in Old Delhi, inhabiting the model of the Prophet itself is something that is important to many Muslims in Old Delhi.

Abida and other members of the Muslim Club have also adopted forms of *purdah* that set them apart from many Muslim women in Old Delhi. Many Muslim women in Old Delhi practice some form of veiling, often throwing a chador over their head and shoulders when they step out, or wearing a burqa and covering their head with a scarf with or without a veil across their faces. Women in the Muslim Club not only donned a burqa and headscarf, but some, like Abida, Tanveer, and Raisa, distinguished themselves by wearing gloves and socks to cover everything except their eyes. Tanveer told me that covering one's hands and feet is not required, but it is something that she and some others in the Muslim Club have chosen to do.

If we understand that the subject is a "performative accomplishment" (Butler 1990, 271), then such acts can be seen as among the many ways that a person comes to embody a particular subjectivity "through acts over time" (274). As Saba Mahmood notes in her work on women in the mosque movement in Cairo, veiling is an act through which these women inhabit the virtue of modesty that they are trying to embody (2005, 51, 156–61). The veil can also be seen as a sign that communicates to the world something about who a person is and how she should be related to. As Laura Ring notes in her work on Muslim women in Karachi, the veil also encodes messages that are readily understood by others who share these understandings, about who one is, how one views others, and how others should relate to one (2006, 141–43). Indeed, the use of the veil to index relationships of deference or distance is common in North India among women across the religious spectrum—Hindu, Sikh, and Muslim (Jeffery and Jeffery 2018, 9–10; Jeffery 2000, 6). The forms of veiling adopted by Muslim Club women mark them as particular kinds of subjects—pious certainly, but also as knowledgeable Muslims with the authority to disseminate their ideas to others and to inhabit public space in ways that most Muslim women in Old Delhi did not.

That religion and performances of piety provide a space for women of all religions to engage in the public sphere and exercise authority is something that several scholars have noted in other contexts (in South Asia see Knight 2011; K. Menon 2010; Flueckiger 2006; Khandelwal 2004; Basu 1995; outside South Asia see Deeb 2006; Frederick 2003). In the case of women in the Muslim Club, their status as pious women engaged in *dawa* allowed them to enter people's homes without invitation and request permission to talk to them about religion. Here, their self-presentation and religious work not only gave members of the Muslim Club a means to speak with authority, to shape others, and to shape their worlds in ways that may not have been available otherwise, but also it created a way for them to expand their networks and social mobility. Indeed, as A. Afzar Moin has noted in his discussion of Farhat Hashmi and her followers in Pakistan, since "religious rituals often provide a space for women to meet, socialize and get around the social barriers to mobility," religion is often viewed by many women as a positive force in their lives (2018, 83).

Veiling was a subject often broached by members of the Muslim Club in encounters with other Muslims. On one such occasion, after asking to address a group of women she had not met before, Abida informed them that there were six points of *hijab* (covering), required for Muslim women, five of which are also expected of men. She said the expectations for covering vary only in what must be covered for men and women—men are only required to cover from "navel to knee." However, she asserted, both men and women are prohibited from wearing tight clothes, those that are transparent, those that are not gender appropriate, and those made of attractive colors and fabrics. Additionally, both men and women are prohibited from adorning themselves with the dress, jewelry, or signs associated with another religion. But, she said, "when it comes to *hijab*, we strictly discipline women, but not men. But in the Quran, men are addressed first. Allah Tala says first that when a man sees a woman, after the first look he should lower his gaze. The first look is forgiven. But to look again is *haram*. The first veil on the gaze [*nazar ka hijab*] is on men. Then on women."

Abida's description of the six points of *hijab* is almost identical to that found in a book by Zakir Naik (2011, 45–46), which was among several books by him that she gave me as a gift at the end of a yearlong stay in Old Delhi. She viewed Naik as a teacher. She said she had many teachers, but the ones she mentioned most to me and to others in Old Delhi were Zakir Naik and Farhat Hashmi. Internationally known but controversial figures among South Asian Muslims, both assert that Muslims today should live only according to the prescriptions of the Quran and of the texts detailing the life of the Prophet and his companions. Naik in particular is well known to many in Old Delhi, beyond the Muslim Club, because several people watched his program on Peace TV, which he founded. A physician and Islamic teacher formerly based in Mumbai, where he founded the Islamic Research Foundation, Naik now resides in Malaysia since his passport was revoked by the Government of India.[3] Neatly turned out in a Western suit, articulate in English, able to quote from several religious texts including the Bible and the Vedas, and passionate about defending Islam from the global stereotypes that position Muslims as out of touch with the modern, Naik is popular among many young, educated Muslims. Indeed, it is perhaps because he does not present himself as the quintessential Islamic cleric, draws on his authority as a physician to present the Quran as a text that foreshadows scientific insights, and speaks to the dual aspirations of Muslim youth to be both modern and Muslim that Naik is so appealing to urban, educated youth in places like Delhi (see T. Khan 2015).

Farhat Hashmi, now based in Canada, is the founder of Al Huda in Pakistan, an Islamic school for women that tends toward a "literal interpretation of the Quran . . . and an idealized image of the first Muslim community" (S. Ahmad 2009, 40). While her critics note Hashmi's "ahistorical and problematic use of religious sources to construct a religious or legal opinion" (Moin 2018, 81), her followers see her as a source of "authentic" knowledge. As Maqsood observes in her work on followers of Hashmi in Pakistan, many "mention her doctorate in Hadith Sciences from a foreign university . . . as proof of her extensive knowledge . . . [and] as evidence of sectarian neutrality" (2017, 95). Abida drew heavily on the writings and lectures of Hashmi and Naik to "authenticate" her particular understanding and practice of Islam. Abida was also very active online, querying other "teachers" around the world who she believed had "true" knowledge on a variety of issues.

Following the teachings of such figures, members of the Muslim Club asserted that Muslims should only follow those practices that have been prescribed in the Quran and "authentic" Hadith. Abida told me,

> Our Prophet said himself before his death [*inteqal*], that I am leaving this world. I will leave two things and go. He held two things: the Quran and his Sunnat. . . . The speech of Allah and my way. Whoever holds on to these two things, they will go straight to paradise. And those who

> leave these two things will be in hell. People have left both these things, taken short cuts. . . . That is not Islam.[4]

Abida used the internet, which enabled intercontinental discussions on a range of issues of concern to Muslims, to access sources of knowledge such as Hashmi's lectures or the life histories of the Prophet's companions, which were instrumental to her own religious education, her analysis of what was "authentic" and not, and her understanding of the Islam practiced by the Prophet and his companions in seventh-century Arabia. The process of verification emphasized by Abida and other members of the Muslim Club, the need to build one's understanding on textual evidence, and the importance of rational processes as a basis for religious acts are very reminiscent of the processes of authentication that Lara Deeb describes (2006, 20–21) as central to the "enchanted modern" of Lebanese Shias with its "dual emphasis on both spiritual and material progress as necessary to modern-ness" (6). Most importantly, understanding the ways in which Abida used technology (the internet, YouTube, podcasts, and messaging apps on her mobile phone) to draw on understandings of Islam produced in different parts of the world (from Canada to Pakistan, and Saudi Arabia to Mumbai) to shape herself, those around her, and the spaces she inhabited, enables us to see Old Delhi itself as what Purnima Mankekar refers to as a nodal space, "produced through the traffic in peoples, commodities, and media" (2015, 10). Drawing on Paolo Favero, who argues that a "long history of dialogue between local and foreign influences" has produced Delhi, Mankekar suggests that Delhi is a space that can only be understood through a transnational framework (Favero 2005, 197, cited in Mankekar 2015, 10). Indeed, the activities of the Muslim Club require us to use a transnational perspective to understand how Indian Muslims make place for themselves in Old Delhi today.

Islam and Modernity

Nowhere is this transnational perspective more necessary than to understand the frequent references to modernity made by members of the Muslim Club and the Islamic scholars that they draw on. Members of the Muslim Club are deeply aware of constructions in India and abroad of Islam and Muslims as outside of, or antithetical to, modernity. In their conversations and lectures, they frequently draw on the ideas of Islamic scholars such as Zakir Naik to construct Islam as a religion for the modern world and themselves as modern Muslim subjects. An important reference was Zakir Naik's book *Rights of Women in Islam: Modern or Outmoded?*, which clearly addresses global stereotypes about Islam and Muslims while also establishing a new way for readers to understand Islam in places like Old Delhi. Referencing the Oxford and Webster dictionaries in his book, Naik says, "In short, modernizing is a process of updating or opting for the betterment of the present status itself; it is not the present modern status itself" (Naik 2011, 7). He continues:

> Now the question is, can we modernize ourselves to master our problems, and to realize a new way of life for the whole human race? I am not concerned about the modern ideas, the conclusions and categorical statements made by scientists and inexperienced armchair experts as to how a life should be lived by a woman. I am going to base my conclusions and considerations on truth, which can be proved by experience. Experience and unbiased factual holistic analysis is the sure test between the gold of truth and the glitter of theory. (7–8)

Here Naik insists on the primacy of experience, suggesting that unlike the "glitter of theory" it is based on an unmediated, incontestable truth. Of course, experience, as Joan Scott argues, "is at once already an interpretation and something that needs to be interpreted. What counts as experience is neither self evident nor straightforward; it is always contested and always therefore political" (Scott 1991, 797). However, Naik clearly attributes an "authenticity" to experience, suggesting that it is not marked by the flaws, limits, and political interests that inflect theory. What does this have to do with his understanding of women's rights? Naik asserts that if one were to believe portrayals of women's rights in Islam in the Western media, then one would have to agree that Islam is "outdated" when it comes to women's rights (2011, 8). But in fact, he argues, "the Western talk of women's liberation is actually a disguised form of exploitation of her body, deprivation of her honour, and degradation of her soul" (8). In contrast, he continues, "Islam's radical revolutionary support gave women their due right and status in the days of ignorance . . . 1,400 years ago. Islam's objective was, which continues to be, to modernize our thinking, our living, our seeing, our hearing, our feeling and striving for the women's upliftment and their emancipation in the society" (8). After insisting that women's rights in Islam must be determined by an understanding of textual sources, not based on what Muslim societies in existence today practice, he discusses at length what the texts say about women, their status, rights, and obligations (8–13). It is not hard to see why these ideas would appeal to many Muslims in Old Delhi who have to contend with local and global stereotypes about Muslim women and Islam and who aspire to reconcile their religious commitments with their desire to be understood as modern Muslims (T. Khan 2015).

Drawing on Naik's ideas, members of the Muslim Club often argued that there was nothing in Islam that contradicted science or logic. "Our religion is a logical religion," Abida told women at one gathering at Rabiya Baji's house. The insistence that there is nothing in Islam that is against logic or science is a major concern of several of Naik's publications. Indeed, Naik is well known for his arguments about the "scientific" validity of the Quran (see also Maqsood 2017, 115; Hansen 2001, 176–77). Naik asserts, "For any book to claim that it is a Revelation from Almighty God, it should stand the test of time" (2010b, 39). He insists, "There is not a single verse [of the Quran] which is against the established science" (92). Naik claims that 1,400 years ago, the Quran discussed the big bang theory, the rotation of planets, and the water cycle (2010a, 8–10). He also says that Quranic knowledge about embryology was not only well ahead of the rest of the world but that it continues to stand the test of science (2010a, 12; 2010b, 49). Trained as a physician, Naik's writings discuss the health benefits of Islamic practices such as the daily prayer (2010a, 17) and the monthlong fast (22–23). These are issues that greatly appeal to Abida, a science teacher, and often make their way into her discussions and lectures. At one gathering during Ramzan, for instance, she spoke at length about the health benefits of bodily movements during prayer and the nutritional benefits of the date that Muslims break their fast with to make the point that Islamic prescriptions have scientific validity.

The religious subjectivities of women like Abida, Raisa, Tanveer, and others in Old Delhi are shaped and enabled by the forces and flows of the modern world—science, the internet, global and local Islamophobia and violence, and the economic and political inequalities and inequities that mark the neoliberal landscape. While they might advocate a return to a way of life modeled by the Prophet and his companions in the seventh century, they do not reject the "modern" and instead strive to reshape it. Indeed, being modern was no less important than being Muslim for Abida and inflected her understanding of how to be a good Muslim. As such, understanding her words and deeds requires us to think about Abida as a plural subject, compelled by multiple and competing hegemonies.[5] It is useful to think about the religiosity of women like Abida as "bring[ing] together a variety of aspirations" (Maqsood 2017, 12). In her work on Islamic movements in contemporary Lahore, Maqsood notes that the call for an "authentic" Islam could be understood as a way of positioning oneself in relation to others, "a way to critique the privileged position of those higher . . . in the . . . social hierarchy" (64), while the "emphasis on education, generalized rationalization, and scientific thinking . . . cater to the needs and disciplinary demands of middle-class life" (12). Maqsood shows how conversations on how to be a "good" Muslim among those she worked with in Lahore "reveal an array of complex motivations, including both the desire for spiritual progress and an aspiration for becoming—and appearing to be—modern in relation to the wider moral universe" (149). This was certainly also the case among women in the Muslim

Club in Old Delhi who also draw on many of the same sources of authority as Maqsood's interlocuters in Lahore to make their arguments.

To understand women in the Muslim Club, it is important not to privilege European or U.S. experiences of modernity as a prototype for the world. Indeed, as we shall see below, if one were to do this, one could not understand Abida's tendency to situate her subjectivity and practices within the modern. To counter this trend, many scholars have made the case for "multiple modernities" and "alternative modernities."[6] While such formulations have been central to challenging a singular construct of the modern, Lara Deeb argues, "We need to explore not only local understandings of being modern, but also how these understandings are employed and deployed in various contexts and to what effects, and how these uses relate to dominant global and transnational discourses about modern-ness, including western ones" (2006, 15). Furthermore, people often deploy multiple understandings of the modern at the same time, and the "tensions among different understandings of modern-ness" reflect "the power relations of the contemporary world" (15). Therefore, Deeb suggests, "rather than pluralizing the concept . . . it [is] more useful to recognize the plurality of experience, interpretation, and understanding of this notion" (15).

Mustapha Kamal Pasha argues that there is a tendency to place Islam itself "outside the global modern," a strategy that "ensures both the global domestication of Islam and the concealment of the darker side of globalization" (2010, 175). Instead, he insists, we should be wary of understanding Islam, Muslims, movements, or violence as somehow "removed from history's current compulsions" (180) and instead understand how these become "intelligible principally as a constitutive aspect of modernity" (182). In the Indian case, Irfan Ahmad's work reveals the extent to which Islamic ideas and actions in India in the twentieth century were shaped by colonial and postcolonial modernities (2017b, 2009). Ahmad shows that the push for a "pure" Islam untainted by local customs, by figures such as Maulana Maududi in the context of struggles for independence in the twentieth century, were related to insecurities about the loss of Muslim distinctiveness amid the "majoritarian, assimilationist democracy of the Congress" and challenged the Muslim politics of both the Muslim League and the Jamiat Ulema-e-Hind (95–97). In the postcolonial context, Ahmad shows how the radicalism of Islamic groups such as the Student Islamic Movement of India (SIMI) is a reaction to "the radicalism of Hindutva and the erosion of Indian secularism" and not some ahistorical enactment of Islamic doctrine (Irfan Ahmad 2009, 164).[7] Responding very differently to the same historical circumstances, the Student Islamic Organization of India (SIO), affiliated with the Jamaat-e-Islami, advocated *dawa* for "the propagation of Islam's message of peace" to counter the destruction of the Babri Masjid and the Gujarat Pogrom

(148). While such responses might have the effect of marking the distinction between Muslims and others, they are still very much responses to the political circumstances that Muslims find themselves in (see Haniffa 2013).

The variegated efforts of Islamic modernists since the colonial period in India illuminate their efforts to reconcile their ideas with their experiences and understandings of modernity. From Sir Sayyid, who established Aligarh Muslim University so that Muslims could have access to European knowledge (Lelyveld 1978), to Maulana Maududi, the founder of the Jamaat-e-Islami, who believed that scientific knowledge had bolstered the power of the British in India (Irfan Ahmad 2009, 53), Muslim reformers in India have not eschewed science and modernity in India, even as they may have called for a return to a "pure" or "authentic" Islam. And indeed, as Irfan Ahmad argues in his analysis of Maududi, this "pure" Islam "bears the indelible signature of modernity" (50). Francis Robinson has argued that many eighteenth-century and nineteenth-century Islamic reform movements "drove a coach and horses through the old authority resting on a connectedness to a 'sacred past' and created new forms, future-oriented forms, which could be regularly remoulded" (2013, 35). Islamic reformers like Muhammad Iqbal and Sir Sayyid Ahmad Khan emphasized the importance of human action in transforming the world (36) and transforming the self through self-reflection (37–39). The emphasis on following the prescriptions of the foundational texts by many Islamic reformers "rationalized Islamic belief and practice" while attacking Sufi practices that implied immanence of spiritual power, or *barakat*, and the intercession of saints (40).

These insights are important to understanding the religious practices and subjectivities of members of the Muslim Club and illustrate parallels with earlier traditions of Islamic reform in India. Muslim Club women argue that Muslims must model their lives on the foundational texts of Islam: the Quran and the Sunna. At the same time, they see these works as texts for the modern world, containing a modernizing vision that all Muslims should work toward achieving. They do not believe that Islam is incompatible with modernity. This is also true of many other Old Delhi Muslims who are not part of the Muslim Club. For instance, Rafiq Sahib once told me that Islam is an "ultra-modern religion" because "it was valid then, it is valid now, and it will be valid in the future." Both Abida's words and Naik's writings negotiate with local understandings of modernity and attempt to situate their own ideas and understandings of self and religion within these frameworks. Through their *dawa*, members of the Muslim Club challenge the Islamophobia and stereotypes about Muslims that affect their lives and worlds. Their visible practices of piety, while marking their distinction, can also be understood as a form of place making, an assertion of presence in a country that is increasingly inhospitable to Muslims. Their efforts to discourage other Muslims from engaging in practices that they believe are "innovations" or "cultural accretions," and to mark their own distinction from others in their worlds, are reminiscent of earlier traditions of reform in India and advance a particular, though contested, Muslim politics amid fears of erasure or assimilation in Hindu majoritarian India. Indeed, their words and deeds are historically contingent responses to the particular social and political circumstances of modern India.

Debating Islam

Members of the Muslim Club insisted that it was important for individual Muslims to read the Quran, not just in Arabic, which most Old Delhi Muslims could not understand, but in translation and using the interpretations of scholars they considered to have "authentic" knowledge. Emphasizing the importance of using one's own knowledge of the texts to determine religious practice, they were very critical of any identification by *maslak*, and of the tendency to base one's religious practice on the teachings of particular *maslaks*.[8] For instance, Tanveer informed me that she told women not to identify by *maslak*: "I say, Allah has said I won't tolerate divisions, I won't forgive divisions, so then you should not do divisions." The various *maslaks* in South Asia are connected to different schools of Islamic reform—Deobandi, Barelvi, and Ahl-e-Hadis—which have different "normative orientations" (Tareen 2020).[9] While these names mark the boundaries between different *maslaks*, it is important to be aware of "subjective flexibility" and avoid assuming that a tradition reflects a "fixed set of views and positions" or "conflat[ing] the conceptual aspects of these movements or sectarian affiliations with the lived experience of its followers" (Maqsood 2017, 149). It is also important to take seriously how people represent and understand themselves because this might reveal religious priorities that are important to individual constructions of self. While many in Old Delhi associated Muslim Club women with Ahl-e-Hadith teachings because of their insistence on the primacy of the Quran and the Sunna, on unmediated access to them, and their rejection of all four schools of Sunni law, rejecting any identification with *maslak* was clearly important for the self-understandings of Muslim Club women.[10]

Muslim Club women were particularly critical of the practices and traditions of Deobandis and Barelvis who form the majority of Old Delhi Muslims. They were quick to denounce those Muslims who pray at the *mazars* (tombs) of Sufi saints to intercede with God on their behalf. During a conversation after a gathering at Rabiya Baji's home, Abida said to a handful of women who remained, "It is mentioned in the Quran that Allah Tala said these people who are lying in graves—the bodies of *pirs*, *walis*, *faqirs*—they are like the wings of a mosquito, like the skin of a date seed that is so fragile that even the wind can tear them. They are like that, these dead bodies. And you are telling them to intercede with Allah on your behalf?"[11] Abida recited the *Ayat-ul-Kursi* (Quran 2:255) in Arabic and said, "Who is there who can intercede with Allah? No one can intercede with Allah, leave one: Muhammad Rasulallah. Even he won't speak until Allah says, Muhammad what do you want to say? He will only speak when Allah tells him to. Only him. And you are saying that dead bodies in graves will speak with him?" Rabiya Baji, listening intently to Abida's words added, "Allah Tala says, In the world you need things. But I say to you, whatever you want, ask me for. Do not ask anyone else."

Such statements are deeply critical of contemporary Muslim practices in India, especially those that might suggest the immanence, rather than the transcendence, of spiritual power (Robinson 2013, 29). Sufism has been a central force in Indian Islam, not only accounting for the largest numbers of converts historically (Eaton 1993) but also making India a center of pilgrimage for many Muslims. The *barakat* (blessings) of Sufi saints is understood to be literally embedded in the places where they were buried and enshrined, making India sacred space for many and connecting Indian Muslims to transnational Muslim spaces (Green 2012, 2–4, 27–28). And of course, the power of the saint draws not just Muslims but people of different religions to Sufi shrines in India. Indian Sufi practices have been critiqued by various Islamic reform movements, especially in conjunction with an increasing interest in sacred texts since the eighteenth century, which became centrally important to the Islamic reform movements of the nineteenth century (Pernau 2013, 46, 50–51). Margrit Pernau argues that it is in this period that we see a shift from an "identity formed in relation to a center, a person, towards one which placed greater emphasis on religious doctrines and tended to view the boundary lines as more clearly defined" (55). Such shifts, as Pernau contends, are very much connected to the rise of the Muslim middle classes in Delhi after 1857. Especially in the period after 1857, when Indian Muslims unequally bore the brunt of British repression and the last remnants of the Mughal state were dismantled, these middle classes sought to inhabit positions of authority left vacant by a now decimated Muslim aristocracy. Pernau shows that the assertion of new forms of piety associated with Islamic reform movements by middle-class Muslims was very much part of this process (424–25, 430).

The tensions between the various traditions of Islam in India today show that these debates have not been resolved, and the conflicts over interpretation, sectarian affiliation, Sufi teachings, scriptural authority, and schools of jurisprudence continue to shape religious life and practice in the country. Muslim Club members intervene in this politics by arguing against dominant traditions of

Islam in Old Delhi. They position their religious practices as "authentic" Islam, based in scripture and rid of local accretions. It is important to note here that while many reform movements in India may construct themselves as adhering to scriptural prescriptions while critiquing Sufi traditions for their embeddedness in local culture, we must be wary of such characterizations. We must be equally wary of the tendency to celebrate Sufi traditions in South Asia while constructing Islamic reform movements as foreign (Osella and Osella 2013, iv–v). Both illuminate the "discursive tradition of Islam" (Asad 1986), both are inflected by transnational connections, and both are embedded in the cultural, social, and political realities of India (see, for instance, Pernau 2013; Green 2012; Irfan Ahmad 2009).

That said, Muslim Club members understand their practices to be "authentic" Islam, beyond sectarian divisions and schools of jurisprudence. Adding eschatological power to their position, they insist that any other religious practice amounts to disobeying God, the consequences of which will catch up with individuals on judgment day. Abida said,

> Our religion emphasizes unity. Live as one. Leave all the *maslaks*. . . . The Quran says, . . . Say you are Muslim. . . . Do not divide into sects. It is *haram*. But people do not listen. So Allah Tala said, Muhammad, I will give them *hidayat* [guidance] from above. I will show them the line. So do not cry for these people. Because the Prophet would cry a lot. I will give them *hidayat*. But if they do not listen to your guidance—like after I have said do not divide in sects and they still divide themselves—I will say, have you delivered my message? Yes? Your duty is over. On the day of *qiyamat* I will ask them, . . . Why did you divide into sects? When they say, I didn't know, I will call you as a witness and ask them, Why did you ignore his words? They can't say that.

Positioning their understandings of Islam as "authentic" and dismissing other practices as un-Islamic, members of the Muslim Club often got pushback from women who listened to their lectures at gatherings with a diverse membership. Tanveer said that this is why how they communicate their lessons about Islam is as important as the lessons themselves. She said:

> If you say something with anger, then they won't understand. If you say things gently, then it sits in their heart. I tell them, do research on this yourself. Find out which books are authentic, which Hadis are authentic. Learn for yourself. Don't just believe what I say. That I have come and said this is wrong and this is right. Those people say this is what we have learnt from our fathers. We have seen our elders do this so how

> can we change? I say, OK, don't change. But study for yourself. Learn for yourself what Allah Tala says and what Allah's messenger said. If what they said is the same as what you do then you are right. Otherwise you are wrong.[12]

Conflicting ideas of how to be a good Muslim are not unusual in South Asian Islam and often reflect the differences in *maslak* in South Asian Islam and the sources of religious authority followed by each. Examining tensions between different traditions of Islam in Pakistan, Naveeda Khan argues that they grow out of long traditions of debate in Islam on what it means to be Muslim (2012, 10–11) and are best understood through the lens of "striving" to be a better Muslim in the world (57). Ultimately, the insistence that Indian Muslims follow "authentic" Islam, and the adoption of religious practices that members of the Muslim Club believe can be traced to the Quran and the Prophet Muhammad in the seventh century, must be understood in the context of contemporary struggles to define what it means to be a good Muslim in India today. Tanveer echoes what I heard from many members of the Muslim Club—that part of being a good Muslim is not blindly following tradition, or even listening to other members of the Muslim Club, but rather engaging one's mind and intellect to verify whether one's practices were based in the foundational texts. They emphasized the importance of reading translations of the Quran and the commentaries of well-known teachers. Most importantly, for Muslim Club women, individual engagement in self-improvement was an essential requirement for those seeking to become better Muslims in the world.

The Struggle to Be "Good"

The process of fashioning oneself into a "good" Muslim can be fraught, especially since there are various understandings of ideal religious subjectivity in Old Delhi. Consequently, many members of the Muslim Club spoke of how their path had not been easy. Their efforts to be "good" Muslims, which entailed diligently following what they believed were the prescriptions of the foundational texts, were not uniformly viewed as such. While they found support in each other, they often struggled with their families and communities in everyday life. Raisa, a schoolteacher at Roshanara School in Old Delhi who commutes there daily from Jamia Nagar, has struggled against members of her family to practice her form of Islam.[13] She spoke of these struggles to women assembled at one of the Muslim Club gatherings in Old Delhi that she often attends after school. She said that in her Muslim neighborhood in Jamia Nagar

> even married women do not wear burqas. Since I wear a burqa even though I am unmarried, they ask, What has happened to you? Why do you wear it? In the beginning, even my mother and sister used to fight with me. Why do you wear it? There will be no marriage proposals. *Hamdulillah* [praise God], they finally understood. But my neighbors still feel this way. . . . *Hamdulillah* I think, Allah, show them the right path. Today, *Mashallah* [God wills it], after some time a few women in my area have begun to wear burqas.

Raisa's words highlight the questioning that she faced in her own community and from her family for her decision to cover.[14] In her narrative, Raisa notes that time has brought with it what she views as positive change, marked by Muslim women in her neighborhood adopting the burqa and hijab. For her, their acts are situated in a logic of progression that has, in her eyes at least, improved her community. Her own insistence on maintaining her practices despite criticism from others, and her attempts to encourage other women in her own neighborhood and in Old Delhi to adopt these practices, are part of her efforts to be a better Muslim in the world.

While most of the women they encounter are other Muslims, Muslim Club members are enthusiastic about non-Muslims who show an interest in them. For them, Islam is the one true religion. As Rabiya Baji told me, "Allah Tala says, You are the children of the same father. I am the one who created all of you. I created Adam, and Adam propagated children." When I interjected to ask whether she meant all Muslims or all people, she responded, "Allah is not saying people of all religions. Everyone. Muslims. There are no religions, only Islam. . . . Differentiation happened because some people lost their way." For Rabiya Baji, human life provides an opportunity for each individual to follow God's command. But it is up to each individual to make the decision to do so. She said, "The reality is that Allah has left it to humans to make judgments. He does not say, Follow me. He has said, I have given you the straight path. If you do not follow me you will get lost."

Because Muslim Club women believe that straying from the path that Allah has revealed has dire consequences for humans, unlike most other Muslims I worked with in Old Delhi, they felt duty bound to save others from these consequences. Abida explained this to me by referring to the example of the Prophet: "The Prophet, whenever he sees someone who is not Muslim, meaning someone who does not follow Allah, he cries. . . . He says, I feel scared that on the day of *qiyamat*, in . . . hell, they will burn. . . . How will they bear it? So the Prophet would cry a lot—not because they were not Muslim. It made no difference to him if they were Muslim or not." Abida then added, "It does not matter to me if someone is Muslim or not. But I speak about this wherever I go."

For Abida, Raisa, Tanveer, and Rabiya Baji, telling others how to follow what they understand to be the correct path is not just about the salvation of others. It is also about doing the right thing themselves, should they be called upon as witnesses on Judgment Day. Once, when I expressed my gratitude to Abida for spending so much time taking me to gatherings, introducing me to others, and inviting me to her home, she responded, "No, no. This is our opportunity—that we could talk to you. On the day of *qiyamat* we can be your witnesses [laughs]." Then after reciting a verse from the Quran (2:256) in Arabic, she added, "There is no compulsion in religion. You cannot force anyone to do anything. It is *haram*. If you force someone to recite the *kalma*, it is *haram*—until you want to do it. There is no compulsion in religion. . . . It is our duty to tell you. It is your choice."

Sometimes the struggle to be a good Muslim is with oneself rather than others. This was certainly the case with Tanveer. Born and raised in the Ballimaran neighborhood and married at seventeen to a machinist, Tanveer never finished school. Tanveer, her husband, and her daughter live in an apartment that her parents left to her and her sister Mariam, also a member of the Muslim Club. Unlike Mariam, who was vivacious, self-confident, and had the distinction among her peers of being a *hafiz* (one who has memorized the Quran), Tanveer was very shy and diffident when I first met her in 2013. Tanveer told me that going for *waz* (religious sermon) gave her life a direction and purpose that she did not feel she had before. Saying that the paths of individuals who go to *waz* are lined with the wings of angels, she explained that it stimulated her interest in the Muslim Club. She said,

> Because of Allah I was taken there and I started going there. *Waz* happens in many places, but there I received a purpose to live for. That I have come into the world for a purpose. Allah Tala did not create me with no purpose. I discovered the real reason why Allah Tala put me in this world. *Al Hamdulillah*, I am grateful to Allah that I was joined with my *din* [religion].

Tanveer teaches other women how to recite the Quran with the correct pronunciation. She insists, "You must read the whole Quran with *tajvid* [pronunciation]. You must recite every word with the right *tajvid*, in the right way." However, as a diffident person, she did not like speaking at Muslim Club events and had to be coaxed by Abida to recite *duas* (prayers) at gatherings. Like many young women in Old Delhi across religions and classes, especially those with less formal schooling, Tanveer was not socialized to assert herself or to speak authoritatively about subjects like religion. In the years since 2013, Tanveer has clearly struggled to overcome her diffidence in public forums and has become more confident and assertive about her religious knowledge. This was apparent when she took me to a *waz* at Kauser Apa's well-appointed home during Ramzan in 2016. After Kauser Apa had read out a number of hadith and explained these to the diverse group of women gathered there, Tanveer, with a confidence I had not seen before, told Kauser Apa that since it was *Shab-e-Qadr,* she should also give a lecture about that. Kauser Apa suggested that Tanveer do it instead. To my surprise, Tanveer agreed without hesitation and lectured to those present about the importance of praying during this time. Praying on *Shab-e-Qadr,* when the first verses of the Quran were revealed to the Prophet Muhammad, "is equivalent to the prayers of a thousand months," she said, and sometimes you might even feel pins and needles and see your hair stand on end because "the angels are holding your hands." As women listened to her with rapt attention, I realized that Tanveer was no longer the woman I had met in 2013, who had to be coaxed into speaking in public. Tanveer's religious work had given her not only a sense of purpose but also a lot more self-confidence in her dealings with others. Her religious work had provided the space for her to learn to inhabit a particular kind of Muslim subjectivity, even if she had to struggle with her inner demons every day to become the person she aspired to be.

While Tanveer struggled with gendered inhibitions, Abida struggled with desires that interfered with her aspirations. She once told me, "When I take the metro, I pray: Allah guide them [*sabko hidayat de*]. Show them the straight path [*seedha rasta*]. Guide me. I also stray a little bit. Because I have not yet controlled my *nafs—nafs* meaning desires." Ultimately for women like Abida and Tanveer, being a good Muslim was not just about teaching others, but also about constantly improving the self, becoming better Muslims, and regulating their own fears and desires in a world filled with challenges and temptations. Their struggles to overcome perceived limitations are perhaps best understood in terms of what Naveeda Khan calls Muslim aspiration—where individuals are constantly striving toward "self-perfectibility" rather than "perfection" in the context of a future that is open rather than fixed (2012, 203). Nowhere is this more apparent than in Abida's story, which I discuss in the next section.

Ultimately, the lessons of the Muslim Club must also be understood as making place for Muslims in places like Old Delhi. Whether instructing Muslim women to adopt visible practices of piety such as veiling, inviting women to attend prayers in congregation, holding and attending religious lectures, explaining their practices to the uninitiated, contesting stereotypes about Islam, and making time to talk to anthropologists like me, the members of the Muslim Club not only embed a particular form of Islam in Old Delhi, but also, by inviting others to adopt its practices of piety, they increase the visibility of Muslims. When such practices raise questions or discomfort, members of the Muslim Club do not suggest retreating to safe spaces; rather, they advocate making place for Muslims in neighborhoods that might be less hospitable to them. For instance, when Abida was explaining the six points of *hijab* to the gathering mentioned earlier, a woman interjected to say that it was difficult for her to conform to those prescriptions because she lived in a non-Muslim neighborhood. Abida immediately responded that she herself had lived in a non-Muslim neighborhood for many years and had encountered many questions from its non-Muslim denizens. She insisted that she saw these questions as an opportunity to explain why she wore the hijab. In other words, while Abida understood the hijab as a necessary part of her religious practice, she also saw it as a visible artifact that enabled her to make place for herself among the non-Muslims she lived with. As such, religious practice is not just about the divine and transcendental (see Fadil and Fernando 2015), but also about the anxieties and concerns of Muslims traversing the landscapes of everyday life in India today.

Self-Making in Everyday Life

While the lessons of the Muslim Club are central to how women like Raisa, Abida, and Tanveer understand what it means to be a good Muslim, religion is not the only force operating in their lives. They are not just religious subjects. They are gendered subjects, they are class subjects, they are ethnic subjects, and they are national subjects. As such, their everyday lives are shot through with competing hegemonies that variously compel them, discipline them, repel them, or render them "other" as they traverse the fraught politics that inflects their worlds. Therefore, fashioning self and identity is an ongoing process that operates in the context of competing hegemonies, conflicting aspirations, and complex sociopolitical forces. It is useful to think about identity, as Nida Kirmani does, as "shifting contextual processes of situating oneself in relation to various 'others' rather than as indicative of any stable, fixed categorizations" (2013, 15). Identities, in her view, are "processes that come into being—although never fully—through narration" (15). In this last section, I relate Abida's story to reveal how she draws on the lessons of the Muslim Club. And yet the constructions of self and identity in her narrative cannot be understood only in terms of religion. Her narrative illuminates her struggle to be a good Muslim at the intersection of the complex forces and aspirations operating in her life.

Abida's Story

Abida taught science and math at Roshanara School, an Islamic girls school in Old Delhi that caters to children of privileged families. She holds bachelor of science, bachelor of education, and master of science degrees. She has also completed the requirements for a master's in Islamic studies and is keen to earn a PhD in this field. Demonstrating how her religiosity reflects multiple aspirations (Maqsood 2017, 12, 149), Abida insisted that religious education must be accompanied by what she terms "secular knowledge." Dismissing those who believe they do not need secular knowledge and only need to "read the scriptures" as people who have no "logic," she said that an "educated mind cannot be fooled."

The daughter of an Afghan refugee who married an Indian woman, Abida was born in Ghaziabad, Uttar Pradesh, and moved to Old Delhi when she got married to a Deobandi Muslim. She saw her life as a journey toward higher religious knowledge. In 2013, when I interviewed Abida at length about what drew her to her religious path and the Muslim Club, she told me, "I was very modern." She said that she only began to wear a burqa and hijab after her marriage. She said her mother encouraged her to be "religious, cover myself properly. But I was modern." She associates her mother's insistence on wearing the burqa with "tradition," saying dismissively that her mother was strongly influenced by "Indian culture." Abida did start covering, but only after she had studied religion for herself. She did not see her decision to cover as a move toward "tradition," but rather as one based on knowledge and deliberation, and consonant with the constructions of Islam and modernity propounded by people like Zakir Naik whose teachings have informed her religiosity. Studying religion changed the course of her life and led her to start the Muslim Club in Old Delhi.

While her work with the Muslim Club and her practices of piety helped her find fulfillment, it also caused problems in her marriage. Her husband at the time was a Deobandi Muslim who found her new religiosity difficult to accept. She said, "My husband, he does not like I should wear this hijab. . . . He does not take me with him. He says, Make yourself smart and come. Then I will take you with me. But I said, It is your choice. If you want to go with me, I have to wear, because it is compulsory in Islam." Her husband also objected to her frequent absences from the house on Sundays, the only day he was home. If Abida heard there was a marriage celebration or a funeral in Old Delhi, she would immediately drop everything and go there to counsel people on the importance of following the foundational texts rather than what she dismissively called "Indian culture." If such events fell on a Sunday, she felt compelled to go even if her husband wanted her to stay at home. She said, "My husband does not like this. [He says,] Sunday is only for me. You will not go anywhere. I say, I have to go, . . . because all this [local practices] is not there [in the foundational texts]. I want to go. My teacher says, Go when you are called."

In 2013 Abida was still trying to make her marriage work, even as she consistently challenged her husband's attempts to make her conform to his expectations of a wife. However, when I met her again a year and a half later, she had moved out and was trying to get a divorce. She told me, "Our minds do not meet." By 2016 she had married a man who shared her religious views and had moved to Mumbai. Sylvia Vatuk argues that examining why marriages fail enables us to understand "the challenges that men and women face when trying to conform in their daily life to the prescriptions and norms of their religion, and the difficulties they experience when trying to perform to one another's satisfaction their assigned gendered roles" (2015, 191). Abida and her husband not only had different understandings of the centrality of religious prescription in everyday life, but also different views on how to be a good Muslim and a good wife. The instructions that accompany the model marriage contract created by the All India Muslim Personal Law Board in 2005 say that a wife must "obey her husband . . . in all religiously permissible matters. . . . She must not leave the house without his permission" (Vatuk 2015, 199–200). Abida, however, schooled by her teachers to read the foundational texts for herself and follow their instructions literally (or her teachers' commentaries on their instructions), believed otherwise.

The last time I met Abida was in December 2014 when she had left her husband and was living on her own with her youngest son, having sent her older son and daughter to a religious school run by the Jamaat-e-Islami in Uttar Pradesh. She was clearly having a difficult time: with her husband who did not want to grant her the divorce, with her children who were unhappy at the breakup, and with the societal scrutiny she was under as a woman living on her own and continuing her religious work. These concerns found their way into a lecture she gave later that day at a gathering at Rabiya Baji's house. Her lecture was remarkable in revealing how her narrative wove together her religious and personal concerns. I quote excerpts from it:

> The ignorant among the people will say, "What caused them to turn away from their former *Qibla* [direction of prayer] towards which they used to turn?" Say, "To Allah belongs the East and the West. He guides whom he wills towards the Right Path." (Quran 2:142, recited in Arabic; translation by Majid Fakhry)
>
> Because of Allah's orders, the direction [of prayer] changed. . . .
>
> People began to criticize the messenger. They made fun of him. They criticized him so much that Allah Tala said, Tell these people if

they want to live their life according to my instructions they must do as I say. This is *change management*. . . .

We must have patience [*sabr*] and tolerance to withstand these changes. Otherwise it will be very difficult. . . . Whatever changes come, these are tests. Allah says, till your death I will keep testing you. . . .

When things happen in your life and you have to take a step, people will criticize you. . . .

The things that are out of our control, we should not run after them too much. We can only try and pray. After that we should leave it. Think of it as Allah's wish. Whatever changes happen in our life are temporary. Just think, What did Allah's *rasul* [messenger] do? . . . Because Allah's *rasul* went through all the troubles we go through in life. And Allah's *rasul* tells us the solution to all these things. Allah's *rasul* said, When your sorrows cause you too much tension, remember me once and your sorrows will seem smaller. People tell me, people are so critical of me, my family is so critical of me. Allah's *rasul* had eleven uncles. Only two had accepted Islam. The others criticized him. People say we have no money, my in-laws trouble me. Allah's *rasul* faced social boycott for three years. When his wife Khadija had nothing to feed her children, he had to pluck leaves to feed them. . . . When we think of all our hassles in life, we should think about how much Allah's *rasul* was harassed. He was even beaten, till blood flowed. . . .

Death ends all troubles. Whenever we face change, we must hold on to patience. Whenever we have changes, we need to be patient and strengthen ourselves with prayer. . . . Just remember: Allah, you have given me these troubles. You alone will end them. Once you understand that, even if the world tries to destroy you, they cannot do anything.

Sabr, meaning OK, let it be. Let it happen. How much will people say? How much will they trouble you? One day they will give up. . . . And one day they will come to you and say, You are right. . . . That day will definitely come. But you need patience. Not that if someone treats you badly you treat them badly. If someone spoils your character then you spoil their character. You should be silent. No answer. No justification. Sit quietly. Let them say what they want, do what they want. Silence is such an important weapon for the *momin* [believer]. . . .

Whatever Allah said, that is what you should do. Religion does not mean you apply it whenever it suits you. Do what you like and leave what you do not. Embrace religion fully. . . .

When people behave badly we have to show our own pious, true character. We should not also behave badly. . . . You should remember

> that Allah is watching too. Make yourself strong through prayer and patience. . . .
>
> We must prepare for our end. Remember the day of judgment when we are standing in front of Allah. There we will have to give an accounting. The trials in our lives are about this, so Allah can check on us. Allah says, . . . I have made life and death for this reason, to test which of you is good and which is bad. I made life for this reason. Every moment we are being tested. Two angels are sitting and noting down each thing and a book is being prepared. . . . At *qiyamat* we are told to open our books. The angels will open the book and say, Allah, they have only done so many good things and done so many bad things. At that time, we will be out of time. . . .
>
> We must think about those who are criticizing. What is their standard? How thoughtful are they? . . .
>
> When I sit with religious people and tell them what I am doing, they always say, That is absolutely correct, because I am following religion. . . . And those who do not follow religion, they have so many questions. . . . This is why we need to check the standard of those who are saying things. Some people are very religious, very intelligent. When they say something we think, Maybe I have done something wrong. But it could be jealousy. . . . If some religious, good people are criticizing you, it is possible it is because they are jealous. . . .
>
> These changes in life come from Allah—no one else. Whatever difficulties, big or small, remember no one can give you these troubles. These can only come from Allah. . . .
>
> A Muslim is someone who does not cause trouble to others, by their lineage or by their hands.[15]

As I listened to her thirty-eight-minute lecture, I was reminded of our conversation earlier that day when she had spoken to me about her marriage and difficulties. It seemed to me that her own struggles had inflected her lecture that day. The women she was addressing knew Abida and were aware of her current circumstances. Interestingly, after her talk she said to those gathered that she was experiencing difficulties and asked them to say a prayer for her. One woman remarked that she had heard that Abida had left her home (*ghar chod diya*). Abida did not respond to her or say anything further on the subject. Perhaps she was following her own instructions about silence, the weapon of the believer.

In her narrative, Abida sought to make place for herself in Old Delhi as a pious, modern, Muslim woman who aspired to live the life she wanted. However, while Abida's actions might conform to her religious understandings, they challenged gender expectations that also inform her life. As a woman who had left her husband and taken her children with her, was insisting on a divorce that he did not want to give, and was living on her own under nobody's protection, she was violating the prevailing norms of female subjectivity in Old Delhi, particularly, but certainly not only, among Muslims. As Patricia Jeffery and Roger Jeffery have shown in their work in Bijnor, women's experiences and gendered expectations of marriage can be quite similar across religions and classes (2018). In Old Delhi too, across religions, classes, and castes, it is not easy for women to forge a life that goes against familial and gendered expectations. As such, Abida's struggles resonate with those of other women who have sought to leave their marriages and have felt the weight of patriarchal expectations from their husbands, consanguineal and natal families, and from the social circles they belong to. Under scrutiny and facing criticism from others, Abida was struggling against dominant understandings of what a good woman would do—and since religion and gender are mutually constitutive, what a good Muslim woman would do. In her lecture, she used religious discourse and her religious authority to defiantly position herself as a good Muslim woman who was patiently waiting out the criticism, with the understanding that, ultimately, others would come to understand that she was right.

Abida's work not only illuminates how particular notions of piety and gender inform her life but also reveals her aspiration to be modern, to inhabit forms of middle-class religiosity that reflect the contemporary privileging of science and rationality, and to position herself as a global citizen in an inhospitable world. Her projection of herself as a modern woman who valued both religious and secular education, her reliance on "teachers" around the world, her frequent use of the internet to verify her practices, her efforts to encourage other Indian Muslims to practice what she saw as "authentic" Islam, and her challenge to Islamophobia in India and abroad revealed how national and transnational forces and flows shaped her everyday life and who she aspired to be. Such forces and flows, what Purnima Mankekar calls "transnational public cultures," enable us to see places like Old Delhi, and indeed national contexts like India, as "extroverted," rather than insular (2015, 10, citing Massey 1991, 27, 29). Mankekar argues that notions of India and Indianness, while neither singular nor uniform, are shaped by "transnational public cultures" that construct "India as an archive of affect and temporality" (2015, 32). As Mankekar notes, "Subjects are not where affect originates; rather affect produces subjects through the traces it leaves upon them" (13). The transnational public cultures that are part of Abida's world also produce her as a particular kind of subject. As a Muslim woman in India experiencing the resurgence of the Hindu right and its exclusionary understandings of nation and subject, transnational public cultures can exclude and marginalize her. At the same time, other transnational public cultures enable her to intervene in debates about

Islam in South Asia, to correct Islamophobic constructions of Islam and Muslims in India and abroad, to disseminate her particular understandings of Islam in Old Delhi, and to make place for herself in her community as a pious woman negotiating the particular circumstances of her life in India today.

Conclusion

For women in the Muslim Club, their religious work reflects who they are, who they aspire to be, and the kind of world they want to live in. Deeply critical of the practices of many Indian Muslims, they insist on returning to the foundational texts and the practices of the Prophet and his companions in the seventh century. Yet they live in the contemporary world, have multiple and complex aspirations, and must craft self and identity as plural subjects negotiating competing hegemonies and contradictory pulls. They strive to live up to their constructions of good Muslims in a world that is not always good to them and in which they often have to struggle against expectations, desires, needs, and aspirations that trouble their efforts and understandings. While often deemed exceptional by others in Old Delhi, they are in fact like anyone else in the city, or anywhere in the world for that matter: they are complex, contradictory, and plural subjects.

The stories these women tell about their lives provide a window into their struggles to be, and to be perceived as, good Muslims in contemporary India. Like the narratives of many other Muslims that I discuss in the remainder of this book, they are stories through which members of the Muslim Club make place for themselves in Old Delhi today and disseminate their understandings of Islam and proper Muslim subjectivity in their communities. Inflected by transnational cultures and affective regimes, their stories, their religious discourses, and their acts of piety allow us to see Old Delhi as a confluence of multiple hegemonies—of gender, class, religion, and nation—that are local, national, regional, and transnational, amid which individuals construct both self and place. They force us to understand Old Delhi as a place that is "extroverted" (Massey 1991) and cosmopolitan, one that is not just linked to transnational forces and flows but is in fact produced and enabled by them.

At a historical moment when anti-Muslim sentiment is on the rise in India and across the world, the narratives and practices of women in the Muslim Club are one, albeit contested, way to make place for Muslims in contemporary India. Their religious views are colored by the anxieties, expectations, fears, and aspirations that inform their lives, and are very much in conversation with the politically fraught circumstances that inflect their worlds. Challenging reductive understandings of Muslim identity, we need to situate their words and deeds within the sociopolitical context of their performance. As the place for Muslims shrinks amid the majoritarian impulses of Indian politics, Muslim Club members insist on visibility, on disseminating particular understandings of Islam that challenge local and global Islamophobias, and on maintaining their distinction from those around them. In this they are not unlike many Muslim reformers who preceded them. Fearing erasure and experiencing disavowal amid Hindu majoritarianism and violence, many have sought to mark Muslim identity and presence in India, to assert their political claims. However, as I show in the rest of this book, this is not the only way to make place in the face of exclusionary nationalism.

4

LIVING WITH DIFFERENCE

With my heart in my mouth, I ducked under the restless horse standing amid the crowds on Hamilton Road near Kashmiri Gate and followed Sakina to the other side. "Crouch lower," the horse minder told me urgently, concerned that my head would touch the horse's underbelly and alarm it. While I was terrified of being kicked in the face, Sakina was not scared at all. For her this was not a horse, but Dhul Dhul Maula, a representation of the steed Zuljinah, who took Imam Husain out to the battlefield and brought his body home to his grieving relatives on Ashura, the tenth day of the Islamic month of Muharram. Sakina, like many others, believed that Dhul Dhul Maula was carrying Imam Husain, his *ruh* (spirit) invisible above the saddle that was bedecked with flowers. The cloth covering the animal was spattered with "blood" and covered with the arrows that had hit Zuljinah on the battlefield. Zehra Baji, Sakina's mother, touched Dhul Dhul Maula and brought her fingers to her heart and lips but chose not to go under it. "It is too restless," she said. In retrospect, I wished that I had followed her lead instead of Sakina's.

We pushed our way down Hamilton Road through crowds of mourners dressed in black, stopping to pay our respects to Husain's bier and his *alam*, or standard (see figure 4.1). We paused briefly by a group of young men stripped to the waist and engaged in *zanzeer matam* (self-flagellation with blades) as those gathered around sprayed them with rose water, before continuing on our way to Panja Sharif, the Shii *dargah* where the procession was headed. Unlike the men who lingered on or joined the procession, many of the women preferred to move on quickly to Panja Sharif to secure a place to sit on one of the upper levels and watch the proceedings

FIGURE 4.1. Paying respects to Imam Husain's bier on Hamilton Road. Photograph by the author.

below. There is perhaps no other event that marks sectarian difference as clearly as Ashura, when Husain and seventy-two of his followers were killed on the battlefield by the caliph's forces, initiating the sectarian split that divides Muslims today.

Muharram is a time of heightened sectarian tension in much of South Asia, which sometimes bubbles over into confrontation and violence. Indeed, especially during Muharram, histories of tension and violence between Shias and Sunnis in South Asia are repeatedly recounted, accompanying stories of the latest incidents of violence. And yet it was also a moment when many in Old Delhi highlighted points of commonality between Shias and Sunnis instead of dwelling on the differences that are the stuff of conflict, newspaper headlines, and television reports. While tensions do inform relationships between Shias and Sunnis in Old Delhi during Muharram, here I focus on everyday attempts to bridge difference, diffuse tensions, and enable broader understandings of community among Old Delhi's Muslims, and between Muslims and Hindus, during this period.

What people say may belie what they do. However, their representations of self and community are important discursive practices that reveal what they hold to be important, how they want to be viewed, and how they want to situate themselves in the world. I examine how religious practices and discourses during and immediately after the Islamic month of Muharram provide an arena for new ways of positioning Shias in Old Delhi and in India today. I argue that Shii rituals and discourses during Muharram, while marking religious and sectarian distinctions, simultaneously enable forms of identity that challenge exclusionary constructions of community and nation and allow Old Delhi's diverse communities to *live with difference* in contemporary India.

In her work on the city of Ajmer, Shail Mayaram highlights the importance of examining how communities live with difference. She says, "The question of Hindu-Muslim conflict has often been addressed by counterposing it with ideas of 'communal harmony,' which to my mind, are quite illusory. The question with respect to a multicultural center such as Ajmer is how people live with and manage difference" (2005, 160). We can extend this question to Old Delhi, a place that is home to people of many religions, classes, ethnicities, and languages. It is a place that is not immune to the communal tensions that have plagued India in recent years, or to the sectarian and ideological tensions that have affected South Asian Muslims.[1] And yet it is a place where people of multiple religions and sects live together, are economically interdependent, and use each other's services during important religious and social events. How do people live with difference in Old Delhi? While in the next chapter I examine how other groups of Muslims in Old Delhi articulate identity and community, here I focus on Old Delhi's Shias to explore how they construct community across religious and sectarian lines, forging common cultures (Visweswaran 2010) to live with others in contemporary India.

Shias in Old Delhi

Of the 14.23 percent of Indians who identify as Muslims, the majority are Sunni, making Shias a small minority in the country. Muslims account for 12.86 percent of the population of Delhi and 33.4 percent of the population of Central Delhi, where Old Delhi is located.[2] The census does not provide a breakdown of sectarian affiliation, but researchers put the percentage of Indian Shias at about 10 percent of the Muslim population (D'Souza 2012, 71; Bard 2005, 159). There are significant differences among Shias, a product of varying traditions, histories, and networks of different Shii communities in India (F. Robinson 2014). All the Shias I worked with were Twelver Shias, and most were migrants from the North Indian states of Uttar Pradesh and Bihar. While the majority were economically underprivileged migrants who came to Delhi as part of the "depeasantisation" of rural India (G. Menon 2018), a few were well off, claiming aristocratic connections and, in one case, tracing descent to the Persian troops called to support Emperor Humayun (1508–1556) during his reign.

Most Shias I worked with resided in different parts of Old Delhi, while a few lived elsewhere but led or sponsored events there. Some were highly educated, some were Delhi's cultural and economic elite, and many had minimal or no formal education and lived in one-room tenements in Old Delhi. My work with Shias was greatly facilitated by Zehra Baji, whom I met through her daughter, who chanced upon me at a Sunni neighbor's house in Shahganj and took me to her one-room home nearby to meet her mother. It was Zehra Baji who patiently taught me how to dress and comport myself during Muharram, generously invited me to accompany her to events, introduced me to her extended family and neighbors, and even enabled my acceptance beyond her networks. For instance, on the ninth of Muharram a relative of the erstwhile Nawab of Rampur, who sponsors events at Old Delhi's Panja Sharif Dargah, noticing my black clothing, said, "I commend you on your choice of colors this evening," and invited me to participate in the proceedings with his family. Indeed, Zehra Baji's schooling helped me gain acceptance among Shias, even those with far more education, wealth, and status in Old Delhi than her.

While residing in different parts of Old Delhi, many Shias I worked with hailed from regions that were once part of (or influenced by) the former princely state of Awadh, located in what is today the state of Uttar Pradesh. Awadh was an important cultural and political center for Shias in North India, and it has been influential not just regionally but also in Iran and beyond (M. Khan 2014, 398, 401). The global influence of Awadhi Shii practices was very important to some of my interlocutors, most notably Hasan Jafri, a member of Delhi's Shii elite and a well-known personality on Delhi's cultural scene, who insisted that Awadhi Shii practices during Muharram had been influential in places like Iran and Iraq. The transnational flows of Awadhi Shii practices indicate that we need to pay more attention to the global impact of South Asian Islamic traditions and decenter the focus on the Middle East in Islamic studies.

The religious practices of Old Delhi Shias make place for Muslims in India today by enabling a vision of community that troubles religious and sectarian boundaries. Highlighting the blurred boundaries between religious traditions in India (see Hirst and Zavos 2005), Jafri Sahib said that some Shii practices illuminated the shared religious worlds of places like Awadh, where Hinduism and Islam have influenced each other for centuries. By way of example, Jafri Sahib said that Shii women break their glass bangles on the first of Muharram as an act of mourning, a gesture reminiscent of the practices of many North Indian Hindu widows upon their husband's death.[3] Important in terms of understanding Old Delhi Shias, one feature of Shii narratives produced in this region, according to Justin Jones, is that they "universalize[d] Husain's message beyond the Shia themselves, to all of humankind" (2014, 422). Indeed, as I will show below, such traditions of positioning Shias with non-Shias continue to be important in Old Delhi, and they provide a way to construct common cultures that enable people to forge alliances and affiliations across divisions and boundaries (Visweswaran 2010, 8, 16). At a historical moment when religious and sectarian conflict often dominates the headlines in South Asia, I examine how Old Delhi's Shias draw meaning from their traditions to construct self and identity and to articulate broader understandings of community that embrace difference in contemporary India.

However, while many Shii traditions might speak to such cultural commons and shared religious worlds, it is important to recognize that the relationship Old Delhi Shias have with other groups, including Sunnis, is complicated. Indeed, there are variegated articulations of belonging among Old Delhi's Muslims that require a nuanced reading of shared religious worlds in South Asia, rather than an uncritical celebration of religious pluralism (Gold 2014; C. Mahmood 1993). While cultural commons can be forged across religious and sectarian boundaries in certain circumstances, they can also be premised on particular exclusions that warn against any celebratory reading of these. So, for instance, Jafri Sahib in particular, while highlighting commonalities between Hindus, Shias, and Barelvi Sunni Muslims, could be deeply critical of Deobandi Sunni Muslims, dismissively labeling them "Wahabis" who were intolerant of Shias.[4] However, while it was the case that some Deobandis were critical of Shii practices, other Old Delhi Deobandi Muslims actively forged alliances with Shias and Hindus across sectarian and religious boundaries.

The complexities in the relationships between Shias, Sunnis, and Hindus in Old Delhi emerge from the multiple forces at work in these communities that sometimes draw people together, while dividing them at other times. Shias live in close proximity with these other groups in Old Delhi, a fact that sometimes sparks tensions while also creating the need to find ways for Shias, Sunnis, and Hindus to live with each other. Panja Sharif Dargah, where many Muharram commemorations take place, is surrounded by shops owned by Sikhs and Hindus, many of whom are from families who came to Delhi during the partition. Their relationships with Muslims were historically fraught, and they continue to be tense in a country fractured by the violent politics of the Hindu right. Both Sunnis and Shias have experienced prejudice and violence at the hands of the Hindu right and have suffered discrimination in a Hindu-majoritarian state (Chatterji, Hansen, and Jaffrelot 2019; Ghassem-Fachandi 2012; K. Menon 2010; Jaffrelot 2007; Brass 2003; Hansen 1999; Kakar 1996). Their common experience of violence and discrimination at the hands of the Hindu majority has often led Muslims to see commonalities among themselves despite sectarian differences.

At the same time, other forces have exacerbated sectarian tensions, while enabling alliances across religious boundaries. Sunni piety movements have actively called on people to return to the prescriptions of the foundational texts, a move that has created tension between Shias and Sunnis in neighborhoods like Zehra Baji's where Shias are a small minority. Other sectarian tensions have sometimes led Shias to emphasize connections between themselves and non-Muslims and to construct India as a refuge despite rising Hindu-Muslim conflicts (Eisenlohr 2015, 691–92). Indeed, for some Old Delhi Shias, especially when Shia-Sunni tensions rise in South Asia, sectarian difference can be more important than religious difference. A couple told me that they would rather live in a Hindu-majoritarian state than a Sunni one. Although he subsequently quit because of differences with Narendra Modi, Jafri Sahib even held a powerful position in the Delhi BJP, whose Hindu-chauvinist views few Muslims I worked with supported. It is amid such complex histories, alliances, and politics that Old Delhi's Muslims live with each other and construct community in contemporary India.

Of course, religious identity is not the only force operational in people's lives. Class can be a factor that fractures cultural commons and that informs people's actions and affiliations. This was particularly apparent in my interactions with those from wealthy and well-connected backgrounds. Given my own class positioning as an educated, urban, English-speaking, upper-middle-class Indian, many of these interlocutors welcomed me into their lives and homes but were less willing to include other Shias from less-privileged backgrounds. For instance, Jafri Sahib's wife, Meena Jafri, invited me to sit with her family for Muharram commemorations but was clear that she did not want me to bring any of my companions from Old Delhi with me. While Meena Jafri and her husband were well-educated, upper-class, Delhi urbanites, my companions at these events were all economically underprivileged Shii women with minimal or no formal schooling, who found themselves in Delhi because of India's agrarian crisis. Such instances forced me to recognize class as a gulf that sometimes seemed less bridgeable than religious difference.

In her work on modern Muslim subjectivity in Pakistan, Katherine Pratt Ewing argues that the subject is constituted at the interstices of competing hegemonies, "unexamined ideologies and habits" that influence the subject in particular contexts (1997, 35–36). Narratives reveal not only how individuals align themselves with particular subject positions in particular contexts, but also the conflicts and inconsistencies that are the product of being caught between multiple and competing hegemonies (6). Identities, of course, are not static but "processes that come into being" in narratives, and they are inflected by the historical events that shape those narratives (Kirmani 2013, 15, 85). For Shias in Old Delhi and elsewhere, historical events and relationships from the past and the present shape their constructions of self and identity in contemporary India. As such, for Shias, and indeed for all Muslims, how they understand themselves, their relationships with others, and their place in the nation is structured by colonial legacies, postcolonial violence, and the pasts and presents of "living together separately" (Mayaram 2008, 11).

Muharram in Old Delhi

Muharram is the first month of the Islamic calendar and, as many Muslims of all sects were quick to tell me, a time of sadness for Muslims because it is the month when Husain, the grandson of the Prophet Muhammad, and the younger son of his daughter Fatima and son-in-law Ali was killed at Karbala, in present-day Iraq. Husain was killed on Ashura, the tenth day of Muharram. Having refused to pledge allegiance to the caliph Yazid, Husain, along with his family and companions, decided to move to Kufa, where he had been invited and where there had been unrest during the reign of Yazid's father, Muawiya (Hyder 2006, 87–88). Viewed as a threat and a potential source of more upheaval in the region, Yazid's forces intercepted the group at Karbala, where Husain and seventy-two of his supporters, including his half-brother Abbas, and his sons Ali Akbar and six-month-old Ali Asghar were killed (88). By nightfall on Ashura, only a few had survived, led by the forceful presence of Husain's grieving sister Zainab, a major figure in Shii commemorations during Muharram (193).

Old Delhi holds a special place for many Shias in the city during Muharram and the months that follow it. It is the site of some of the largest Muharram commemorations in the city. Old Delhi is also the place where two major Shii processions begin, carrying the *taziya* (replica of Husain's tomb) from Old Delhi to the Shii "Karbala" located at Shah-e-Mardan Dargah in Jorbagh, New Delhi—one marking the fortieth day of Imam Husain's death (*Chehlum* or *Safed Taziya*), and the other marking the end of the two months and eight days of mourning (*Kala Taziya*). While *majalis* (mourning gatherings; singular *majlis*) are held throughout Delhi, few compare to the one held on Ashura at Panja Sharif Dargah, where thousands gather from all over the greater metropolitan area of Delhi to mourn the death of Husain and his companions (see figure 4.2). Panja Sharif near Kashmiri Gate is one of the oldest Shii shrines in Delhi and, along with Shah-e-Mardan in Jorbagh, is one of only two in the city dating back to the Mughal period that survived colonial rule (Singh 2006, 281). Historically, Panja Sharif has attracted people of all religious and sectarian traditions (291–92). In our conversation at Panja Sharif, Maulana Asghar Ali said that this is also true today, since many from the surrounding market attend events during Muharram, including many Hindus. Although it was hard to determine religious affiliation in the crowds that had gathered, the maulana's claim was corroborated by the

FIGURE 4.2. Women and men at Panja Sharif Dargah on Ashura. Photograph by the author.

presence of a Hindu holy man, prominent in his saffron robes, at one of the Ashura events at Panja Sharif. Maulana Asghar Ali also showed me the handprints (*panja*) of Ali that make this *dargah* famous and mark it as a sacred place. Nalini Singh asserts that people believe that the Mughal emperor Bahadur Shah Zafar would walk to the *dargah* from the Red Fort to pray (288). Such histories, imagined or otherwise, along with Ali's handprints, mark Panja Sharif, and indeed Old Delhi, as a special place for many Shias.

On Ashura, thousands from all over the city gather between the Shii Jama Masjid and Panja Sharif Dargah in Old Delhi for the *azadari* or mourning procession, when blood and rose water seep into the ground every year, becoming part of the place, as mourners make their slow progression down Hamilton Road performing *matam* (ritual mourning) with hands, blades, chains, and knives. Jafri Sahib and his wife, Meena Jafri, told me that the mourners were protected by the power of their imams; their wounds, only treated with rose water, never get infected. Many of the male mourners who participated in the procession belonged to various Shii *anjumans* (organizations). Upon arriving at Panja Sharif, each *anjuman* would read its *nauhas* (dirges) and perform *matam* in the open courtyard as thousands watched from the balconies above.

While most refrained from making overt political statements, some *anjumans* used the ritual occasion to pronounce their solidarity with groups they understood to be oppressed. For instance, one of the Kashmiri *anjumans* engaged in a call and response, naming various beleaguered groups, including Palestinians, followed by the crowd response, "We are with you" (*hum tumhare saath hain*). While some enthusiastically joined the call and response, others, wary of the media presence and potential repercussions, were critical of the politicization of the ritual occasion. To me, the call and response illuminated how ritual occasions provide an arena to transcend boundaries, including sectarian, religious, and national ones, and construct alliances with people—in this case, through the common experience of suffering. It also beautifully illustrated how the Karbala narrative provides Shias with a framework for understanding their lives in the contemporary world. Husain's suffering becomes their suffering—as Shias marginalized by the Sunni majority, as Muslims marginalized by Hindu majoritarianism and violence, and as a beleaguered people marginalized by the politics of nation-states.

Indeed, Muharram provides a privileged lens to examine how Shias construct their past and present, and articulate particular understandings of identity and community. This was powerfully demonstrated at a *majlis* held at Panja Sharif Dargah commemorating *Sham-e-Ghariban* (night of the dispossessed), the night after Husain's death at Karbala. As night fell on Ashura, the *dargah* was enveloped in darkness broken only by the wavering light of candles and the haunting words of *Ghabrayegi Zainab*, a famous *nauha* that speaks of Zainab's grief.[5] The words underscore the transition of Husain's struggle to his sister, for, as Hyder notes, "the day belonged to Husain; the night to Zainab" (2006, 194). Husain's struggles and Zainab's suffering and commitment to her brother's cause provide a framework for Shias in Old Delhi and elsewhere to understand their lives and struggles in the present.

That night after the *nauha*, Maulana Kalbe Rushaid recited the last of his many *masaibs* (remembrance of the sufferings of the Prophet's family) during Muharram at Panja Sharif.[6] Addressing the audience, he said, "Usually I do not say anything at the *majlis-e-Sham-e-Ghariban* apart from the *masaib*. But conditions are such that I want to spend a few minutes on those martyrs . . . who were killed only because they lift the coffin [*tabut*] of Husain, who were killed only because they lift the *taziya* [replica of the tomb] of Husain, who were killed only because they lift the standard [*alam*] of Husain." He referred to a Tehrik-e-Taliban attack on a Muharram procession in Dera Ismail Khan, Pakistan, the day before, in which eight people had been killed and several wounded: "I want to say, what kind of Islam is it to kill such victimized people?"[7] Then, inviting those "who think this is Islam," presumably, the instigators of the attack, to come to the battlefield, he said, "You see what you do and we'll see what we do. You bring a bomb and come. We will bring an *alam* and come [audience praise]. You will come to kill. We will come to die. And the world will decide after many years who were the killers [*maarnewale*] and who were those killed [*marnewale*]." It will be clear, he said, that those who killed were the same as "those who killed Husain in the field of Karbala." He proclaimed, pointedly noting his departure from Urdu to use the Hindi/Hindu word *shraddhanjali*, that he wants to pay tribute and give *salam* [salute] to those who died and to their mothers. Then, highlighting the perpetuity of Husain's message, he said, "Nobody could kill Husain then, nobody can kill Husain today. Nobody could destroy Husainiyat (Husain's ethics) then, nobody can destroy Husainiyat today. Yazid [voice raised], drowned in the darkness of the night. Husain is alive even today. . . . Wherever there is humanity [*insaniyat*], there is Husainiyat." The maulana then launched into his *masaib*, which focused on remembering the women of the Prophet's family who, he said, lost everything on this night. His tone switched from anger to a mournful lament delivered in a melodious voice. He wept, and the audience wept with him.

Maulana Kalbe Rushaid is a powerful speaker, and his words deeply impacted the audience. To understand the power of his words, we need to recognize that the *taziyas* carried in Muharram processions are not just symbolic objects. For Shias, they are items that "emanate potent grace and [the] sanctified power [*baraka*]" of the martyr (Ruffle 2011, 32). To carry them is to participate in the dissemination of their power in the world, especially among those who come to perform *ziyarat* [pilgrimage] to them. While many Muslims, like the women in the Muslim Club, would critique such practices and emphasize instead transcendent power and textual prescriptions (Robinson 2013), it is the belief that spiritual power is immanent in these objects that draws many, Shias and others, to these processions.[8] The *ziyarat* of women I attended Muharram with in Old Delhi involved approaching each of these objects barefooted, respectfully touching them and kissing their fingers, and reciting prayers at each of them.[9] For them the mere presence of the *taziya*, the standard, the bier, and Dhul Dhul Maula made place in Old Delhi for Shias, endowing both people and place with the *barakat* [blessings] of their imams. In part, it is because of the power of these objects that the maulana's reference to acts that desecrated them, and killed or wounded their bearers, evoked such strong reactions among those gathered.

Maulana Kalbe Rushaid's words must also be understood as having the potential to evoke a reaction across sectarian and religious lines, in his condemnation of tragic violence, his fluid insertion of Hindi/Hindu words (*shraddhanjali*), his performative power, and his mastery of affect. Indeed, many were moved by the affect generated at the event because they could relate to the experiences being narrated. Their reactions were not just because of their religious identities, but also because of their positioning in other common cultures—of gender, of motherhood, of performance, and of culture. This was powerfully revealed when one woman began sobbing next to me during one of the *masaibs*. When other women around her started comforting her, she explained that she had lost her son the week before. As a grieving mother, she could relate to the grief of the Karbala survivors in ways that transcended difference—of time, circumstance, culture, religion, or sect. Moreover, as Amy Bard notes, "ritual speech, especially appreciation for poetic speech, accounts in large part for the fluidity with which mourners in South Asia individually navigate the *majlis*' ideal emotional state" (2005, 156). Bard argues that poetic performances at a *majlis* share with other Urdu poetry performances a reliance "upon finely honed, learned sensitivity to allusions and literary conceits, upon heightened personal and communal responsiveness," which "helps explain the impact *majlis* narratives have on many non-Shia'ahs" (157). Thus, the performative and affective dimensions of the maulana's oratory are key to his ability to appeal across sectarian and religious lines, and to narratively and emotionally construct a community of mourners across such boundaries. And as I examine below, the maulana consciously blurs religious and sectarian boundaries by identifying *Husainiyat*, or *Husaini*, ethics (Ruffle 2011, 5), with *insaniyat*, humanity.

Maulana Kalbe Rushaid is greatly respected by Old Delhi Shias who come to listen to him at Panja Sharif year after year. Thus, what he has to say about Shias, and their relationships with others in the past and the present, is listened to by many and, in that sense, is a force in Old Delhi articulations of self and identity.[10] In his *masaib*, the maulana pointed to the sectarian violence and tension that often plague Shii-Sunni relations in South Asia, particularly during Muharram. Most Old Delhi Shias live with the awareness of simmering tensions in everyday life. The tensions, Shii-Sunni difference, and antagonistic understandings of each other were often expressed in conversations I had with Muslims in Old Delhi. Yet it is also important to recognize the effort taken to live with difference in Old Delhi.

Living with Difference in Old Delhi

Shias and Sunnis in Old Delhi certainly live with the awareness of difference, even as they also share common experiences of economic and political marginalization in the country, and are affected by the violence and exclusionary politics accompanying the rise of the Hindu right. During Muharram, this awareness of difference sometimes manifests in a tense atmosphere, but unlike in other parts of India, there has been little outright violence. Indeed, the most discussed episode of Shii-Sunni violence in Old Delhi had little to do with Muharram. Sunnis and Shias told me about a fatal shooting in the Ballimaran area in 2008, when the family of a Sunni groom was attacked by angry men of the Shii bride's family upon their "love marriage" without parental consent.[11] Though overtly about sectarian difference, such gendered violence, as Saadia Toor has argued in her work on Pakistan, is often deeply embedded in the tensions around the defiance of patrilineal authority and control of female sexuality in South Asia (Toor 2011). While some I worked with expressed their disapproval of the practices of the other sect, as often as not they emphasized community across sectarian lines. These inclusive understandings of community manifested in narratives that emphasized solidarities, and in practices like sharing food, assisting one another, and building friendships across these boundaries, even while living with the awareness of difference and occasional tension.

Although ostensibly about difference, the maulana's *masaib* at Panja Sharif was also about these solidarities. In it he constructs Shias as *marne wale*, or those who are killed, as opposed to *maarne wale*, or those who kill. He constructs an identity for Shias that is consonant with humanity, nonviolence, and love for Husain. This is clearly juxtaposed against the violence of the Tehrik-e-Taliban that he insists is against Islamic principles. Here the maulana's articulation of Islam as a religion of peace and against violence is consonant with the narratives of many Old Delhi Muslims of all sectarian affiliations.

Moreover, in his *masaib* he draws on understandings of Husain and the model he presents that are common in South Asia and that cross religious and sectarian boundaries. Karen Ruffle asserts that key to Husaini ethics in South Asia is the idea that Husain and other members of the Prophet's family provide models of ideal conduct for Shias through their willingness to suffer and sacrifice themselves and through their commitment to justice, truth, social welfare, restraint, and peace (2011, 18, 50). This image of Husain has been mobilized in various political movements in South Asia, including by non-Shias such as Muhammad Iqbal and Maulana Azad in their opposition to colonial rule (Jones 2014, 422; Hyder 2006, 150–58), and by Shias presenting themselves as models for humanity in their opposition to religious militancy (Eisenlohr 2015, 699). Beyond South Asia, Mary Elaine Hegland notes how Husain was held up as a "model for emulation" during the Iranian Revolution for his willingness to sacrifice himself to oppose tyranny (1998, 240–41). Here the maulana's narrative does more than position Shias as models worthy of emulation. He insists that a good Muslim—Shia or Sunni—would not engage in violence against innocents, and that a good human being would be compelled by Husainiyat, thereby mobilizing difference to articulate a community defined by its commitment to shared values.

The maulana's construction of Shii identity is one I encountered often in Old Delhi, though not always in a positive light. One Shii maulvi visiting from Lucknow, a city that has seen a lot of Shii-Sunni violence, critiqued Old Delhi Shias for being too "polite."[12] In his view, Old Delhi Shias sacrificed their religious traditions to avoid conflict. Maulana Kalbe Rushaid does not suggest sacrificing Shii practices, but he insists that dying for them is more in the spirit of Husain than engaging in violence over them. Indeed, most of the Shias I met in Old Delhi maintained their religious practices. Women held or attended *majalis* every day during Muharram, and very often in the weeks that followed until the end of the two months and eight days of mourning. While aware of critique from Sunni neighbors, Shias I knew continued to engage in *majlis* and *matam*, wore black clothes, did not wear makeup or jewelry, avoided celebrations of any sort, and did not listen to music or watch television. Occasionally, when they engaged in a ritual that could potentially offend, they were secretive about it. For instance, in a ritual not endorsed by many Shias, a group of Old Delhi Shii families from the same village in Uttar Pradesh, who were related to Zehra Baji and Sakina, burnt an effigy of "Umar" the day after the end of the mourning period. Sakina identified Umar as the person "who killed Imam Husain," suggesting that the effigy was of Umar Ibn Sad who led the attack at Karbala. However, in her description of this ritual in Lucknow, Amy Bard argues that while some said it was Umar Ibn Sad, many claimed it was an effigy of the second caliph (Bard 2010, 174), an identification that many Sunnis would find problematic. Recognizing they could potentially offend, Old Delhi Shias who engaged in this ritual did so quietly, hiding their acts from others, especially their Sunni landlords. They did not want to offend and, as a small minority in Old Delhi, they certainly did not want conflict or violence.

Many Shias insisted that Islam condemns violence, and in this they are very much in agreement with many of the Sunnis I worked with. For instance, Meena Jafri contended that for Shias, violence is only permissible in defense of religion. A story about Ali encapsulated this philosophy for her. She told me that once, in battle, a man spat on Ali's face. When Ali responded by immediately sheathing his sword, his followers asked him why he was risking his life on the battlefield. Ali responded that if he fought now, it would be out of anger at the insult. He would be fighting for himself when his religion only permitted him to fight for God. For Meena Jafri, Ali's example powerfully illustrated the Shii position on violence and explained why many believed that engaging in violence because they had been hurt or insulted was problematic.

Like many Shias in Old Delhi, most Sunnis I met also avoided conflict and strived to maintain good relations with their Shii neighbors. Although some were critical of Shii practices during Muharram in conversations with me, most condemned the violence that sometimes accompanies Muharram commemorations in parts of South Asia. Declaring that "idiots all over the world fight," Rafiq Sahib forged common ground between Shias and Sunnis by insisting that they had a shared understanding of the past. He argued that the real difference between Sunnis and Shias was not over their understanding of Islamic history, but over engaging in *matam*, ritual mourning. He said:

> This history—it is Islamic history. This war happened. . . . In it he [Husain] was tricked and murdered. We have a part in all of this. *It is part of our Islamic history.* These Shias, for a few days they beat their chests. . . . They do *matam* and harm their bodies—cut themselves with knives. . . . Sunnis do not do this, because Sunnis believe that it is against Allah to cause your body harm, because this *body is given by God.*

Here, Rafiq Sahib suggests that the real split between Sunnis and Shias is about how people mourn during Muharram, not the history that resulted in the sectarian split. Other Sunnis expressed similar sentiments. Ameena Baji said that while Sunnis also feel sad about the death of Husain, the Quran only allows three days of mourning. But, she said, Shias engage in *matam* every Muharram. Reading aloud from an Urdu book called *Adab-e-Sharif* to highlight that crying loudly is inappropriate after the first three days of mourning, she said dismissively, "This screaming and wailing is wrong." Like Rafiq Sahib, Ameena Baji also avoided any discussion of the different interpretations of the foundational texts, the question of who was to succeed the Prophet after his death, and the resulting divergence between those who supported the caliphate versus those who supported the imamate. Instead, what she chose to articulate to me was that she did not think the highly emotional expressions of mourning and grief were appropriate. However, she told me that she refrains from raising these disagreements with most Shias she knows.

Interestingly, there is much that Shias like Zehra Baji and Sakina would agree with Ameena Baji about, despite important disagreements on this issue. This became clear to me a few months after Muharram, when Sakina, Zehra Baji, and I were talking about death and grieving in the context of the passing of one of their neighbors. I have transcribed part of the conversation below, because it is revealing of both the convergences and divergences between Shias and Sunnis in Old Delhi:

> SAKINA: We Shias believe that we cannot cry like this for our own people—that we beat ourselves, mess up our hair. We cannot do this for our own *relations*. Among us, we can only cry like this for Imam Husain.
>
> ZEHRA BAJI: Like in Islam, there are only three days of mourning. For *ordinary* people it is only three days. . . .
>
> SAKINA: Yes, yes. In Islam it is said that if you cry, you must cry quietly. Among us, when we cry for Imam Husain, then we do not cry quietly. We cry as openly as we can cry.

In this exchange, it is clear that while Shias like Zehra Baji and Sakina agree with Sunnis like Ameena Baji about controlling expressions of grief, they make exceptions for their imams, especially Imam Husain. To understand this, it is useful to look at some of the tensions between emotional expression and self-control in South Asian Islam. While the ability to use one's *aql* (intellect) rather than be ruled by emotion is emphasized in some traditions (Ring 2006, 109, 113; Marsden 2005, 87–89), others see emotional expression as a site of authenticity (Marsden 2005, 118) or as central to cultural identity (Ring 2006, 117). In a Shii *majlis*, emotional expression is important, especially when listening to narratives of the tragic events at Karbala. Diane D'Souza argues that crying at a *majlis* is important because "a central purpose of the gathering is the sorrowful remembrance of the terrible losses suffered by the Prophet's family" (2012, 146). In fact, feeling uncontrollably sad about this history is part of being Shia. As Amy Bard notes, for Shias, "*majlis* tears change the world and the individual; they demonstrate faith and accrue merit, even as they transform words and memories into something tangible" (2005, 158). Ultimately, emotional expression at a *majlis* is crucial to enabling particular constructions of subjectivity that Shias strive to inhabit. Indeed, crying at a *majlis* is best understood as a performative act, "a regularized and constrained repetition of norms" that "enables a subject and constitutes the temporal condition for the subject" (Butler 1993, 95).

However, clearly these constructions of Muslim subjectivity are not shared by all Muslims. Revealing her sectarian biases, and perhaps the Deobandi influence that shaped the culture of many Old Delhi Muslims, Ameena Baji condemns such emotional expressions. Writing about Deoband reformer Maulana Thanawi's book *Bihishti Zewar*, Barbara Metcalf writes, "The hallmark of the ideal is self-control and discipline, qualities that orient the believer to unfailing fidelity to religious obligations and to rigorous moderation and restraint in all personal encounters" (1990, 164). Under a subsection entitled "Reprehensible Innovations, Bad Customs, and Bad Deeds, Thanawi includes "upon a death, to cry aloud and weep in sorrow; to beat your face and breast; to recount the event and weep" (Metcalf 1990, 75; in classical Islam see Smith and Haddad 2002, 59). Drawing on these traditions, Ameena Baji suggests that such practices are not properly Islamic. Importantly, many other Sunnis might disagree with her, especially those who form their own procession with *taziyas* during Muharram in Old Delhi. However, her words still reveal sectarian tensions in Old Delhi, ever present in Sunni-Shii interactions but often masked by the demands of Old Delhi etiquette and a mutual awareness of Muslim marginalization in India.

While these sentiments were expressed to me privately, most Sunnis were careful to avoid interfering with Shii rituals during Muharram and, usually, did not share their views with Shias. For instance, as I observed the procession carrying the Kala Taziya on the last day of mourning wind its way through the crowded market at Matia Mahal, I noticed the mostly Sunni shopkeepers sitting in their shops and watching the proceedings. Men, women, and children peered out of balconies and windows or lined the streets to watch. There was no space to move on the street. After we performed *ziyarat*, Zehra Baji and I plastered ourselves against a pillar to watch the procession. There was no laughing and joking, no derogatory remark, no undercurrent of tension. Clutching the sleeve of Zehra Baji's burqa so we would not be separated, I recalled the Lucknow maulvi's words. No matter what they may have thought as they watched the procession, people were indeed "polite." However, we must recognize that this may be about more than "politeness." Like Old Delhi Shias, Sunnis watching the procession also have a long history of living with difference in Old Delhi, or elsewhere in India where traditions of pluralism are evident (Gold 2017; Ruffle 2011; Hyder 2006), curbing their responses in deference to the practices of others and constructing community across sectarian lines.

Sometimes Shias did speak of discrimination they experienced or of their hurt when some Sunnis made light of their grief. Sakina said she was hurt when her Sunni tutor's brother made fun of her black clothes. Illustrating how people consciously restrain themselves in moments of heightened tension, Sakina said, "But

I do not say anything. What is the point? There will be a fight." However, far from focusing on these tensions, differences, and potential conflicts, Shias insisted that Muharram commemorations and the ritual mourning of Husain and his family crossed sectarian and religious boundaries. Indeed, scholars have noted the participation of Sunnis, Hindus, and others in Muharram commemorations in South Asia (see Gold 2017; Mohammad 2013; D'Souza 2012, 79; Ruffle 2011, 70; Hyder 2006, 21, 50; Olsen 2005; Pinault 2001). Others have written about the blurred religious boundaries (Bellamy 2011; Flueckiger 2006; Assayag 2004; Sikand 2004) and "polytropy" (Carrithers 2000) in India that inform these acts, and have warned against constructing religious traditions and identities as discrete and mutually exclusive categories (Hirst and Zavos 2005; Gottschalk 2000; Oberoi 1994). What interests me is not that Sunnis and Hindus participate in Muharram commemorations, but how repeatedly this was expressed to me by Shias—male and female, rich and poor, educated and nonliterate—during Muharram, a time when difference is often a source of tension.

A heterogenous community of mourners seemed central to articulations of self and identity for Shias during this period. If indeed it is in narrative that identities are constituted (Kirmani 2013, 15) and that the subject aligns itself within competing hegemonies (Ewing 1997, 35), then this self-conscious reiteration that non-Shias engage in Shii mourning practices is important. While these narratives privilege Shii traditions amid competing hegemonies, and while they are not always borne out in practice, drawing on Ann Gold's work on religious pluralism, these accounts can still be seen to "affirm a plural consciousness" (2014, 116) amid violent visions of exclusion. At a historical moment when religious and sectarian violence is on the rise in South Asia, it is important to recognize how Old Delhi Shias imagine an inclusive community of mourning—one that embraces difference to construct cultural commons.

"In the House of Husain Meet People of All Persuasions"

During Muharram, I asked Shias about their relationships with non-Shias in Old Delhi. Can you tell me about the relationships between Shias and Sunnis in Old Delhi, I asked? What are some of the difficulties that Shias face in everyday life? In response, most refocused our conversation on the events of Karbala, refusing to be drawn into discussions about Shii-Sunni tensions. Maulana Yusuf Ali, a young man from Muzaffarpur, Bihar, undergoing training at Panja Sharif, where he has lived since 2007, spoke to me for an hour about Karbala. However, when I asked about Shii-Sunni relations in Old Delhi, his rather taciturn response was that since he spends minimal time outside the *dargah*, he knows little beyond what I can read in the newspaper. Indeed, that line of conversation seemed decisively closed. While initially discouraged by such closures, I realized on further reflection that the refusal to speak of tension was interesting in itself. One could, of course, contend that as a small minority, Shias might be afraid of the consequences of their words. The Shias I met, however, did not strike me as particularly fearful, especially during Muharram, when their commitment and emotional connection to their martyrs and history of martyrdom is heightened. Instead, I argue here that for my interlocutors this was part of a larger effort to disrupt the focus on difference and situate Shias within a larger community of mourning in which they were linked in word, deed, and emotion to non-Shias. In a country that has witnessed so much religious and sectarian violence, these attempts to reimagine Shii identity and subjectivity are significant. The refusal to speak about tension is in fact an important illustration of what Laura Ring calls the "micromechanics of coexistence," which can engender "everyday peace" among those living with difference in South Asia (2006, 3; see also Williams 2015).

Whether addressing tension or not, most Shias in Old Delhi constructed the martyrdom of Husain as a moment mourned by individuals regardless of religious or sectarian affiliation. Maulana Asghar Ali, a young man who lives at Panja Sharif, asserted that in Delhi and in his village in Uttar Pradesh, Sunnis did more *matam* than Shias because of their love for Husain. When I asked if this was also true of places such as Lucknow, he said that there "is some distance" between Shias and Sunnis there. Later, showing me around Panja Sharif, he pointed out employees of the *dargah* who were Sunnis. He told me that although they are poorly paid, they stayed because of their love for Husain. For the young maulana, love for Husain transcended sectarian divisions in Old Delhi and his village. In response to my question about Sunni-Shii relations in Old Delhi, he said, "Everyone lives together here" (*Sab mil kar rehte hain*). Shii relationships with others, he asserted, were based on their understandings of Islam. He asked Maulana Yusuf Ali, who was sitting nearby, to expand on this. Maulana Yusuf Ali responded, "In the house of Husain meet people of all persuasions. They may be Hindu, Muslim, Sikh, or Christian." Invoking an inclusive vision of Islam, he cited a hadith that he believed was key to Islam:

> Respect your guest, even if they are *kafirs* [unbelievers]. If a *kafir* comes in the form of a guest, then take care of them, respect them, love them. Not that . . . they are not my coreligionist [*mere mazhab wala*] so I won't show respect. If you want to see the authentic religion, what is called authentic Islam, then see if *kafirs* are being respected. Or is it just Muslims who are being respected? Only Shias who are being respected?

> There is no differentiation [*bhedbhav*] here. Here it is that if someone is human, then show respect—even if they are *kafirs*. Our Prophet Muhammad . . . Allah sent him for us. He has brought such a religion for us, where there is love for all people [*tamaam logon*].

Maulana Yusuf Ali insisted, "To be a Muslim, one must be a human first." It is interesting to pay attention to the maulana's narrative here. On the one hand, he uses the term *kafir*, which constructs non-Muslims as "other." On the other hand, he insists on the common humanity of all. He refers to those who are coreligionists and those who are not, but maintains that in Islam "there is love for all people." Elsewhere in our conversation, he used the term *ghair mazhab* (other or different religion) to refer to non-Muslim traditions. Indeed, by simultaneously "othering" and unifying, his narrative maintains distinction even as it situates distinct identities in a common humanity. His narrative suggests that a good Muslim must love and respect others, and it illustrates processes through which "people live with and manage difference" in everyday life rather than gloss over, exclude, or erase it (Mayaram 2005, 160). Indeed, as Carla Bellamy has noted, sometimes "otherness is a foundational concept" (2011, 173), and often people are "keenly aware of otherness, and . . . make explicit and unconsidered use of it" (213). Following Bellamy's analysis, I see the maulana's narrative as using everyday religious differences to articulate a narrative of how one lives and interacts with "others," even as he privileges his own tradition. Here one sees how Muharram provides an occasion to reconfigure "others" as connected to the self, and to emphasize forms of identification that embrace, however fleetingly, everyday religious differences.

For Maulana Asghar Ali, treating everyone with respect is necessary not only because of the hadith but also because one's salvation could hang in the balance. Speaking of the Twelfth Imam, who Shias believe is in occultation, he said that no one knows what form he will come in. Looking at me, he said, "It is possible that it is you. We believe it could be anyone." I asked, "It could be a man or woman?" Maulana Ashghar Ali responded, "We do not know what form." Although not privy to this conversation, Zehra Baji echoed this a few weeks later. Lighting a candle in preparation for the *magrib azaan* (evening call to prayer), she told me that one must never turn away or mistreat those seeking alms because the "Maula"—in this case, the Twelfth Imam—can come in any form. I asked, "What if it is a Hindu?" She responded that it did not matter if they were Hindu, Muslim, or Christian; "the Maula can come in any form."

Ultimately, respecting others and living with difference seemed important to Shii constructions of self in Old Delhi. An eminent maulana said, "*You cannot show any Shia* who is engaged in an occupation that is against the nation. . . . [A

Shia] . . . is against falsity . . . against oppression . . . against . . . a policy that is against humanity. Shias give a lot of importance to *law of land*." The maulana then related the following story. Apparently, Ayatollah Khomeini, during a visit to Paris, saw a Muslim sacrificing a goat on the street during Bakra Eid (Eid al-Adha), when Muslims ritually commemorate Ibrahim's willingness to sacrifice his son Ishmael. Khomeini told the man that his act was *haram* "not because you are sacrificing a goat . . . [but] because in France there are special places to sacrifice goats, a slaughter area. Outside that area, outside your house, you are sacrificing the goat. This is against the *law of land*." The maulana insisted that Shias must ensure that others were not troubled by their acts. In this view, to live with others, to live with difference, is central to Shii practice, even though it is not, according to the maulana, a religious rule.

All of these narratives articulate community across religious and sectarian boundaries, and urge Shias to respect and live with difference. Of course, one purpose of such narratives could be to privilege Shias as a community that is more tolerant and accepting than others in a social context where multiple traditions are vying for power and influence. Or perhaps my Hindu name in the context of Hindu chauvinism in India prompted my interlocutors to position themselves in a broader and more inclusive community. Or maybe because it was Muharram and a time of heightened sectarian tension, Shias I met repeated these inclusive understandings of community in which Husain was the focus of love across sectarian lines, and in which being Muslim meant engaging in acts of humanitarianism, charity, and respect across religious lines. Whatever their primary purpose, it was clear that a commitment to embracing those of all religions, and treating them with respect and care, was central to how Shias I met represented, if not always lived, their religion in everyday life.

While people do not always do what they say, and certainly religion does not determine people's choices and behavior, drawing attention to such narratives is important, because as Shail Mayaram has argued, we are so used to thinking about the "cleaving myth[s]" in our discussions of religious groups that "we ignore the shared myths between communities" (2005,157; see also Hirst and Zavos 2005). Narratives of living with difference can enable alternative imaginaries and provide insights into how people can and do coexist even as scholarly analyses tend to pay disproportionate attention to conflict (Ring 2006, 5–6). Indeed, we need to pay more attention to how people "live together separately" (Hasan and Roy 2005; Mayaram 2005) and how they participate in shared religious worlds (Taneja 2018; Bellamy 2011) even with the awareness of difference. Urban contexts are often sites of violence, riots, and intercommunal strife, but as Mayaram says, "Cities have also manifested the ethical idea of living together with strangers" (2008, 9). Old Delhi is certainly a place with a long history of articulating community across religious and sectarian lines, and of living with difference in everyday life.

It is also important to understand that we cannot simply reduce people to their religious or sectarian identities, or indeed construct religion itself as exclusively "otherworldly" (Fadil and Fernando 2015, 70). As I have shown, people in Old Delhi have multiple and overlapping identities—as workers and employees, as villagers and Delhiites, as friends and neighbors, and indeed as people committed to upholding cultures forged in plural religious worlds. These multiple identities are indicative of what Andrew Willford calls a "plural modality of being" that persists amid, and despite, the "monocultural imaginaries" of nations and nationalisms (2018, 4, 6). Not only do the narratives of Old Delhi Shias make place for these multiple identities, but they also illustrate how the religious encompasses multiple concerns, interests, and desires that are very much part of the lives and worlds people inhabit and that inflect the "ethical subjectivity" they seek to cultivate (see Fadil and Fernando 2015, 64). For many of the Shias I worked with, from Zehra Baji to Maulana Asghar Ali, their village identity, and the plural traditions practiced there, were central to their articulations of self, even if they had lived all their lives in Old Delhi. Zehra Baji is close friends with Farhana Baji, a Sunni Muslim who can be critical of Shii mourning rituals, illustrating how individuals can have deep and intimate connections with those they might disagree with on some issues. In fact, friendship can be a powerful force in people's lives, one that brings with it its own demands and expectations (Chambers 2020), wherein a desire for intimacy can lead individuals to violate gendered or religious expectations in their lives (Ring 2006). That most of those who worked at Panja Sharif, and indeed most of those employed by Jafri Sahib, were Sunnis who were deeply loyal to their employers again shows how religious and sectarian identity cannot be understood to determine all aspects of people's lives. Not only are people plural subjects, but also religion itself articulates with multiple aspirations (Maqsood 2017, 12) that are not all "abstract and otherworldly" (Fadil and Fernando 2015, 70, 76).

Ultimately, living with difference is about making place for oneself and one's community in a world shared with others. As they interact with "others" from different religious, sectarian, or class backgrounds, and as they find themselves emotionally or financially involved or dependent on them, individuals construct narratives that transcend difference, even if only momentarily and inconsistently. Against the rising tide of right-wing nationalisms the world over that seek to marginalize, exclude, expel, or destroy those who are different, the Old Delhi Shias I spoke to creatively imagined shared cultures that forged alliances between themselves and those they lived with. Their narratives enable us to think about religion and culture as material forces that can imagine, if not enable, other ways of inhabiting the diverse landscapes of the modern world.

Conclusion

With the rise of the Hindu right, there has been a tremendous upsurge of religious violence in India. The destruction of the Babri Masjid, the pogrom against Muslims in Gujarat, anti-Christian violence in Orissa and Madhya Pradesh, attacks on Christian institutions in the Delhi area, the disturbing frequency of beef-related lynchings of Muslims and Dalits in many northern states, and the pogrom in Delhi in 2020 in which fifty-three people, the majority Muslim, lost their lives, highlight the violent rending of the social fabric in contemporary India. But narratives of violence and exclusion are not the only stories that can be told about the country. Often drowned out by the immediacy and urgency of violence, there are many inclusionary practices of nation and community that still play out in the everyday. This was made abundantly clear at Shaheen Bagh in Delhi, where thousands gathered for a hundred days to peacefully protest the Modi government's discriminatory Citizenship Amendment Act passed in December 2019. While led by Muslim women, especially the *dadis* (grandmothers) of Shaheen Bagh, they were joined by Hindus, Sikhs, and Christians of all ages fighting to uphold the principles of the Indian Constitution (see Mustafa 2020). Such narratives and practices that forge cultural commons in the face of conflict and difference have a long history in South Asia. In places like Old Delhi they are articulated by individuals from all religious and sectarian groups. In a country where the prevailing narrative expounded by the political establishment, by the media, and by many scholars is about difference, tension, and violence, it is important to pay attention to the narratives of Old Delhi's Shias, who construct inclusive communities of mourning. These narratives provide an alternative to the exclusionary visions of the Hindu right, blur boundaries increasingly hardened by rising sectarian violence in South Asia, and belie Islamophobic images of Muslims common in the world today.

I have argued that during the months of mourning, broader visions of community seemed ingrained in Shii articulations of how people should conduct themselves and relate to others in Old Delhi. In response to my questions premised upon religious difference, my Shii interlocutors gently but insistently narrated communities of mourning that embraced religious and sectarian difference. Differences and tensions do exist in Old Delhi between Shias and Sunnis, and between Muslims and Hindus. Yet to focus only on difference is to ignore the consistent articulations of identities that marginalize difference and blur boundaries between groups. It replicates the categories of religious difference that have become entrenched in our conversations about religion in South Asia and beyond, and imagines religious communities as mutually exclusive groups. It marginalizes the shared traditions that make place for Muslims in a country besieged by Hindu chauvinists. And it disregards narratives and practices of inclusion that are deeply ingrained in South Asian religious worlds, and certainly in places like Old Delhi. Everyday life in South Asia is marked by moments of inclusion and moments of violent separation in the past and the present. In a country and region fraught with violent conflicts over identity and exclusionary visions of community, we must pay attention when individuals blur the lines between groups, negotiate tensions, and live with difference in everyday life. Narratives articulating a community of mourning that crosses religious and sectarian lines, and practices such as the refusal to dwell on difference, can illuminate how the shredded fabric of our social worlds might be sewn back together, however slowly, tentatively, and perhaps, inadequately.

5

LIFE AFTER DEATH

It was the second day of Bakra Eid, the festival marking Ibrahim's willingness to sacrifice his son, Ishmael, to God, and also the end of the Haj, the pilgrimage to Mecca. I had spent the day before celebrating Eid with Farhana Baji, her husband Irfan Bhai, and their children. My phone rang as I was eating breakfast the next morning. It was Sania, Farhana Baji's younger sister, telling me to come immediately because Irfan Bhai had died. Still in shock, breakfast half finished, I rushed to Farhana Baji's house in Old Delhi. Having lost her husband, Farhana Baji, in her early forties, was now entering her *iddat*, a "waiting" period of four lunar months and ten days observed by many Muslim widows.[1] Although it is not universally observed, during her *iddat* a Muslim woman in Old Delhi is typically expected to remain in seclusion from all marriageable men.[2] However, other women are encouraged to visit, condole, provide companionship, and engage in rituals such as reading the Quran on behalf of the deceased.

Here I explore how the death of her husband not only irrevocably changed Farhana Baji's life but also became a moment when various understandings of what it means to be a good Muslim were articulated. I examine some of the tensions that emerged during the three days of mourning at Farhana Baji's house in Old Delhi and in the period of *iddat* that followed. I suggest that the divergent views expressed about how to appropriately mourn reflect various constructions of religious subjectivity, womanhood, and Islam among Old Delhi's Muslims. These views also articulate multiple understandings of self and belonging that root Muslims in different kinds of places and communities. I argue that tensions about rituals of death are very much about life, as diverse groups of Indian

Muslims negotiate the complexities and conflicts of being Muslim in India today. Indeed, articulations of Islam and Muslim identity in Old Delhi are inflected by forces and ideologies that extend far beyond the old city, and by the vicissitudes of forging a life amid pluralism, shared histories, and, indeed, exclusionary nationalism and communal strife.

While religious practice and narrative clearly invoke religious ideologies and worlds, they are also, as Arjun Appadurai has argued, deeply implicated in the processes of fashioning subjects from whose actions localities are emergent (1996). Thus mourning rituals are not just about the afterlife of the deceased and the funerary obligations of the bereaved; they are also fundamentally about people, communities, and places that are very much alive. Mourning rituals help individuals navigate moments of loss and grief, and they provide a space for people to come together to express condolence and show support. If, as Purnima Mankekar (2015) argues, affect produces subjects, then mourning rituals as sites of powerful affect can be understood to produce not just religious subjects but also subjects of an affective commons enabled by grief and commiseration, and potentially transcending other axes of difference.

Performed amid the ebb and flow of everyday life in particular places and communities, mourning rituals also bear the traces of complex histories, religious interactions, and cultural influences that can be local, regional, national, and transnational. Connected to powerful discourses, these traces also contain within them variegated possibilities that can enable multiple subject positions. In Old Delhi, Muslim mourning practices can bear the traces of the city's cosmopolitan pasts and anxious presents. Examining discourses about death, conflicts over appropriate grieving practices, and rituals of mourning among different groups of Muslims, I analyze how mourning enables alternative forms of subjectification. Forging cultural commons and building community across boundaries and over differences, Muslims variously make place for themselves amid the exclusionary nationalism of a revanchist Hindu right. Such practices require us to think about Islam as a "historical and human phenomenon" (S. Ahmed 2016, 72), inseparable from politics and entangled in multiple and complex anxieties, interests, and aspirations (Maqsood 2017; Fadil and Fernando 2015; N. Khan 2012).

Bidat or Tradition? Divergent Ways of Being an Indian Muslim

In this book I have looked at Old Delhi Muslims in all their diversity. Representing a range of classes, occupations, politics, and educational levels, my interlocutors belonged to different sectarian traditions (Shia, Sunni) and followed different *maslaks* (Deobandi, Barelvi, Ahl-e-Hadis). While some were deeply attached to Old Delhi, others were recent migrants with deep connections to other places. I have suggested that while such differences can engender conflicts, other historical circumstances enable solidarities, however temporal and contingent, that blur sectarian, class, or even religious boundaries. Even as some reminisce about a bygone era marked by shared cultural and religious worlds, today many Old Delhi Muslims are deeply aware of tensions between them and their Hindu, Jain, and Sikh neighbors. Such tensions have only been exacerbated in the past few decades as Indian Muslims have had to contend with the extreme violence of the Hindu right that imagines India as a Hindu nation (K. Menon 2018, 2010; R. Robinson 2013; Ghassem-Fachandi 2012; Jaffrelot 2007; Hansen 1999), and increasing suspicion and surveillance by the state, while also becoming the targets of extrajudicial killings, arrests, and detention under antiterrorism laws (Irfan Ahmad 2017a; Sethi 2014; JTSA 2012). It is amid these historical forces that individuals forge understandings of self and belonging, envision religious identity and practice, and live their everyday lives. Following scholars who have highlighted the inseparability of religion, power, and politics, I suggest that mourning rituals among Old Delhi's diverse Muslim communities are inflected by the anxieties they face and by their efforts to negotiate difference and construct belonging in contemporary India.[3]

I begin with a moment of tension that emerged among different groups of Sunni Muslims during the rituals following Irfan Bhai's passing (*inteqal*). Many Islamic traditions allow for three days of mourning for all except the widow (Dessing 2001, 173), although in India ceremonies for the deceased often take place after this period.[4] Upon hearing the news about Farhana Baji's husband, female relatives and acquaintances came to her house to read chapters from the Quran and to recite the *kalma*, the confession of faith, 125,000 times (*sava lakh kalma*).[5] When I asked why, I was told that since this was the number of recitations of the *kalma* expected of all Muslims in their lifetimes, the mourners recited this on behalf of the deceased. Someone had procured a tin with 125,000 seeds from the local mosque, which women were using to count their recitations of the *kalma*. Some men who were permitted to be there, such as Farhana Baji's sons, joined the women in their endeavors. I was told that for the first forty days after Irfan Bhai's passing, every Thursday night, *juma raat*, a complete Quranic reading would be finished through these combined efforts and "sent" on behalf of the deceased. On the fifth Thursday night, which, several women informed me, coincided with the fortieth day after his passing, tea and snacks were given to those present after the ritual had been completed. Many women participated in these rituals at Farhana Baji's house. However, they were a point of tension among Old Delhi's Sunni Muslims.

This tension first emerged on the *teeja* (the third day of mourning), when three women entered the house and sat down among the other female mourners reciting the *kalma* and reading the Quran in the *dalan* (interior verandah) off the courtyard. Two were dressed differently from the other women in the room; in addition to burqas and hijabs, they also wore elbow-length black gloves and socks. This was my first encounter with Abida, the founder of Old Delhi's Muslim Club (see chapter 3). Abida introduced herself to other women in the room as a student of Zakir Naik's and Farhat Hashmi's, and she asked to address them. Ostensibly drawing on the teachings of these two influential but also controversial Islamic scholars, especially their insistence that Muslims today should live only according to the prescriptions of the foundational texts, Abida proceeded to critique the mourning rituals women were engaged in by talking about *shirk* (attributing a partner to God), *bidat* (religious innovation), and "un-Islamic" practices among Indian Muslims. Abida's privileging of textual traditions and her dismissal of practices not found therein are deeply reminiscent of ideas articulated by many reform movements associated with Islamic modernity in South Asia, which have sought to "rationalize" tradition through a return to the foundational texts (F. Robinson 2013, 40) and mark boundaries that have facilitated modern, bounded, forms of identification (Willford 2018; Pernau 2013; Anderson 1998).

Addressing the women, Abida said, "There should only be three days of mourning. But here people extend their mourning with ceremonies on the fortieth day. They keep reading the Quran for days." She continued:

> Why do we do this? All this is because of Hindu influences. It is Hindus who have a ritual after sixteen days, after forty days, after one year. There is nothing about this in the Quran. Hindus do all this because they believe the *ruh* [spirit] is still around. In Islam the *ruh* does not stay. It is gone. So there is no need for all this. It is all *shirk*, and people should not do it. . . . The reading of the Quran is not prescribed. People read quickly [*jaldi jaldi*] whether or not they are making mistakes. This is wrong. Of course one should read the Quran. But one should read it from the heart and one should read it correctly. There is no point if one makes mistakes while reading.[6]

She also challenged the recitation of the *kalma*, asking, What is the point of reciting it over and over again? Abida asserted that everything that people needed to know about how to live their lives was in the text—in the Quran, with guidance from the Sunna. Everything else, she argued, was *shirk*. When in doubt, Abida said, ask a scholar from Medina, because the Prophet said that Medina is the "house of knowledge" that can never be corrupt. Instead, she asked, who do we take fatwas (legal decisions) from? "Who is this? Long beard, high pajamas, prays five times, *Mashallah!* Can you give me a fatwa?"

In Abida's view, the practices that women at Farhana Baji's house were engaged in after Irfan Bhai's death illustrated their imbrication in a world shared with Hindus and the entangled cultures of Hindus and Muslims in many parts of India (Taneja 2018; Bellamy 2011; Knight 2011; Flueckiger 2006). As such, they presented a problem. Abida chose instead to emphasize textual forms of religion that enabled her to identify with a transnational Muslim community, and she rejected forms of practice that are seen to be mired in the local and that blur the boundaries between religious communities. It is as important to situate her views in the context of the modern impulse to create bounded identities (Willford 2018; Anderson 1998) and rationalized, standardized forms of religion (F. Robinson 2013) as it is to understand the pull of a global community of belonging in a country that increasingly disavows Muslims and Islam and indeed, in a world where Muslims feel alienated.

Abida's words captivated the imagination of the women who visited Farhana Baji in the months that followed Irfan Bhai's *teeja*. But it was clear in the discussions that ensued that for the mourners at Farhana Baji's house, the problem was Abida and the ideology she represented. The night after the *teeja*, after most of the visitors had left, Huma Khala, an elderly widow and distant relative of Irfan Bhai's, said to Zarin Apa, Farhana Baji's mother, "Those women said we should not read the Quran, but I do not agree." Zarin Apa replied, "I also did not like what they were saying, but I did not want to ask any questions." Suggesting that the traditions Abida was proscribing were ones that had ensured the protection and integrity of her community, Huma Khala continued: "It is reading the Quran that has helped us through bad times." She said that long ago when she was young, there were riots, and there was talk of Hindus attacking Muslim women. Alone at home, Muslim women began to read their Qurans. Nothing happened. Huma Khala said, "It was because we read the Quran that we were safe." For Huma Khala, experiences of communal violence in Old Delhi during which she had viewed the Quran as her only source of hope, solace, and protection reinforced her belief in its power in times of crisis, even if the specific ritual had not been prescribed by the foundational texts. Importantly, although the rituals Huma Khala endorses are the very ones that Abida proscribes, both women's acts must be understood within the context of the anxieties, concerns, and desires that inflect their lives.

Women's criticisms of Abida's lecture continued through the months of *iddat*. One Thursday night, Farhana Baji noted that though it was customary to complete readings of the Quran on Irfan Bhai's behalf on Thursday evenings, very few women had been coming to do this. Her friend Rizwana responded, "It is because of those women. They said that we should not do this, that it was *bidat* and *haram* (forbidden). This is our tradition [*riwaj*] and they want to change this. I do not like it." Another time, Zarin Apa told some women who had dropped by for a visit, "You know they said not to send *fatiha* [prayer] on Thursday nights and not to recite the *kalma*. How can reciting the *kalma* ever be bad?"[7] On the fifth Thursday after Irfan Bhai's death, his sister Laila, who knew the three women said, "They are Ahl-e-Hadis. My husband told me, Stay away from those women." Laila proclaimed, "How can reading the Quran be wrong?" Importantly, such criticisms were not reserved for the three women who came to Irfan Bhai's *teeja*. Once, several months later when I was chatting with Zarin Apa about funerary practices in Old Delhi, she told me that "*jamaatis*" have also told people to avoid practices like feeding all the mourners at the *teeja*.[8] Not dismissing their reasoning, she said, "I think that while this is correct, we should still do something. Isn't it? If a person has gone, then?"

Whether critical of the "*jamaatis*" or of Abida and members of her Muslim Club, overt questioning of their pronouncements was rare. While the women who visited Farhana Baji during her *iddat* represented a variety of class backgrounds and educational levels, few felt as well versed in religious texts as Abida was. When I asked Farhana Baji why none of the women had challenged Abida at Irfan Bhai's *teeja*, she responded, "If you do not know enough to challenge what they are saying, then it is best to be quiet." Farhana Baji recognized the power inherent in Abida's proscription of the mourning practices at her house. Indeed, as Talal Asad argues, claims to orthodoxy, attempts to enforce or regulate "correct practices" and proscribe "incorrect" ones, are always indicative of power relationships (1986, 15). Abida's education, religious knowledge, and affiliation with well-known Islamic teachers allowed her to speak to women about their ritual practices without public challenge. Her religious authority allowed her to occupy a powerful role in the public sphere. However, the consistent condemnation of her views over the months of *iddat*, and the refusal by many to follow her prescriptions, illustrated that powerful discourses and authority can be destabilized in multiple ways. Interestingly, on the day of the *teeja*, Abida and her companions had barely left Farhana Baji's courtyard before women had picked up their Qurans and started reading again and reciting the *kalma*. The speed with which they resumed their mourning rituals spoke volumes about their opinion of Abida's words.

Several months later I reconnected with Abida. By this point I had learned from Laila that she and the other two women, Noorjahan and Raisa, were teachers at the highly respected Roshanara Girls School in Old Delhi. Although their work—at the school and through their *dawa* as members of the Muslim Club—brought Abida, Noorjahan, and Raisa together, the three women came from different backgrounds and represented different histories in Old Delhi. Noorjahan came from an affluent Old Delhi family whose beautiful and large *haveli* in Ballimaran was the site of anticolonial meetings attended by such figures as Nehru and Gandhi. Raisa lived in Okhla in South Delhi and commuted to Old Delhi for her job. Abida, who identified with her Afghan father, moved to Old Delhi from Ghaziabad in Uttar Pradesh when she got married. In all three cases, their families did not share their particular understanding and practice of Islam. Both wealth and education separated the three women from Farhana Baji, who stopped studying at seventeen to marry Irfan Bhai and supplemented the modest income he made from electrical work doing home-based work.

Although several months had passed and it was one of many that she had attended, Abida remembered coming to Irfan Bhai's *teeja*. Sometimes, as in the case of Irfan Bhai's *teeja*, she heard of such events through acquaintances or colleagues like Laila. At other times, it was the loudspeaker announcement from the local mosque of a *namaz-e-janaza*, a special prayer for the deceased offered by male members of the community, that instigated her visit to women engaged in funerary rituals in the home. In Old Delhi, while men offer these prayers in congregation at the mosque, women, usually relatives and friends who hear from those who know the family, tend to read the Quran or recite the *kalma* at the home of the deceased. I asked Abida why she told women at Irfan Bhai's *teeja* not to recite the *kalma* or read the Quran. She responded, "*Uper vale ko counting nahin chahiye, quality chahiye*" (God wants quality not counting). She said dismissively,

> This is all *culture*. I'll tell you, those people [Hindus] read the Hanuman Chalisa, they read it seven times, they read it forty times. In truth, in India many people converted to Islam. But they also bring their *culture* with them. So instead of the Hanuman Chalisa, they [Muslims] say, We will read this *sura* [chapter of the Quran] forty times. They say, *chalo* [OK], they have *teeja* on the third day, we will also do this. . . . They have tenth-day, twentieth-day, and fortieth-day ceremonies. We will also have four Thursday nights and a fortieth-day ceremony. . . . Just like there they [Hindus] read a whole story [*katha*], we will read the Quran. They follow the same *non-Muslim culture* because that is where they are from.[9]

Abida's words eloquently express her anxieties about the blurred boundaries between Hindus and Muslims in a cultural context in which Hinduism and Islam have been entangled for centuries, enabling what Aamir Sahib referred to at the beginning of this book as the "Ganga-Jamni culture" of Old Delhi. Aware that most Indian Muslims are Hindu converts, it is precisely the close links between Hindus and Muslims, the proximity of their Hindu past, and the ever present specter of the cultural commons that concerns Abida. As Andrew Willford has noted in his work on Bangalore, "It is the intimacy of the Other" that is threatening to modern, bounded identities, "precisely because this intimacy points to the impossibility of exclusivity" (2018, 159; see also Hansen 2001; Anderson 1998). But importantly, as Willford notes, while the specter of common culture can instigate attempts to further delineate or exclude, as we see in the case of the Sangh Parivar's efforts to construct Muslims as an "other," or indeed in Abida's proscription of the mourning practices at Farhana Baji's house, its traces continue to challenge exclusionary forms of identification through everyday religious practices in places like Old Delhi (see Willford 2018, 161).

For Abida it was not just the funeral rituals but also the practice of *iddat* among women in Old Delhi that revealed a misunderstanding of Islam. Abida insisted that in fact the strictures on women to stay at home were not only during *iddat* but at all times. She said, "[Going out] is forbidden anyway among us, . . . because the worst place in sight for Allah is the marketplace." Although Abida has a job, regularly visits homes where there has been a death, and gives religious lectures in public and private venues, she claims that she only leaves the house, "on necessary work." She explained, "If you are going to teach, if you are going to study, if you have to go to the doctor, you have to follow this during *iddat* too. But these people, they lock the woman in the house during *iddat* and leave her there." Abida told me that one of her colleagues at the school taught during her *iddat*. When she was done with school she would go home and stay there.

It is not only members of the Muslim Club who are critical of the way that women like Farhana Baji practice *iddat*. Farhat Begum, a sixty-two-year-old woman from a relatively privileged background who used to be a schoolteacher, was also very critical of such practices even though she did not share Abida's religious views. When I told Farhat Begum and her daughter Nazia that I had just visited a woman who was in *iddat* and had not left her home, Farhat Begum said, "When my husband died, I observed four o'clock *iddat*. *Mazhab* [religion] makes an allowance for women who need to be out of the house, for work or for other reasons. It was not possible for me to observe complete *iddat*, so I did a four o'clock *iddat*. I was at home every evening by four." Nazia, who works in an NGO that focuses on gender and sexuality, interjected, "I do not understand why she did not do something like this. If *mazhab* makes a provision for you, why shouldn't you take it?" Caught off-guard, I said rather lamely that her family was conservative and that this might set tongues wagging. But mother and daughter were adamant that this was unnecessary—especially when the woman in question had children to take care of. Such views notwithstanding, Farhana Baji, whose circumstances, concerns, and understandings of piety were different, never left the house during her *iddat*. Indeed, Farhana Baji did not even talk on the phone to men who were not natal kin during her *iddat*. Once I had to speak with a male bank manager on the phone on her behalf about a stolen credit card because she told me she was maintaining *awaaz ka parda* (voice purdah). However, according to her, this purdah did not extend to emails and text messages, revealing how modern technology permits the manipulation of ritual boundaries.

Abida's visit to Irfan Bhai's *teeja* along with other members her Muslim Club was a key moment to understand constructions of religious subjectivity among Sunni Muslims in Old Delhi who belong to different *maslaks*. Most members of Farhana Baji's family identify as Deobandi. They were often critical of the practices that Barelvi Muslims engaged in at Sufi shrines. For them such practices amounted to *shirk* and revealed Hindu influences.[10] A week before her husband's passing, Farhana Baji and I were at the Jama Masjid in Delhi. Articulating her critique of Barelvi Muslims, she said, "Our religion says that there is only one God, and God is the only person you can ask for help. But many people who go to *pirs* (Sufi saints) think they can ask them for things. This is wrong." But those belonging to Ahl-e-Hadis believe that Deobandis also engage in problematic practices. Although Deobandis, like Ahl-e-Hadis, tend to emphasize the foundational texts of Islam (Quran, Sunna), Sufi teachings continue to be important to Deobandis (Zaman 2009, 226), and they follow Hanafi law. In contrast, Ahl-e-Hadis reject "the authority of the medieval schools of law" and emphasize "unmediated access to the foundational texts" (226). However, revealing the fluidity between these categories in everyday life, some Deobandis in Old Delhi asserted that they were similar to Ahl-e-Hadis but said they offered *namaz* [daily prayer] a little differently.

Although Laila and others claimed that Abida was Ahl-e-Hadis, she consistently refused to identify as such. Abida's religious practice, such as the way she offered *namaz*, was indeed different from that of the Deobandi teachers at her school. Yet as I have already noted, in our many interactions she refused to identify by *maslak*. When I asked her what *maslak* Noorjahan and Raisa belonged to, she responded in English, "Not *maslak*. They believe that they are Muslims. . . . Muslim means those who follow the commandment of God." She said that rather than follow a *maslak*, they read the text themselves. Insisting that the first Islamic community should be the only model for Muslims today, Abida asserted, "That is the beauty of Islam. Everything is 1,400 years back. Everything is preserved, even the Quran."

Adamant that Muslims do exactly what was prescribed in the foundational texts on Irfan Bhai's *teeja*, Abida told the women mourners a story. She said that on Judgment Day, the angels presented God with a few men whose foreheads were shining brightly because of all the extra prayers they had done. Abida explained that people believed their prayers could be seen by God on their bodies.

God told the angels to put the men in hell. The angels questioned God's decision, saying that the men were so pure that they were shining from all the prayers they had offered. According to Abida, God explained to the angels, "They did not follow the Quran. They did more than what I told them to do." Abida used this story to enjoin the women gathered to follow God's teachings in the Quran exactly.

Abida believed that the recitation of the *kalma* and the readings of the Quran at Farhana Baji's house were *bidat*, religious innovations and Hindu accretions that testified to an incomplete conversion to a new subjectivity.[11] However, for Farhana Baji's neighbors and relatives, Abida's critique of their practices was problematic. In their conversations, they never claimed their practices were in the Quran or the Sunna. In fact, many of them were aware that they were not. Instead, they argued that these practices were their *riwaj*, their tradition. For women like Rizwana and Huma Khala, these traditions were an articulation of their identity as Indian Muslims, even if they distinguished them from Abida's "authentic" Muslims from Medina. They did not see their practices as problematic, saying that while such acts did not always conform to Islamic rules, they embodied the spirit behind them. Ultimately, the tensions between members of the Muslim Club and the mourners at Farhana Baji's house are about different understandings of piety, of "striving" to be a good Muslim (N. Khan 2012, 57) amid not just multiple traditions of Islam in South Asia but also innumerable local, national, and transnational forces and discourses that affect and influence them.

That many in Old Delhi think being a good Muslim is compatible with engaging in practices that mark them as Indian Muslims is consistent with the fact that, as Muzaffar Alam has asserted, from the beginning, "Islam appropriated and welcomed ideas from the world outside" (2004, 24). Women's insistence on reciting the *kalma* 125,000 times, their weekly readings of the Quran on Irfan Bhai's behalf, and their ritual marking of his *teeja* and fortieth day are indicative of how notions of self and belonging are forged amid competing hegemonies (Ewing 1997, 6), including those of sect, of *maslak*, of transnational articulations of religion, of culture, and of nation. In their conversations about *riwaj*, the women subtly contested exclusionary understandings of religion—whether those of religious purists like Abida, or of Hindu chauvinists who cast Muslims and Islam as foreign, as suspect, and as "other." Resonating with the work of so many scholars who have urged us to look at the alternative views, transgressions, and challenges embedded in the stories people tell (Gold and Gujar 2002; Raheja and Gold 1994; Wadley 1994; James Scott 1990), here religious narrative and practice provide a means to disrupt existing hegemonies and to claim one's place in Old Delhi and India. Indeed, the practices of Farhana Baji's neighbors, acquaintances, and relatives can be understood as rituals of belonging that situate Old Delhi's Muslims firmly within the national imaginary and challenge the stereotypes and antipathies about Indian Muslims that are prevalent in the country today. And if, as Arjun Appadurai (1996, 198) has argued, locality is emergent from the practices of ordinary people struggling against myriad local, national, and global forces, then it is through such articulations and practices of self, through such rituals of belonging, that Old Delhi emerges as a locality where Muslims unquestionably have a place.

Sectarian Tensions and the Making and Unmaking of Communities

Religious narratives and practices around death and mourning clearly provide an arena for constructing alternative communities and illustrate the extent to which religion and culture are sites of struggle in Old Delhi. Abida's teachings reflected her desire to forge community with her coreligionists in Medina, as also with other South Asian Muslims inspired by the teachings of Zakir Naik or Farhat Hashmi. Meanwhile, mourners at Farhana Baji's house articulated belonging with other Indian Muslims whose traditions were forged in the subcontinent and inflected by a long history of living in community with Hindus in India. However, they still saw themselves as belonging to a transnational community of believers committed to following the word of God and the model of the Prophet. Indeed, individuals can forge connections with multiple, sometimes overlapping, and sometimes conflicting communities at once. And even for those who aspire to inhabit exclusive forms of identity, the traces of a common culture remain a specter, an ever present threat that must, continuously, be kept at bay.

Communities, of course, can include and forge connections even as they exclude and articulate disjuncture and difference. Kamala Visweswaran critiques the tendency of anthropologists to focus on articulating cultural difference rather than tracing "cultural commons or affinities" (2010, 8). Warning against "culturalisms," Visweswaran says that scholars must be wary of treating "culture as a residuum or limit point for understanding communities, rather than as a site of multiple determinations working to produce the 'effects' of culture or community" (10). She urges scholars to understand culture as a "site of debate or contestation," a sign of "cultures engaged in definitional and political struggle," and to pay attention to how common culture can be forged to build alliances (16).

Funerary rituals and narratives about death, while defining religious and sectarian difference, can also illustrate how individuals empathize, sympathize, and build affinities and community across religion, sect, and tradition. Through engaging in ritual practices that position them in shared religious worlds, and by condoling and commiserating with one another in moments of profound grief and loss, people build cultural and affective commons that can transcend religious and sectarian difference. In the discussion below, I compare the rituals and narratives around death and mourning of two groups of Muslims living in Shahganj. One was a group of Sunnis who identified as Deobandi and had long roots in Old Delhi. The other was a group of Shias who were all from the same village in Uttar Pradesh and maintained close ties with their village. Since individuals construct self and community at the intersection of multiple ideological systems and forms of subjectification, even as sectarian boundaries were defined and sparked tension, I show how they could also be set aside, transgressed, or transcended in various ways. Ultimately, I suggest that rituals and narratives of death provided an opportunity to articulate other forms of community and belonging, even as they marked sectarian difference.

Two different narratives about Shab-e-Barat, a night that falls on the fifteenth of the Islamic month of Shaban, illustrate the conjunctions and the disjunctions between these two groups of Muslims in Old Delhi. Several months after Irfan Bhai's passing, days before Shab-e-Barat, a night many Shias and Sunnis in India spend praying, Farhana Baji told me that Muslims believe there is a tree on whose leaves each person's name is written. If a leaf falls on Shab-e-Barat, the person named on it will die that year. Although this is not a story found in Quranic sources, in Farhana Baji's conception her husband's death had been foretold by a falling leaf on the previous Shab-e-Barat.[12] I asked, "On this night do you pray that Allah does not take you or your loved ones?" "No," Farhana Baji said. "A true Muslim is not scared of death. It is a happy day, because you are going to Allah." Farhana Baji's response to my question echoed something she often said over the months of her *iddat*—that even in grief one should not question why God took someone from you. This is in keeping with conceptions of the divine in the Quran which insist that God is the creator of everything and that any event is a product of God's wisdom and plan (Smith and Haddad 2002, 2). Explaining why she prayed on Shab-e-Barat, she said, "We believe that on that night, Allah Pak comes down to the first heaven. He hears everything. This is why it is a night of *dua* [prayer]. We pray for various things . . . because it is believed that Allah is close by and will hear your *dua*."

Many Muslims believe that their destinies are written on Shab-e-Barat, and they pray for forgiveness through the night. For others, it is a time to remember those who died the previous year and distribute *halwa* [sweet], though Zarin Apa told me that many have stopped doing this because of the influence of "*jamaatis*." When I joined Farhana Baji and her family on Shab-e-Barat at Old Delhi's Jama Masjid, where they planned to stay till dawn to offer prayers, the place was packed (see figure 5.1). It is the one night in the year when women can remain

FIGURE 5.1. Men and women at the Jama Masjid for Shab-e-Barat. Photograph by the author.

after *magrib* (evening) prayers, so many families choose to pray there. Others, put off by the crowds and noise, stay home. Several will fast the following day, although according to Jamal, a Sunni man, it is not required. Farhana Baji and her family found a place to sit in one of the quiet covered areas on the sides of the grand mosque. There they offered prayers and read the Sura Yasin (a chapter of the Quran), pausing to eat and rest.

Many Shias in Old Delhi also observe Shab-e-Barat and narrate a similar story about its significance. Fatima Baji, whose husband had recently passed away, told me, "All Muslims believe that there is a tree in *Khuda's* [God's] house. And on this night it loses leaves and gains leaves. Each leaf it loses represents one person who will die. Each leaf that it gains represents one person who will be born." Fatima Baji, however, offered a slightly different explanation for why she prayed on Shab-e-Barat. Unlike Farhana Baji, Fatima Baji said, "We pray that God protects our loved ones. Does not take anyone from us." While the men pray at the mosque, Fatima Baji, her daughters, and other women in their *mohalla* usually gather at her sister-in-law Yasmeen's home next door to pray together until *fajr namaz* (morning prayers). In addition to offering *namaz*, they also listen to Urdu texts, relying on Yasmeen, who can read Urdu, to read on their behalf. Fatima Baji's daughter Kulsum told me that the following morning they keep *roza* (fast) and open it with a *niyaz* (petition) for the Twelfth Imam, "the one who is hidden," who was born that day. Both Shab-e-Barat and the birth anniversary of the Twelfth Imam fall on the fifteenth of Shaban that begins at sunset. According to Kulsum, many Shias visit the banks of the Yamuna River during the day and make requests of the Twelfth Imam, which they write down with the help of a maulana, wrap in *atta* (dough), and throw in the river. If a request is granted, as Kulsum's had been the previous year, the person must visit the river on the fifteenth of Shaban the following year.

The two narratives have obvious convergences, but they are also different in important ways. While both families offer prayers and ask for help and forgiveness through the night on Shab-e-Barat, the fact that Fatima Baji's family observed the birth of the Twelfth Imam on the following morning is a clear marker of sectarian difference. There are other differences in the narratives, but it is important to recognize that not all can be reduced to sectarian affiliation or religion. While Farhana Baji's family has strong connections to Old Delhi, having lived there since "Mughal times," Fatima Baji's family, although they have lived in Old Delhi since before independence, continue to maintain very close ties to the village in Uttar Pradesh where their extended family still resides, returning there for funerals and important religious occasions such as Ashura. While most of those in Fatima Baji's family lack formal schooling, live in rented homes, and cannot read or write, most in Farhana Baji's family live in homes they own and have been to school or college. Indeed, Yasmeen is among a handful of women in Fatima Baji's family who can read, while everyone in Farhana Baji's family can read some Arabic, Urdu and/or Hindi, and English. Consequently, it is important to understand that sectarian differences are also inflected by other factors, including class, educational levels, and regional backgrounds.

Indeed, various common cultures that people are rooted in inflect and inform sectarian differences in important ways. The petitions by Shias at the banks of the Yamuna River sacred to many Hindus (see Haberman 2006) speak to centuries of living with Hindus in the village from which they hail. Zehra Baji told me that Hindus and Shias lived in shared religious worlds in their village, with Hindus joining in Muhurram commemorations or making accommodations for their Shii neighbors if Ashura happened to coincide with Diwali. The common cultures of North Indian Muslims (and Pakistanis), both Shia and Sunni, also inflect sectarian difference. Some Sunnis in Old Delhi, like those in Farhana Baji's family, no longer use *Khuda*, the Persian/Urdu word for God, preferring, for instance, *Allah Hafiz* instead of the more commonly used *Khuda Hafiz* (God protect you) when taking leave. Fatima Baji's use of *Khuda* and *Khuda Hafiz* reveals the Persian inheritance of many North Indian Muslims, both Sunni and Shia. It also speaks to the continuing close ties of Indian Shias with Iran. In fact, most Shias I met in Old Delhi, from a range of economic and educational backgrounds, articulated the transnational connections between India and Iran through the centuries. As I have already suggested, some clearly situated Indian Shias as a force in the global Shii community, insisting that not only had Persian culture shaped Indian Shii practice but also that Indian culture had influenced the Shii world. The use of Urdu texts in their ritual practice illustrates the Indian roots of this Shii community and its potential influence on the culture of Shias beyond the region. Farhana Baji's family's repudiation of the word *Khuda*, and their insistence on using *Allah Hafiz*, a term most closely associated with piety movements in Pakistan since the 1980s, also reveals a transnational community, but one that tends to be Sunni.[13]

Making and unmaking sectarian differences, funerary practices create spaces in which various identities inflected by alignments of class and region are activated, sometimes in very gendered ways. When Fatima Baji's husband, Muhammad Asghar, died at fifty-six after a prolonged battle with tuberculosis, many of the rituals his family engaged in were similar to those I witnessed after Irfan Bhai's passing. Others clearly illustrated divergences that highlighted sectarian boundaries. At the same time, as I discuss below, even as such differences generated tensions between individuals from different sectarian backgrounds, they also provided an opportunity for some to work across difference, to build commonality across divides. As complex subjects whose understandings of self were forged at the intersection of multiple hegemonies and subject positions, these individuals encountered many points of convergence that encouraged them to bridge divides and construct community amid tension and difference. It is therefore worth considering both the intersections and the differences to examine how death is also about life—of the widow, of the bereaved, and of the communities they belong to.

Much as I had witnessed at Farhana Baji's house, after Muhammad Asghar's passing there were three days of mourning when no food was cooked in the house. Fatima Baji also secluded herself for her *iddat* for four months and ten days and removed all her jewelry after her husband died. There were ceremonies on the *teeja*, and on the tenth, twentieth, and fortieth days, also marked by many Sunnis in Old Delhi. These are all occasions for the gathering of community, not unlike rituals of mourning in other religious traditions, and among people the world over. Among both Shias and Sunnis in Old Delhi, it is not just relatives but neighbors who have a "duty" to take care of the bereaved. Zehra Baji, a neighbor and distant relative, visited Fatima Baji multiple times a day, considering this a neighborly obligation. In fact, on the day of Muhammad Asghar's *teeja*, even though I found Zehra Baji lying down at home because she was feeling unwell, she picked herself up to read the chapter of the Quran that had been sent to her that morning, and to accompany me next door to visit. As a neighbor she did not want to be criticized for not condoling adequately. Such neighborly obligations ensured that the widow was never alone. In the case of Fatima Baji's community where all the close female relatives stay at home for the first forty days, it also guaranteed that the bereaved have support and company during these initial weeks.

At the same time, a daily *majlis* for women at the widow's house recalling the sufferings of the Prophet's family marked sectarian difference. Men did not engage in a daily majlis, but they did organize them at the mosque on the *teeja* and on the tenth, twentieth, and fortieth days. In Fatima Baji's case, for forty days, female relatives and neighbors gathered at her house to remember the sufferings of the Prophet's family, to read *nauhas* (dirges), and to perform *matam*. Prayers in Arabic were offered; however, much of what was read at the *majlis* was in Urdu and Hindi, indicating the use of local texts and marking an important departure from Sunni practices. And, of course, the daily recollection during the *majlis* of the sufferings of the Prophet's family at Karbala, where his grandson Husain and his followers were killed by Yazid's forces (680 CE), was also a daily reminder of Shii-Sunni difference (D'Souza 2012, 26–29; see also Hyder 2006).

Mourning rituals also provided an arena for commentary on sectarian differences. Zehra Baji, who knew Farhana Baji well, often remarked on these differences to me. There was tension between them when Zehra Baji learned that on completing her *iddat*, Farhana Baji would be presented with new sets of clothes and would wear bangles and a nose pin again. Fatima Baji and Kulsum told me that Shias do not give clothes, jewelry, or other gifts to the widow after her *iddat* is complete. Instead, the end of *iddat* is marked by a *niyaz*, the sharing of food, and, in some cases, giving to charity. Many widows avoid the jewelry they wore as unmarried and married women, such as nose pins and bangles, despite the fact that Shii women told me that widow remarriage was not an issue. Gesturing to widowed women at a *majlis* at Fatima Baji's house, Zehra Baji pointed out that none of them were wearing nose pins. Articulating her views on ideal Muslim womanhood, she said, "For Farhana they put all this back on. We do not do that. They [Sunnis] do a lot of things wrong." Once she had greatly upset Farhana Baji by saying this to her. Huma Khala, who was visiting Farhana Baji at the time, responded curtly, "After her *iddat*, Farhana can wear anything she wants." Farhana Baji and Huma Khala see no reason to continue to bear the signs of mourning after the period of *iddat*, especially since another marriage is permissible. In this they are supported by the writings of Maulana Thanawi, an influential colonial-era Deobandi reformer, who dismissed strictures on widows as Hindu accretions in Indian Islam (Metcalf 1990, 145).

To be clear, while Zehra Baji used such practices to mark sectarian difference, it was not only Shias who expressed such views. Once, a Sunni neighbor of Farhana Baji's who was also a widow annoyed her by asking if she was going to wear new clothes for a function she was attending that evening. Farhana Baji told me later as we were returning to her house, "Did you notice how she asked me if I was wearing new clothes tonight? . . . . She thinks because I am a widow I should not wear any new clothes or dress up at all. People here are like this. This is why I keep my distance from them." Others dismissed such attitudes, with Huma Khala once telling Farhana Baji, "Do not worry about what others will say. Do what is right." To understand this, it is important to see these practices as marking both sectarian boundaries and boundaries between different groups of Sunni Muslims hailing from a range of *maslaks* and backgrounds. Moreover, such complexities show that even as difference is mobilized by individuals and groups to mark sectarian and other boundaries, it is important to understand the shifting and contingent nature of such boundaries in everyday life and to recognize "subjective flexibility" (Maqsood 2017, 149).

In Zehra Baji's and Farhana Baji's interactions, constructions of gender marked sectarian boundaries but also enabled convergences that bridged differences among Muslims in Old Delhi. Indeed, despite the tensions discussed above, sectarian differences were often secondary to other forms of community that included both Sunnis and Shias. As Syed Akbar Hyder asserts (2006, 6), in Islamic history "identities other than those grounded in religion . . . often tended to outweigh the religious ones." In Old Delhi, whether Shia or Sunni, women were deeply sympathetic to the issues that widows faced, and they did what they could to help. Once, upon learning that Farhana Baji's toilet was blocked and unusable, Zehra Baji, cognizant of the challenge this presented to a woman in *iddat* who could not leave her home, immediately sent her husband to find someone to clear it. Thus, even as death created an arena to mark sectarian difference and to air Shia-Sunni tensions, it also enabled the creation of a community—in this case of women—that occasionally transcended it.

Women in Old Delhi, regardless of religious and sectarian background, share similar gendered vulnerabilities, enabling empathies and community across difference. For instance, women recognize the gendered vulnerability of widows who no longer have the security provided by their husbands during their married years. After Irfan Bhai's death, Zehra Baji often expressed concern about Farhana Baji, wondering how she would manage on her own. Her concern articulated her recognition of the vulnerability of single women living without a husband in places like Old Delhi. In fact, although she eventually left him, Zehra Baji once told me that she only remained with her violent and abusive husband because of the difficulties she felt she would face as a woman without a husband. The one time she temporarily left him, it was to live with her best friend, a Hindu woman who provided her shelter and companionship during this trying period.

In her work on single women, Sarah Lamb has noted the extent to which "marriage is a compulsory norm" for Indian women (2018, 49). Illuminating the difficulties faced by unattached women of all backgrounds in Old Delhi because of this norm, Zarin Apa, a widow who lives with her youngest son and his wife, once said to me in a conversation we were having about Sunni funerary practices, "This is the way the world works. A woman needs the support of a man, even if she is earning for herself. . . . Respect is given to a married woman." I asked, "Here women do not live by themselves?" Zarin Apa responded, "Yes, they do not live alone. And if they are alone, then people say *ulti-sidhi bat*" (i.e., they cast aspersions). Indeed, as her *iddat* came to an end, Farhana Baji worried that she would no longer have the freedom to wander around as much as she used to when Irfan Bhai was alive. Everyone in Old Delhi talks, she told me. She said that men think a widow is like a piece of "*chocolate*" with no owner. "Everyone is aware that she has no owner. There is no protection," she insisted. This is why everyone wants to keep her, she said. Of course, recognition of gendered vulnerability does not mean that women do not forge their own paths, imagine alternative lives, and question and resist gender norms (see Jamil 2018; Raheja and Gold 1994). Farhana Baji dreamed of living like Wahida Apa, an elderly lady a few houses down from her who never married, lives independently in a house with a lovely courtyard filled with plants and a guava tree, and gives tuitions at home to make a living.

There are other gendered vulnerabilities that many in Old Delhi recognize, such as the financial difficulties that many widows encounter after their husband's passing. Some are unable to work because of *iddat*, others lose a source of financial support, and still others are burdened by the debts left behind by the deceased. Fatima Baji's husband left her with gambling debts that caused her family financial distress. In addition to this, Zehra Baji told me that the cost of food alone for the various funeral ceremonies over forty days amounted to about Rs. 20,000. Additional expenses were incurred for burial and transportation costs, since the family returned to their village to bury Muhammad Asghar. This is a lot for a family surviving on the meager income of offspring working in the informal sector. While more financially secure than Fatima Baji and her family, Farhana Baji too was left with financial difficulties, since she had relied on both her income from home-based work and her husband's income to pay the expenses of feeding and educating her children. Although there are various government schemes to assist widows—such as a pension of Rs. 3,000 every three months, or money to pay for their daughters' weddings—not everyone is aware of these schemes, and not all can avail of them. For women in *iddat*, who are unable to leave the home, availing of this assistance can be difficult, for it often requires filling out paperwork at the appropriate government office, a circumstance that reveals how "structural violence is enacted through the everyday practices of bureaucracies" (A. Gupta 2012, 33). Filing the paperwork to receive this pension also requires furnishing various forms of ID that many women, including widows of all religions and castes, do not have. Indeed, as Tarangini Sriraman notes, the ID document regimes through which the state governs and administers its subjects can foster "deep social inequalities and disadvantages," including those of gender, caste, and religion (2018, 277, 280). Farhana Baji was only able to fill out this paperwork after her *iddat*, and she was unable to collect money for the months she missed.

Recognizing these difficulties, many in Old Delhi did what they could to help widows they knew or encountered. Zehra Baji, although facing financial constraints herself, and despite a difficult relationship with her husband, often sent food she had cooked, or fruit from the stock her husband had bought for his juice cart, to Farhana Baji's house. Although Farhana Baji had received warnings from family to be wary of food sent by Shias, she ignored these and graciously accepted the food sent by her friend. Their friendship, and their recognition of each other's gendered vulnerabilities, enabled them to transcend their sectarian disagreements and religious differences; this reveals the importance of recognizing alternative communities of belonging. Meanwhile, Raza Sahib, who declared he was a communist, could often be found at the local councillors office (then affiliated with the Congress Party) helping widows submit their paperwork and collect their pension checks without regard to sectarian, religious, or party affiliation. This was especially important for those women in Old Delhi who were unable to read or write and therefore could not file their paperwork. In these instances, people like Zehra Baji and Raza Sahib actively transcended sectarian and religious boundaries to help others in need. In so doing they forged community across boundaries that could be quite visible in everyday life.

Ultimately, despite tensions and conflicts over religion and sect, my interlocutors in this book cannot simply be reduced to their religious or sectarian identities; they must be understood as complex subjects pulled by competing subjectivities, ideologies, desires, interests, demands, and aspirations. While they may aspire to be good Muslims, they also aspire to be other things—good parents, good teachers, good workers, good women, good friends, good citizens, good neighbors, and occasionally, good communists. Their understandings of self were shaped by discourses of gender, nation, region, politics, class, and education as much as they were affected by religious or sectarian identity. Even their attempts to inhabit bounded, singular subjectivities when pulled by particular religious movements were continuously imperiled by traces of the commons, of other identities, and "others" who have shared their worlds for centuries (Willford 2018; Nandy 2000). As plural subjects traversing the diverse landscapes of contemporary India, they were necessarily caught up in rapidly changing and powerful global and transnational flows that they had to negotiate in everyday life and that inflected their understandings of self and belonging. It is in such multifaceted contexts that mourning rituals were performed and became implicated in debates about identity. And indeed, it is amid these competing pulls and hegemonies that individuals make and unmake communities of belonging, forge common cultures across boundaries that are perhaps less rigid than they might at first appear, and make place for themselves in modern India. In so doing, they make place for Muslims in Hindu-majoritarian India, where a resurgent Hindu right has violently sought to displace Muslims and remake India as a Hindu nation.

Conclusion

"Tradition," as Muhammad Qasim Zaman argues, is "often the product of bitter and continuing conflicts within a culture," and "appeals to [it] . . . are not necessarily a way of opposing change but can equally facilitate change" (2002, 3). Rizwana's insistence that the mourning practices she and other women were engaged in at Farhana Baji's house were part of her tradition can be viewed not just as a statement of how she constructs the past of her community, but also as a discursive practice that positions her in the world she inhabits today and hopes to inhabit in the future. The statements of Sunnis like Rizwana and Huma Khala, and of Shias like Zehra Baji, can also be understood as a form of what Irfan Ahmad calls immanent critique, "a form of criticism that uses tenets, histories, principles and vocabularies of a tradition to criticize it in its own terms" (2011, 109). For Ahmad, tradition here refers not just to Talal Asad's (1986) notion of the "discursive tradition"—namely, the foundational texts of Islam—but also to other oral and written texts that remain important to the everyday lives and conversations of Muslims (Ahmad 2011, 110). Recently, Shahab Ahmed has noted the importance of what he calls the "Con-Text" of revelation, the "complex or vocabulary of meanings of Revelation that have been produced in the course of the human and historical engagement with Revelation . . . [and are] already present as Islam" (2016, 356). In his view, "Con-Text" includes not just textual discourse but also "various individual and collective practices (both experiential and ritual) that constitute action made meaningful to the actor in terms of Islam"—such things as marriage ceremonies, funeral traditions, styles of dress, and modes of interaction (357). For women like Huma Khala, Rizwana, and Zehra Baji, the "Con-Text" of their understanding of Islam included practices and traditions that some might deem "un-Islamic" and "Hindu" or that index

Shia-Sunni tensions. Understanding ritual and religious practice as deeply imbricated in the politics of communities, or as modes of self-fashioning at particular historical and political moments (S. Mahmood 2009), I see these practices as rituals of belonging that variously make place for Old Delhi's Muslims in contemporary India.

For Rizwana and Huma Khala, how one mourns illustrates who one is. In their ritual acts, they construct Muslim identity as different from that of Hindus and sometimes oppositional to it, but clearly rooted in a place where Hindus and Muslims are "embedded" with one another (Jairath 2011, 3). Talal Asad has argued that when writing about "culturally distinctive actors," we must "translate and represent the historically-situated discourses of such actors as responses to the discourses of others" (1986, 7). Building on Asad's insights, Vinod Jairath contends that we should understand the "beliefs, practices, and political actions of Muslim communities . . . as embedded in dynamic local and wider social, economic, and political contexts" in India (Jairath 2011, 3). While these contexts have been shaped by shared religious and cultural worlds, they have also been shaped by the experience of extreme violence and what Rowena Robinson calls an "ideologically accepted Otherness . . . [that] seeps into the practices and taken-for-granted assumptions of everyday life" (2011, 249). In the conversations above, while Rizwana illustrates how Indian Muslim "traditions" have been shaped by living together with Hindus and belonging to shared religious and cultural worlds, Huma Khala highlights the specter of violence, ever present in these worlds, that also shapes identity, tradition, and belonging.[14] Together they illustrate how many Indian Muslims understand their place in India, as "embedded but separate," to quote Rowena Robinson (249).

Ultimately, rituals of death can provide an arena to think about life, to articulate constructions of self and belonging, and to make place for Muslims in contemporary India. Whether constructing themselves as "Indian Muslims" or as "Indian Shias," my interlocutors subtly undermined the prevailing tendency in the country to cast Muslims as "foreign" or "other." While Abida and members of her Muslim Club eschewed what they saw as "Hindu" practices, through their *dawa* they too attempted to ingrain transnational discourses of Islam in the everyday lives and practices of those they encountered, making place for these ideas in Old Delhi today. Such religious narratives and practices performatively construct locality in Old Delhi in ways that embed Muslims in place, even in Hindu-majoritarian India. The religious narratives and practices discussed in this chapter also force us to understand culture as something that circulates, mingling with and inflecting different people and places rather than imprisoned within national boundaries (Visweswaran 2010, 3, 8). Twelver Shias like Zehra Baji and Deobandis like Farhana Baji belong to traditions of South Asian Islam that not only have shaped Indian and South Asian culture and practices of etiquette but also have crossed national boundaries and forged transnational communities of practice in ways that force us to recognize not just how "Muslim" Indians are, but also how "Indian" and "South Asian" Muslims can be. Indeed, not only do such practices make place for Muslims in contemporary India; they make place for India and South Asia in the world in ways that challenge both the Middle East–centric scholarship on the Muslim world and the Hindu-centric view of India in the world.

CONCLUSION

"Yes. It is bad. But what can we do? Will wait for five year again. ☹"

I received this message on WhatsApp on May 24, the day after the results of the 2019 general elections in India were declared. In a campaign that had focused on the figure of Narendra Modi, rather than the party he belonged to, the BJP had won by an even greater margin than in 2014. I had been staying in Delhi in the weeks before the election, and everyone I knew in Old Delhi was planning to go out and vote. Even the elderly who rarely left their homes for fear of having to tackle the steep staircases up on their way back were determined to cast their ballot. Iqbal Sahib, very frail and just out of hospital, declared his intention to go out despite the precipitous stairs from his top-floor apartment that had me clutching the handrail every time I had to descend. Zarin Apa, whose arthritic knees prevented her from tackling the many flights to her apartment on the fourth floor except for emergencies, seemed surprised that I even had to ask if she planned to go.

The last five years had been grueling for Indian Muslims, as lynching became the stuff of everyday news. Critics of the ruling party had been systematically targeted by the government, investigated by its various departments, sent to prison on trumped-up charges, or simply killed by right-wing vigilantes. In New Delhi's Defence Colony, the tony neighborhood dominated by Hindus and Sikhs that I was staying in, many said in conversations with me in the weeks preceding the elections, "Who else is there to vote for?" This was not a question I ever heard among Muslims in Old Delhi. To ask the question is a reflection of one's privilege: to be safe from lynching, to be safe from being forced to say, "Jai Shri Ram," to be safe from being charged with sedition for expressing dissent, and to be safe from being shot outside your home by vigilantes. On May 24, 2019, when the BJP's resounding victory suggested that many had voted for the ruling party despite its divisive communal rhetoric and the surge in anti-Muslim violence, it seemed that the place for Muslims in India had shrunk a little more. And yet amid the depressed texts and WhatsApp messages I received on a day when nobody I knew actually wanted to talk to anyone else, there was this message—of perseverance, if not quite hope.

Voting is also a way to make place, even when one is voting in a district in which one's voice will be a minority. With the exception of the southern states of Tamil Nadu and Kerala, which gave no seats to the ruling party, many in the rest of India voted for the BJP despite the fact that the material conditions of their lives had become significantly more challenging under its regime. Many of the working poor voted for the BJP even though unemployment was at a forty-five-year high in 2019. Despite the fact that farmers had been reeling under probusiness agricultural policies that had further indebted them, triggering large-scale protests and tragic suicides, many farmers voted for the BJP. Indeed, when one has lived through decades of systemic violence and seen very little change despite different parties taking over the government, it might appear reasonable to give the ruling party another shot at governance. However, according to the CSDS-Lokniti Post-Poll Survey, while 44 percent of Hindu voters, in an unprecedented consolidation of the Hindu vote across castes and classes, voted for the BJP (51 percent for the NDA coalition it formed), only 8 percent of Muslims voted for the BJP nationwide.[1] For the vast majority of Indian Muslims, then, it was not reasonable to think that the BJP was the same as every other political party, and they registered that opinion on election day.

Making place is not about winning an election. As I have shown throughout this book, places are made through the everyday acts of individuals; they are the residua, the traces left behind. Such traces are left through narratives that materialize particular understandings of the past and the present, through religious acts that operationalize distinct visions of community and belonging, and through cultural performances and gestures that situate individuals firmly in place. Voting against the grain, registering an opinion when the odds are stacked against you, expressing political opposition at a time when dissent has become dangerous, these too are ways to make place for oneself in a country under the grip of majoritarianism. Making place when one is staring at what one hopes is rock bottom is about refusing erasure and waiting for the next time—"again."

Old Delhi is a place that still bears the residua of the city that Emperor Shah Jahan built, even as its streets are marked by the traces of many others who came after him. It is a city that, to recall Narayani Gupta's words, has died many times and yet continues to bear the ethos of Shahjahanabad (1981, 55, 1). Its Muslim denizens have been crushed many times too: after the revolt of 1857, during the partition in 1947, during the Emergency years from 1975 to 1977, and since the right-wing resurgence from the 1980s to the present moment. And yet life goes on even in difficult times. People continue to assert their understandings of self and community and articulate belonging in the face of exclusion. And places are kept alive through everyday religious, cultural, and political acts despite the overwhelming force of majoritarian understandings of India.

I have argued in this book that although securitization discourses, Islamophobia, prejudice, and violence have "secured" Muslims in places like Old Delhi, and while economic forces capitalize on the politics of religion, class, caste, gender, and place to make some rich at the expense of others, people continue to live, love, and build community in the face of marginalization, alienation, and dispossession. Some articulate transnational religious communities that defy the singular and insular claims of the nation-state, forcing us to understand place as "extroverted," variegated, and marked by the traces of multiple histories, places, cultural flows, people, and movements (Mankekar 2015; Massey 1991). Some highlight boundaries and difference, making themselves visible and laying claim to place in a country in which violent disavowals of Islam and Muslims are increasingly frequent, and valorized. Others narrate religious histories, cultures, identities, and communities that disrupt religious and sectarian boundaries and forge community across bitter divides. And still others engage in rituals of belonging that resist understandings of religious identity as mutually exclusive, rooting people in place against the tide of Hindu chauvinism and exclusionary understandings of nation and belonging. I see such efforts as forms of place making, tenacious acts through which Indian Muslims make place for themselves in contemporary India.

At no time in the history of independent India have these efforts been more visible than they are today, in the wake of the discriminatory Citizenship Amendment Act (CAA) passed by the Indian Parliament in December 2019, which provides a path to citizenship for migrants from Afghanistan, Pakistan, and Bangladesh as long as they are not Muslim. Nonviolent protests, spearheaded by young students, spread across Delhi and all over India. On December 15, 2019, when students at Jamia Millia Islamia in New Delhi were brutalized by police trying to violently crush this movement, their mothers and grandmothers took over the streets at Shaheen Bagh. Following their lead, people poured out into the streets calling for the protection of the rights promised by the Indian Constitution. The women who protested for a hundred days at Shaheen Bagh before a global pandemic enabled the government to shut them down and paint over every last trace of their resistance were not there only as Muslims. They were there as Indians defending the Indian Constitution against those seeking to rewrite and undermine its promise of equality. They were there as mothers and grandmothers calling out police brutality against their children in an increasingly authoritarian state. They led many others of all genders, religions, castes, classes, and regions in the largest nonviolent mass movement the country has experienced since the struggle for independence from British colonial rule. And as in the years leading to 1947, the streets echoed with calls for *azadi* (freedom), once again from an antidemocratic state.

To those who saw the very public presence of Muslim women as extraordinary, the women at Shaheen Bagh said, "We simply came out on the roads to support and protect our children who were being attacked in colleges and universities all over, when nobody else did. The attacks on the youth were extraordinary. Our response was not extraordinary. If we had stayed silent—that would have been extraordinary" (Mustafa 2020). These women inspired many who had remained silent during the lynchings of Muslims and Dalits since 2014, remained silent through the final dismemberment of any semblance of Kashmiri sovereignty with the revocation of Article 370 and Article 35A in August 2019, and remained silent when the Supreme Court verdict of November 2019 handed over the grounds of the Babri Masjid to those who had destroyed it, to finally take a stand against the drift toward authoritarianism in India. A verse penned by the late Rahat Indori, which I have used as the epigraph for this book, was held up on placards at Shaheen Bagh, at "Shaheen Baghs" throughout the city, all over India, and all over the world, including in Chicago where I live: "*Sab ka khoon shamil hai yahan ki mitti mein, Kisi ke baap ka Hindustan thodi hai*" (Everyone's blood is part of the soil of this place, Hindustan is not anyone's personal property). Shaheen Bagh was about making place in the face of the threat of erasure and exclusion, even under the shadow of violence.[2]

Visibly and vocally claiming place in Modi's India is a dangerous act, especially for Muslims. Indeed, the claim to place voiced in the anti-CAA protests was met with violent retribution. Hours after the BJP's Kapil Mishra threatened to call on his supporters to shut down a nonviolent protest near the Jafrabad Metro Station, North East Delhi erupted in anti-Muslim violence in February 2020. According to the report of the Fact-Finding Committee of the Delhi Minorities Commission on the North East Delhi riots of February 2020, Kapil Mishra's speech "clearly incited violence in words and intent" (Delhi Minorities Commission 2020, 30). In an eerie reminder of the Gujarat Pogrom of 2002, many reported that the police did nothing to stop the rioters as they destroyed Muslim lives, homes, and property, while others insisted that the police were participants in the violence (Delhi Minorities Commission 2020, passim, see especially 101–104; see also Mustafa 2020).[3] The chairperson of the Fact-Finding Committee notes in his foreword to the report that while the charge sheets filed by the police construct a narrative "of violence on both sides," it was in fact "a pogrom" in which the state was complicit (Delhi Minorities Commission 2020, 13–14). Old Delhi remained peaceful during this period, but Muslims there worried about friends and family who lived in North East Delhi. They made place for them in their already crowded homes, collected food and essential items for the now homeless and dispossessed, and continued their protests.

The Islamophobia and demonization of Muslims that enabled the Delhi violence were further compounded in March and April 2020. Muslims all over the country were accused of spreading COVID-19 after positive virus cases were detected among a global gathering of Tablighi Jamaat members in Delhi. In the weeks that followed, many Muslims feared going to the hospital even if they were sick, concerned about prejudicial treatment, or of being turned away. These concerns continued even as virus cases mounted in the country. When I worriedly suggested to one of my interlocutors via WhatsApp in July 2020 that she visit a doctor when she had a fever, she declared that she would not go to a hospital even if she got sicker. Unwilling to deal with the prejudice against Muslims at hospitals, she said, "I will die at home."

While this example clearly illustrates how the pandemic exacerbated systemic violence against Muslims, COVID-19 also provided a cover for the state to engage in retribution against the many young students and activists who had participated in the protests against the CAA. Despite a Supreme Court directive in March 2020 to decongest jails by granting bail or parole to certain classes of prisoners to contain the spread of COVID-19, and although there was little evidence to indicate their involvement in the Delhi violence, several nonviolent protestors were arrested under the UAPA (Unlawful Activities Prevention Act), a draconian antiterror law that has been used with alarming frequency against people protesting the curtailment of civil liberties. These arrests occurred while the country was in one of the most stringent pandemic lockdowns in the world, thus limiting public outcry, at least in any physical form, over arrests that the United Nations Office of the High Commissioner for Human Rights said were "clearly designed to send a chilling message to India's vibrant civil society that criticism of government policies will not be tolerated."[4] In India, as elsewhere in the world, COVID-19 has enabled authoritarian leaders to use the institutions of the state to further their own antidemocratic interests.

Today, as institutions of the government are increasingly politicized, as the constitution is increasingly under attack, and as the world's largest democracy is increasingly besieged by fascist forces, it is hard to imagine what the future will bring. Indeed, as many of my interlocutors would insist, perhaps it is not for us mere mortals to predict the future. So at the end, I turn to what anthropology does best—rely on ethnography to sketch the possibilities planted by those whose lives have filled the pages of this book. Possibilities, of course, can unfold in multiple ways. And yet they do allow us to sketch those "avenues of hope" that always exist at the interstices of hegemonic forces (Jamil 2017, 182).

Ameena Baji continues to juggle different jobs in the informal economy to ensure that her children can have what she could not—an education. Today, all her children have college degrees, and some are pursuing graduate studies. Ameena Baji hopes that they will get good jobs and be self-sufficient soon. She hopes that one day she will not have to work so hard to make ends meet. She has dreams too. She wants to enroll in an online program through which she can pursue a bachelor's degree to study one of her passions—Urdu.

Zehra Baji, who stayed with her abusive husband for years, finally left him one morning and has now disappeared. Nobody seems to know where she is, including her Hindu best friend with whom she resided the last time she left him. Her daughter Sakina is now married and living with her husband and in-laws in Old Delhi. Although circumstances have led to a hiatus from college, Sakina is determined to get an undergraduate degree from Delhi University and fulfill the dreams that her mother sacrificed so much for.

Rehana has moved from being a salesperson to being the manager of the posh clothing store she has been working in for years. She feels that she understands the business now and has developed a sense for what customers want. She has also learned where to source the material and already knows whom she can hire to do the sewing, embroidery, and handwork. She feels that she is ready to start her own shop. She just needs to put together the money to start up. Once she has done that, she thinks things will go smoothly.

Rafiq Sahib and others continue to work year after year to help young girls and boys in Old Delhi with college admissions, advising them on courses of study that they did not know existed and educating their parents on the value of sending their sons and daughters to college despite high unemployment levels and employment discrimination. People like Rafiq Sahib give their time and money to schools in Old Delhi, keeping them afloat and urging their students to do well. While such actions might increase their standing in the community and bring them prestige and influence, they are also undeniably a labor of love in a place that many others have chosen to forget.

Tariq Sahib continues to write about the religiously plural worlds of Delhi and disseminate the histories of a place that once was. Raza Sahib continues to make time for journalists and scholars to talk about his life in Old Delhi, the friendships that crossed religious boundaries, and the experiences of those who lived through the partition of India in 1947. Iqbal Sahib continues to do research on everything from festivals and traditions in Mughal Delhi to the legacies of Muhammad Iqbal, publishing his articles in Urdu journals and newsletters in the city. All three of them very generously make room for strangers like me to enter into the lives and worlds of a place that they love.

Zafar's family began to wear *tawiz* (amulets) containing verses from the Quran around their necks for protection when blood spatters started mysteriously appearing in their courtyard on Holi, Diwali, and Dusshera—three important Hindu festivals. Although they were not sure who or what was causing this, Zafar's mother explained in 2016, "This only happens when they are trying to get rid of you." When I met them again in 2019, Zafar's mother told me that she had not seen the blood spatters since she had read verses from the Quran over water and blown it in different parts of her courtyard. She had read Manzil Dua, a set of thirty-three verses from the Quran meant to counter the effects of sorcery, jinn, black magic, and shaitan. She believed that these religious acts had enabled her to reclaim her home from inimical forces that sought to displace her.

Syed Sahibs continue to wake up Farhana Baji for *fajr namaz* every morning. Whether jinns or martyrs, they make sure she does not sleep through prayer time, that the *barakat* from her acts continues to permeate Old Delhi. While Syed Sahibs can be good or bad, according to Farhana Baji, the one's in her house are good and never cause any problems. "They take care of us," Farhana Baji tells me. Indeed, when her children have not listened to her or have acted selfishly, the Syed Sahibs in her house have gently made their presence known and shown them the error of their ways. These Syed Sahibs continue to ensure that Old Delhi is filled with people who strive to be good and that it is suffused with *barakat*.

So many I worked with in Old Delhi made protests against the Citizenship Amendment Act part of their daily lives, believing firmly, along with many others throughout the country, that the act violated the Indian Constitution. After a long day at Shaheen Bagh in Delhi where women had been sitting in protest for weeks, one of my interlocuters told me, "Modi has done one good thing unknowingly. At Shaheen Bagh there were no Sunnis, there were no Shias, there were no Barelvis, there were no Deobandis. . . . . Everyone said, we are all Muslims and we are one. There were Hindus there. There were Sikhs there. We were there to protect the constitution."

These small acts can make place. Again.

Glossary

alam ('alam) standard
anjuman organization
apa (āpā) elder sister
azaan (azān) call to prayer
azadari ('azādārī) mourning procession
baji (bājī) elder sister
barakat (barakāt) blessings
bhai (bhā'ī) brother
bidat (bid'at) religious innovation
biradari (birādarī) occupational group
burqa (burqa') veil, overgarment for covering
dalan (dālān) interior verandah
dargah (dargāh) shrine
dawa (da'wā) religious outreach
didi (dīdī) elder sister
dua (du'ā) prayer
dupatta (ḍupaṭṭā) long scarf
fajr namaz (fajr namāz) morning prayers
haram (ḥarām) forbidden
haveli (ḥawelī) house, mansion
hidayat (hidāyat) guidance
ibadat ('ibādat) worship
iddat ('iddat) waiting period observed by Muslim widows
insaniyat (insānīyat) humanity
jinn beings created by God from smokeless fire
juma (jum'a) Friday
kalma the Muslim confession of faith
karkhana workshop
Khuda (Ḵẖudā) God

kurta tunic

kurta-pajama tunic and pants

magrib azaan (magrib aẕān) evening call to prayer

maidan (maidān) open space; field

majalis (majālis) mourning gatherings; singular *majlis*

masaib (maṣā'ib) remembrance of the sufferings of the Prophet's family

masjid mosque

maslak Islamic path; norms associated with Islamic reform movements in South Asia

matam (mātam) ritual mourning

mazars (mazār) tombs

mazhab (maẕhab) religion

mohalla (maḥalla, or more commonly *muḥalla)* neighborhood, quarter

nauha (nauḥa) dirge, lament

nazr (naẕr) vow or offering to God

niyaz (niyāz) petition, prayer

pak (pāk) pure

pareshan (pareshān) troubled

pir (pīr) saint

purdah (parda) veil

qiyamat (qiyāmat) day of resurrection

rasul (rasūl) messenger, the Prophet

riwaj (rawāj, riwāj) tradition, custom

roza fast

rozmarra zindagi (rozmarra zindagī) everyday life

ruh (rūḥ) spirit

sahib (ṣāḥib) sir, mister

shaheed (shahīd) martyr

shahid (shāhid) witness

shairi (shā'irī) poetry

shirk attributing a partner to God

supari (supārī) areca nut, betel nut

tawiz (ta'wīẕ) amulets

taziya (taʿziya) replica of the tomb of Husain or other key Shii figures

teeja (tījā) the third day of mourning

waz (waʿẓ) religious sermon

zakat (zakāt) almsgiving that purifies

ziyarat (ziyārat) pilgrimage

Notes

INTRODUCTION

1. All names in this book are pseudonyms, unless otherwise indicated. Very rarely, I have given the same individual a different name when discussing a sensitive issue, in order to protect their identity from those who might know them.

2. For scholarship that has questioned the focus on difference, see especially the work of Visweswaran 2010; Gottschalk 2000; Hirst and Zavos 2005; Oberoi 1994.

3. Mukesh (also *mukaish*) is a form of metal embroidery.

4. Memories of this past can also be recalled in the present to intervene in contemporary politics in India (see H. Ahmed 2013).

5. Punjab in northwestern India was divided between West Pakistan and India. Bengal in eastern India was divided between East Pakistan and India.

6. There are important Hindu nationalist organizations that are not part of the Sangh Parivar, such as the Shiv Sena (see, for instance, Bedi 2016; Sen 2007). While the Shiv Sena has formed alliances with the BJP, it has also formed alliances with their opposition in some instances.

7. See "Here Is How Your Pin Code Is Decided," *Economic Times*, March 29, 2017, https://economictimes.indiatimes.com/slideshows/nation-world/here-is-how-your-pin-code-is-decided/here-is-the-procedure/slideshow/57889793.cms.

8. For more on the jinn who inhabit the landscapes of Delhi, see Taneja 2018.

9. Shoaib Daniyal, "How Narendra Modi Helped Spread Anti-Beef Hysteria in India," October 7, 2015, https://qz.com/india/518975/how-narendra-modi-helped-spread-anti-beef-hysteria-in-india.

10. See Mahtab Alam, "Why Do Mob Lynchings Still Continue Unabated?" *The Wire*, September 7, 2019, https://thewire.in/communalism/mob-cow-lynching-vigilante.

11. Pehlu Khan, a fifty-five-year-old Muslim dairy farmer, was beaten to death by approximately two hundred people summoned via WhatsApp who believed he was transporting cows for slaughter, even as he pleaded his innocence. In fact, Pehlu Khan was transporting dairy cows he had just purchased at a cattle fair and had receipts to show that he had just spent a considerable sum on them. Despite compelling evidence to the contrary, including videos of the attack, six of those accused of lynching Pehlu Khan were acquitted on August 14, 2019. For more on Pehlu Khan, see Salam 2019 and Ramani 2018. For more on the use of WhatsApp by the BJP to organize violence, see Neyazi 2019.

12. For more on the classification of bovines, see Z. Ahmad 2018, 8.

13. See Avay Shukla, "Kanpur Diary: No More Waiting Till the Cows Come Home," *The Wire*, January 10, 2019, https://thewire.in/communalism/cows-coming-home.

14. Many scholars have examined the ways in which violence has become ingrained in the workings of democracy in India, whether one talks about violence as an exercise of state power (Mahmood 1996), as a form of communication (Hansen 2018, 1087) and voicing protest (Chakrabarty 2007), or of consolidating community (Appadurai 2006) and vote banks (Jaffrelot 2007).

15. Eid is the festival that marks the end of Ramzan (Ramadan), the Islamic month of fasting.

16. For more on Junaid Khan's murder, see Somya Lakhani, "A Boy Called Junaid," *Indian Express*, July 2, 2017, https://indianexpress.com/article/india/faridabad-lynching-train-beef-ban-a-boy-called-junaid-4731198. See also Mander 2019.

17. For more on the construction of the upper-caste Hindu as the normative national subject in India, see Sunder Rajan 2003 and Kapur 2012.

18. See, for instance, Low and Lawrence-Zuniga 2003, 13. See also Massey 2005; Srinivas 2001; Escobar 2001; Moore 1998; Gupta and Ferguson 1997; Basso 1996; Werbner 1996.

19. In the South Asian context, *maslak* refers to particular schools of Islamic reform (such as Barelvi, Deobandi, and Ahl-e-Hadis) and, more specifically "normative orientations" associated with these reform movements (Tareen 2020).

20. Muharram is the first month of the Islamic calendar, during which Muslims, particularly Shias, mourn the death of Hasan and Husain, the grandsons of the Prophet Muhammad. Ashura marks the day of Husain's death, and that of his companions, at Karbala.

1. A PLACE FOR MUSLIMS

1. For scholarship that challenges these stereotypes about veiling in Islam, see Mahmood 2005 and Scott 2007.

2. Ramzan (*Ramadan* in Arabic) is the Muslim month of fasting.

3. A gazetted officer is a senior government official with the authority to issue the official stamp of the government.

4. For a discussion of the ambivalent character of this modernity, see Devji 2013.

5. Laurent Gayer says the Muslim population is most concentrated in Central Delhi, where Old Delhi is located, at 29.88 percent (2012, 217).

6. The *azaan* (*adhan* in Arabic) is the call to prayer. *Nehari* and *korma* are meat preparations that Old Delhi is renowned for. *Naan* and *bakharwadi* are breads.

7. There is a substantial body of scholarship on space and place. See Low and Lawrence-Zuniga 2003, 13; see also Massey 2005; Escobar 2001; Gupta and Ferguson 1997; Deeb 2006; de Certeau 1984.

8. Many Muslims, following the Quran (62:9), attend congregational *Juma* prayers on Fridays.

9. For more on the close connections between politics and religious articulations in postcolonial India, see Irfan Ahmad 2009.

10. Larger homes often have areas where men can receive male visitors. However, as homes have been increasingly divided, space has become an issue. Consequently, young men often meet their friends outside the home, sitting in teashops or perching on scooters and motorcycles parked on the streets.

11. See the website of the National Cadet Corps at https://indiancc.nic.in.

12. Ajmal Kasab was convicted for the attack in Mumbai on November 26, 2008, and hung on November 21, 2012. Many critiqued the secretive nature of the execution, and some believed it was unconstitutional (see Madhubashi Sridhar, "An Act of Constitutional Impropriety" *The Hindu*, November 23, 2012, 12). Afzal Guru was convicted for the December 13, 2001, attack on the Indian Parliament in New Delhi. Although many believed that the evidence against him was shaky, he was hung on February 9, 2013, less than a month after this conversation with Rafiq Sahib (see Arundhati Roy, "A Perfect Day for Democracy," *The Hindu*, February 10, 2013, 12).

13. See "Ishrat Jahan: Terrorist or Innocent," *Hindustan Times*, July 4, 2013, 11. Also see "Ishrat Killed for Promotions?" *Hindustan Times*, July 7, 2013, 10.

14. According to Mahesh Langa, in the 1,500-page document released by the CBI, "The agency said in its first charge sheet on the 2004 case that Ishrat and three others were abducted, kept under illegal confinement, sedated and killed by the cops in a 'fake encounter'" (see "Abducted. Drugged. Shot," *Hindustan Times*, July 4, 2013, 1).

15. The Batla House encounter took place on September 19, 2008, between the special cell of the Delhi police and men suspected of being members of the militant group Indian Mujahideen. Two were killed and two were arrested (see "The Encounter," *Hindustan Times*, September 19, 2012, 3).

16. See "Report Points Fingers at Special Cell," *Hindustan Times*, September 19, 2012, 3.

17. See Arundhati Roy, "A Perfect Day for Democracy," *The Hindu*, February 10, 2013, 12.

18. See "Despite SC's Stance on Sedition, Charge Slapped on JNU's Kanhaiya Kumar, Others," *The Wire*, January 15, 2019, at https://thewire.in/rights/despite-scs-stance-on-sedition-charge-slapped-on-jnus-kanhaiya-kumar-others.

2. GENDER AND PRECARITY

1. Other scholars who have written about the concentration of Muslims in certain neighborhoods include Jamil (2017), Kirmani (2013), and Gayer (2012).

2. The informal economy refers to that part of the national economy that is "bureaucratically invisible" because it is unregulated by the government but in which most individuals participate in some capacity (Shah 2014, 9). According to Maidul Islam, neoliberal reforms include "liberalization, privatization, and globalization with market led economic policies, deregulation of the economy for foreign investments, retreat of the State from major economic activities and greater alignment with United States foreign policy" (2012, 62).

3. See Monika Banerjee, "What Work Choices Are Women Making and Why?" *The Wire*, June 7, 2019, https://thewire.in/women/indian-women-work-care-informal-sector.

4. For scholarship that challenges these stereotypes, see Jamil 2018, Kirmani 2013, Abu-Lughod 2013, and Mohanty 1988.

5. Ranadeep Bhattacharyya, "Silver and Gold—Story of Zardozi," Heritage India, http://heritage-india.com/silver-gold-story-zardozi.

6. People in Old Delhi often intersperse English with Hindi in conversations. The English words are in italics.

7. I am very grateful to Syeda Asia of Delhi University for this insight, provided as part of her discussant comments at the Twenty-Fifth European Conference on South Asian Studies in Paris on July 26, 2018.

8. Diane D'Souza defines *nazr* as "an offering, usually of food which a person makes with a specific intention" (2012, 310n1).

9. See "99.30% of Demonitised Money Back in the System, Says RBI Report," *Economic Times*, August 30, 2018, https://economictimes.indiatimes.com/news/economy/finance/after-almost-two-years-of-counting-rbi-says-99-3-of-demonetised-notes-returned/articleshow/65589904.cms.

10. Manoj Kumar, "GST Impact: Hundreds of Thousands Lose Their Jobs Even as Economy Grows," *The Wire*, September 7, 2018, https://thewire.in/labour/gst-impact-powerlooms-panipat-jobs.

3. PERFECTING THE SELF

1. There are, of course, exceptions to this. For instance, Osella and Osella document men and women at Eid prayers in Kerala (2013, 159).

2. Maqsood's argument is reminiscent of the writings of scholars who have used the work of W. E. B. DuBois on double consciousness to argue that Muslim Americans and Arabs Americans engage in the world with an awareness of how they are perceived by others (Cainkar 2009; Naber 2006; DuBois 1903).

3. While the Malaysian government has granted him permanent residency and has apparently failed to act on an extradition request from India out of fear that he would

not be treated fairly, it has been troubled by speeches that Naik has delivered in Malaysia in which he has commented on racial and religious dynamics in the country. See, for instance, "Malaysia: Zakir Naik Apologizes for Controversial Chinese Remarks," Al Jazeera, August 20, 2019, https://www.aljazeera.com/news/2019/08/20/malaysia-zakir-naik-apologises-for-controversial-chinese-remarks.

4. *Sunnat* in Arabic is *Sunna*.

5. For a discussion of how middle-class aspirations shape religiosity among India's Hindu middle classes, see Fuller and Narasimhan 2014.

6. For discussions of these various theories, see Deeb 2006, 14–15; Grewal 2014, 59.

7. For scholars who have attributed Islamic politics and violence to Islamic doctrine, see Juergensmeyer (2000) and Lewis (2003).

8. Farhat Hashmi and Al Huda women also assert that those who identify with *maslak* lack knowledge (see S. Ahmad 2009, 40).

9. *Maslaks*, associated with the various schools of Islamic reform in South Asia, draw on different sources of religious authority. While some groups, like Ahl-e-Hadis, insist on the primacy of the foundational texts of Islam and on unmediated access to them, Deobandis also accept Sufi teachings and follow Hanafi law, and Barelvis often engage in practices that these other groups claim reveal Hindu influences and amount to *shirk* (attributing a partner to God) (Metcalf 2009, 226).

10. For more on the differences between these groups, see Tareen 2020 and Metcalf 2009.

11. Both *pir* and *wali* are used by Old Delhi Muslims to refer to Sufi saints. *Faqir* refers to a dervish or religious mendicant.

12. *Hadis* in Arabic is *Hadith*.

13. This is a pseudonym for a well-known girls' school in Old Delhi.

14. For a discussion of a similar struggle among members of the Mosque Movement in Egypt, see S. Mahmood 2005.

15. Although I have translated *sabr* elsewhere in this excerpt, I have not translated the term in one instance where she is defining it for her audience.

4. LIVING WITH DIFFERENCE

1. On Shii-Sunni violence in South Asia, see Uzair Hasan Rizvi, "The Rising Threat against Shia Muslims in Pakistan," *The Wire*, June 11, 2016, https://thewire.in/41862/the-rising-threat-against-shia-muslims-in-pakistan. On Hindu-Muslim violence, including Hindu-Shia violence, see Violette Graff and Juliette Galonnier, "Hindu-Muslim Communal Riots in India II (1986–2011)," *Sciences Po*, August 20, 2013, http://www.sciencespo.fr/mass-violence-war-massacre-resistance/en/document/hindu-muslim-communal-riots-india-ii-1986-2011.

2. See the results of the Government of India 2011 Census, available at http://www.censusindia.gov.in/2011census/C-01.html.

3. For evidence of shared religious worlds in Shii ritual and narrative in other parts of India, see Karen Ruffle's work on Hyderabad (2011).

4. Both Deobandi and Ahl-e-Hadis Muslims are often labeled "Wahabi" or are used to point to instances of Wahabi influence in South Asia. However, as Barbara Metcalf warns, it is important to recall, "from colonial times until today . . . [that] the label 'Wahabi' is often used to discredit any reformist or politically active Islamic group" (Metcalf 2006, 270). For how the British used the term "Wahabi," see Mallampalli 2017.

5. It is sometimes attributed to the Hindu poet Munshi Channu Lal (aka Dilgeer Lakhnavi). For Hindu composers of Shia poetic traditions, see Ruffle 2011, 107.

6. This is not a pseudonym, since he was addressing an audience at a public event.

7. See "Muharram 9: Eight people die despite 'stringent' security," *Express Tribune*, November 24, 2012, https://tribune.com.pk/story/470611/muharram-9-live-updates.

8. For a discussion of the tensions between immanence and transcendence, and the rationalizing tendencies in Islamic reform movements, see Robinson 2013, 29, 40–44 (see also Pernau 2013, 38–47).

9. For more on *ziyarat*, see Bard 2010, 176n6.

10. Indeed, his impact may well be felt beyond Delhi, since he said that the event was being broadcast live to 200 countries. He ran as a candidate for the Aam Aadmi Party (AAP) in the 2014 Lok Sabha elections from Amroha.

11. See Jiby Kattakayam, "Death for Five of a Family in 'Honor Killing' Case," *The Hindu*, September 9, 2011, https://www.thehindu.com/todays-paper/death-for-five-of-a-family-in-honour-killing-case/article2437920.ece.

12. See Kunaal Sharma,"Ending Lucknow's Unholy Hatred," *The Hindu*, July 14, 2015, https://www.thehindubusinessline.com/todays-paper/tp-opinion/ending-lucknows-unholy-hatred/article7418732.ece. See also Jones 2012, 230–35.

5. LIFE AFTER DEATH

1. The Quran says, "As for those of you who die leaving wives behind, their wives should observe a waiting period of four months and ten days. When they have completed that period you incur no offence on account of what they may do with themselves in a lawful manner. Allah has knowledge of what you do" (2:234).

2. Exceptions can be made for various reasons, including financial exigency or illness.

3. See, for instance, Deeb 2006; Hirschkind 2006; S. Mahmood 2005; Harding 2001; Hansen 1999; C. Mahmood 1996; van der Veer 1994; Asad 1993.

4. This is also true in other parts of the world. See, for instance, Venhorst 2012, 85; Gardner 2002; Privratsky 2001, 141.

5. For similar practices among South Asian Muslims in Canada, see Regula Qureshi's discussion of *Qur'ankwani* (1996).

6. In the Quran, *ruh* is "the divine spirit . . . the literal breath of life" (Smith and Haddad 2002, 17).

7. *Fatiha* allows the living to perform acts (like reading the Quran) whose rewards are bequeathed to the dead (see Metcalf 1990, 145). *Fatiha* also refers to the opening chapter of the Quran.

8. This is a reference to Sunni Muslim *dawa* groups, including the Tablighi Jamaat.

9. The Hanuman Chalisa is a Hindu hymn that is recited to worship the monkey god Hanuman.

10. For more on the differences and tensions between Barelvis, Deobandis, and Ahl-e-Hadis in South Asia, see Tareen 2020; N. Khan 2012, 1–5; A. Ahmed 2009; S. Ahmad 2009, 26–29).

11. Robert Hefner argues that conversion requires "a commitment to a new kind of moral authority and a new or reconceptualized social identity" (1993, 17).

12. There is a similar story found in some classical texts (eleventh to seventeenth centuries). According to these sources, the angel of death knows when a death is imminent because a leaf with the person's name falls from a tree "beneath the Throne of God" (Smith and Haddad 2002, 35). In these texts, this occurs forty days before the person's death, not on Shab-e-Baraat.

13. For some of the debates surrounding the use of the term "Allah Hafiz," see Nandagopal R. Menon, "The Islam We Do Not Like," *Kafila* (blog), September 20, 2014, https://kafila.online/2014/09/20/the-islam-we-do-not-like-nandgopal-r-menon.

14. For more on "living together" with others, see Mayaram 2004 and Hasan and Roy 2005.

CONCLUSION

1. See Shreyas Sardesai and Vibha Attri, "Post-poll Survey: The 2019 Verdict Is a Manifestation of the Deepening Religious Divide in India," *The Hindu*, May 30, 2019, https://www.thehindu.com/elections/lok-sabha-2019/the-verdict-is-a-manifestation-of-the-deepening-religious-divide-in-india/article27297239.ece.

2. For more on the multiple threats and acts of violence against anti-CAA protestors, see Delhi Minorities Commission 2020, 27–30.

3. See also the report by the Polis Project, *Manufacturing Evidence: How the Police Is Framing and Arresting Constitutional Rights Defenders in India*, August 13, 2020. https://www.thepolisproject.com/manufacturing-evidence-how-the-police-framed-and-arrested-constitutional-right-defenders-in-india/.

4. See the statement released by the United Nations Office of the High Commissioner for Human Rights, "UN Experts Urge India to Release Protest Leaders," June 26, 2020, https://www.ohchr.org/EN/NewsEvents/Pages/DisplayNews.aspx?NewsID=26002&LangID=E.

References

Abu-Lughod, Lila. 2013. *Do Muslim Women Need Saving?* Cambridge, MA: Harvard University Press.

Addock, Cassie S. 2010. "Sacred Cows and Secular History: Cow Protection Debates in Colonial North India." *Comparative Studies of South Asia, Africa, and the Middle East* 30 (2): 297–311.

——. 2016. "Violence, Passion, and the Law: A Brief History of Section 295A and Its Antecedents." Roundtable on Outrage, Scholarship, and the Law in India. *Journal of the American Academy of Religion* 84 (2): 337–51.

Agnes, Flavia. 2012. "From Shah Bano to Kausar Bano: Contextualizing the 'Muslim Woman' within a Communalized Polity." In *South Asian Feminisms*, edited by Ania Loomba and Ritty Lukose, 33–53. Durham, NC: Duke University Press.

Ahmad, Imtiaz. 1978. *Caste and Social Stratification among Muslims in India*. New Delhi: Manohar.

——. 1981. *Ritual and Religion among Muslims in India*. New Delhi: Manohar.

Ahmad, Irfan. 2009. *Islamism and Democracy in India: The Transformation of the Jamaat-e-Islami*. Princeton, NJ: Princeton University Press.

——. 2011. "Immanent Critique and Islam: Anthropological Reflections." *Anthropological Theory* 11 (1): 107–32.

——. 2017a. "Injustice and the New World Order: An Anthropological Perspective on "Terrorism" in India." *Critical Studies on Terrorism* 10 (1): 115–37.

——. 2017b. *Religion as Critique: Islamic Critical Thinking from Mecca to the Marketplace*. Chapel Hill: University of North Carolina Press.

Ahmad, Sadaf. 2009. *Transforming Faith: The Story of Al-Huda and Islamic Revivalism among Urban Pakistani Women*. Syracuse, NY: Syracuse University Press.

Ahmad, Zarin. 2018. *Delhi's Meatscapes: Muslim Butchers in a Transforming Mega-City*. New Delhi: Oxford University Press.

Ahmed, Asad Ali. 2009. "Specters of Macaulay: Blasphemy, the Indian Penal Code, and Pakistan's Postcolonial Predicament." In *Censorship in South Asia: Cultural Regulation from Sedition to Seduction*, edited by Raminder Kaur and William Mazzarella, 172–205. Bloomington: Indiana University Press.

Ahmed, Hilal. 2013. "Mosque as Monument: The Afterlives of Jama Masjid and the Political Memories of a Royal Muslim Past." *South Asian Studies* 29 (1): 51–59.

Ahmed, Shahab. 2016. *What Is Islam? The Importance of Being Islamic*. Princeton, NJ: Princeton University Press.

Alam, Muzaffar. 2004. *The Languages of Political Islam in India, c. 1200–1800*. New Delhi: Permanent Black.

Anderson, Benedict. 1998. *The Spectre of Comparisons: Nationalism, Southeast Asia, and the World*. London: Verso.

Ansari, Ghaus. 1960. *Muslim Caste in Uttar Pradesh: A Study of Culture Contact*. Lucknow, UP: Ethnographic and Folk Culture Society.

Appadurai, Arjun. 1996. *Modernity at Large: Cultural Dimensions of Globalization*. Minneapolis: University of Minnesota Press.

——. 2006. *Fear of Small Numbers: An Essay on the Geography of Anger.* Durham, NC: Duke University Press.

Ardener, Shirley. 2014. "Credit Unions and Money Clubs (ROSCAs)." *Anthropology Today* 30 (4): 3–6.

Asad, Talal. 1986. *The Idea of an Anthropology of Islam.* Washington, DC: Center for Contemporary Arab Studies, Georgetown University.

——. 1993. *Genealogies of Religion: Discipline and Reasons of Power in Christianity and Islam.* Vol. 18. Baltimore: Johns Hopkins University Press.

Assayag, Jackie. 2004. *At the Confluence of Two Rivers: Muslims and Hindus in South India.* New Delhi: Manohar.

Ayyub, Rana. 2016. *Gujarat Files: Anatomy of a Cover Up.* Self-published by Rana Ayyub.

Azim, Firdous. 2012. "Keeping Sexuality on the Agenda: The Sex Workers Movement from Bangladesh." In *South Asian Feminisms,* edited by Ania Loomba and Ritty Lukose, 267–84. Durham, NC: Duke University Press.

Bacchetta, Paola. 2004. *Gender in the Hindu Nation: RSS Women as Ideologues.* New Delhi: Women Unlimited.

Bakker, Isabella. 2007. "Social Reproduction and the Constitution of a Gendered Political Economy." *New Political Economy* 12 (4): 541–56.

Bard, Amy C. 2005. "'No Power of Speech Remains': Tears and Transformation in South Asian Majlis Poetry." In *Holy Tears: Weeping in the Religious Imagination,* edited by Kimberley C. Patton and John S. Hawley, 145–64. Princeton, NJ: Princeton University Press.

——. 2010. "Turning Karbala inside Out: Humor and Ritual Critique in South Asian Muharram Rites." In *Sacred Play: Ritual Levity and Humor in South Asian Religions,* edited by Selva J. Raj and Corinne G. Dempsey, 161–83. Albany, NY: SUNY Press.

Basso, Keith. 1996. *Wisdom Sits in Places: Landscape and Language among the Western Apache.* Albuquerque: University of New Mexico Press.

Basu, Amrita. 1995. "Feminism Inverted: The Gendered Imagery and Real Women of Hindu Nationalism." In *Women and the Hindu Right: A Collection of Essays,* ed. Tanika Sarkar and Urvashi Butalia. 158–80. New Delhi: Kali for Women.

Bedi, Tarini. 2016. *The Dashing Ladies of Shiv Sena: Political Matronage in Urbanizing India.* Albany, NY: SUNY Press.

Bellamy, Carla. 2011. *The Powerful Ephemeral: Everyday Healing in an Ambiguously Islamic Place.* Berkeley: University of California Press.

Beneria, Lourdes. 1979. "Reproduction, Production and the Sexual Division of Labour." *Cambridge Journal of Economics* 3 (3): 203–25.

Bhatt, Chetan. 2001. *The Rashtriya Swayamsevak Sangh's Ordered Society: Hindu Nationalism: Origins, Ideologies, and Modern Myths.* Oxford: Berg.

Bigelow, Anne. 2010. *Sharing the Sacred: Practicing Pluralism in Muslim North India.* Oxford: Oxford University Press.

Bonilla-Silva, E. 2015. "More than Prejudice: Restatement, Reflections, and New Directions in Critical Race Theory." *Sociology of Race and Ethnicity* 1 (1): 73–87.

Bose, Sugata, and Ayesha Jalal. 2004. *Modern South Asia: History, Culture, Political Economy.* 2nd ed. New York: Routledge.

Brass, Paul. 2003. *The Production of Hindu-Muslim Violence in Contemporary India.* Cambridge: Cambridge University Press.

Butler, Judith. 1990. "Performative Acts and Gender Constitution: An Essay in Phenomenology and Feminist Theory." In *Performing Feminisms: Feminist Critical Theory and Theatre,* edited by Sue-Ellen Case, 270–82. Baltimore: Johns Hopkins University Press.

——. 1993. *Bodies That Matter: On the Discursive Limits of "Sex."* New York: Routledge.

——. 2009. *Frames of War: When Is Life Grievable?* London: Verso.

Cainkar, Louise A. 2009. *Homeland Insecurity: The Arab American and Muslim American Experience after 9/11*. New York: Russell Sage Foundation.

Carrithers, Michael. 2000. "On Polytropy: Or the Natural Condition of Spiritual Cosmopolitanism in India: The Digambar Jain Case." *Modern Asian Studies* 34 (4): 831–61.

Chakrabarty, Dipesh. 2007. "'In the Name of Politics': Democracy and the Power of the Multitude in India." *Public Culture* 19 (1): 35–57.

Chambers, Thomas. 2020. *Networks, Labour, and Migration among Indian Muslim Artisans*. London: UCL Press.

Chatterji, Angana, Thomas Blom Hansen, and Chris Jaffrelot. 2019. *Majoritarian State: How Hindu Nationalism Is Changing India*. New Delhi: Oxford University Press.

Chenoy, Shama Mitra. 1998. *Shahjahanabad: A City of Delhi, 1638–1857*. New Delhi: Munshiram Manoharlal Publishers.

Chigateri, Shraddha. 2008. "'Glory to the Cow': Cultural Difference and Social Justice in the Food Hierarchy in India." *South Asia: Journal of South Asian Studies* 31 (1): 10–35.

Collins, Jane. 2014. "A Feminist Approach to Overcoming the Closed Boxes of the Commodity Chain." In *Gendered Commodity Chains: Seeing Women's Work and Households in Global Production*, edited by Wilma Dunaway, 27–37. Stanford, CA: Stanford University Press.

Comaroff, Jean, and John Comaroff. 1991. *Of Revelation and Revolution: Christianity, Colonialism and Consciousness in South Africa*. Chicago: University of Chicago Press.

Cook, David. 2005. *Understanding Jihad*. Berkeley: University of California Press.

——. 2008. *Martyrdom in Islam*. Cambridge: Cambridge University Press.

Crenshaw, Kimberle. 1991. "Mapping the Margins: Intersectionality, Identity Politics, and Violence against Women of Color." *Stanford Law Review* 43 (6): 1241–99.

——. 2011. "Twenty Years of Critical Race Theory: Looking Back to Move Forward." *Connecticut Law Review* 43 (5): 1253–1354.

Das, Veena. 2010. "Engaging the Life of the Other: Love and Everyday Life." In *Ordinary Ethics: Anthropology, Language, and Action*, edited by Michael Lambeck, 376–99. New York: Fordham University Press.

Davis, Richard R. 1996. "The Iconography of Rama's Chariot." In *Contesting the Nation*, edited by David Ludden, 27–54. Philadelphia: University of Pennsylvania Press.

de Certeau, Michel. 1984. *The Practice of Everyday Life*. Translated by Steven Rendall. Berkeley: University of California Press.

Deeb, Lara. 2006. *An Enchanted Modern: Gender and Public Piety in Shi'i Lebanon*. Princeton, NJ: Princeton University Press.

de Genova, Nicholas. 2011. "Spectacle of Terror, Spectacle of Security." In *Accumulating Insecurity: Violence and Dispossession in the Making of Everyday Life*, edited by Shelley Feldman, Charles Geisler, and Gayatri A. Menon, 141–65. Athens: University of Georgia Press.

Dessing, Nathal M. 2001. *Rituals of Birth, Circumcision, Marriage, and Death among Muslims in the Netherlands*. Leuven: Uitgeverij Peeters.

Devji, Faisal. 2013. "The Equivocal History of a Muslim Reformation." In *Islamic Reform in South Asia*, edited by Filippo Osella and Caroline Osella, 3–25. Cambridge: Cambridge University Press.

Doniger, Wendy. 2009. *The Hindus: An Alternate History*. New York: Penguin Books.

——. 2016. "A Response." Roundtable on Outrage, Scholarship, and the Law in India." *Journal of the American Academy of Religion* 84 (2): 364–66.

Douglas, Mary. 1966. *Purity and Danger: An Analysis of the Concepts of Pollution and Taboo*. London: Routledge and Kegan Paul.

D'Souza, Diane. 2012. *Shia Women: Muslim Faith and Practice*. New Delhi: Zubaan.

DuBois, W. E. B. 1903. *The Souls of Black Folk*. New York: Dover.

Dunaway, Wilma. 2014. Introduction to *Gendered Commodity Chains: Seeing Women's Work and Households in Global Production*, edited by Wilma Dunaway, 1–24. Stanford, CA: Stanford University Press.

Durham, Martin, and Margaret Power. 2010. *New Perspectives on the Transnational Right*. New York: Palgrave Macmillan.

Durkheim, Emile. 1915. *The Elementary Forms of the Religious Life*. New York: Macmillan.

Eaton, Richard. 1993. *The Rise of Islam and the Bengal Frontier, 1204–1760*. Berkeley: University of California Press.

Eisenlohr, Patrick. 2015. "Media, Citizenship, and Religious Mobilization: The Muharram Awareness Campaign in Mumbai." *Journal of Asian Studies* 74 (3): 687–710.

Escobar, Arturo. 2001. "Culture Sits in Places: Reflections on Globalism and Subaltern Strategies of Localization." *Political Geography* 20:139–74.

Ewing, Katherine Pratt. 1997. *Arguing Sainthood: Modernity, Psychoanalysis, and Islam*. Durham, NC: Duke University Press.

Fadil, Nadia, and Mayanthi Fernando. 2015. "Rediscovering the 'Everyday' Muslim: Notes on an Anthropological Divide." *HAU: Journal of Ethnographic Theory* 5 (2): 59–88.

Fakhry, Majid, trans. 2004. *An Interpretation of the Qur'an*. New York: New York University Press.

Farooqui, Mahmood. 2010. *Besieged: Voices from Delhi 1857*. New Delhi: Penguin India.

Favero, Paolo. 2005. *India Dreams: Cultural Identity among Young Middle Class Men in New Delhi*. Stockholm: Stockholm University Press.

Feldman, Shelley, Gayatri A. Menon, and Charles Geisler. 2011. "Introduction: A New Politics of Containment." In *Accumulating Insecurity: Violence and Dispossession in the Making of Everyday Life*, edited by Shelley Feldman, Charles Geisler, and Gayatri A. Menon, 1–23. Athens: University of Georgia Press.

Flueckiger, Joyce. 2006. *In Amma's Healing Room: Gender and Vernacular Islam in South India*. Bloomington: Indiana University Press.

Foucault, Michel. 1982. "The Subject and Power." *Critical Inquiry* 8 (4): 777–95.

Frederick, Marla F. 2003. *Between Sundays: Black Women and Everyday Struggles of Faith*. Berkeley: University of California Press.

Fuller, C. J., and Haripriya Narasimhan. 2014. *Tamil Brahmans: The Making of a Middle-Class Caste*. Chicago: University of Chicago Press.

Galonnier, Juliette. 2014. "The Enclave, the Citadel, and the Ghetto: The Three-Fold Segregation of Upper-Class Muslims in India." *International Journal of Urban and Regional Research* 39 (1): 92–111.

Gardner, Katy. 2002. "Death of a Migrant: Transnational Death Rituals and Gender among British Sylhetis." *Global Networks* 2 (3): 191–204.

Gayer, Laurent. 2012. "Safe and Sound: Searching for a 'Good Environment' in Abul Fazl Enclave, Delhi." In *Muslims in Indian Cities: Trajectories of Marginalisation*, edited by Laurent Gayer and Christophe Jaffrelot, 213–36. New York: Columbia University Press.

Gayer, Laurent, and Christophe Jaffrelot. 2012. *Muslims in Indian Cities: Trajectories of Marginalisation*. New York: Columbia University Press.

Ghassem-Fachandi, Parvis. 2012. *Pogrom in Gujarat: Hindu Nationalism and Anti-Muslim Violence in India*. Princeton, NJ: Princeton University Press.

Ghose, Toorjo. 2012. "Politicizing Political Society: Mobilizing among Sex Workers in Sonagachi, India." In *South Asian Feminisms*, edited by Ania Loomba and Ritty Lukose, 285–305. Durham, NC: Duke University Press.

Gold, Ann Grodzins. 2014. "Sweetness and Light: The Bright Side of Pluralism in a Rajasthan Town." In *Religious Pluralism, State, and Society in Asia*, edited by Chiara Formichi, 113–37. New York: Routledge.

——. 2017. *Shiptown: Between Rural and Urban North India*. Philadelphia: University of Pennsylvania Press.

Gold, Ann Grodzins, and Bhoju Ram Gujar. 2002. *In the Time of Trees and Sorrows: Nature, Power, and Memory in Rajasthan*. Durham, NC: Duke University Press.

Goodfriend, Douglas E. 1983. "Changing Concepts of Caste and Status among Old Delhi Muslims." In *Modernization and Social Change among Muslims in India*, edited by Imtiaz Ahmad, 119–52. New Delhi: Manohar.

Gottschalk, Peter. 2000. *Beyond Hindu and Muslim: Multiple Identity Narratives from Village India*. New York: Oxford University Press.

——. 2011. "A Science of Defining Boundaries: Classification, Categorization, and the Census of India." In *Engaging South Asian Religions: Boundaries, Appropriations, and Resistances*, edited by Mathew N. Schmalz and Peter Gottschalk, 21–37. Albany, NY: SUNY Press.

Gottschalk, Peter, and Gabriel Greenberg. 2018. *Islamophobia and Anti-Muslim Sentiment: Picturing the Enemy*. 2nd ed. Lanham, MD: Rowman & Littlefield Publishers.

Govindrajan, Radhika. 2018. *Animal Intimacies: Interspecies Relatedness in India's Central Himalayas*. Chicago: University of Chicago Press.

Graff, Agnieszka, Ratna Kapur, and Suzanna Danuta Walters. 2019. "Introduction: Gender and the Rise of the Global Right." *Signs: Journal of Women in Culture and Society* 44 (3): 541–60.

Green, Nile. 2012. *Making Space: Sufis and Settlers in Early Modern India*. New Delhi: Oxford University Press.

Grewal, Zareena. 2014. *Islam Is a Foreign Country: American Muslims and the Global Crisis of Authority*. New York: New York University Press.

Gupta, Akhil. 2012. *Red Tape: Bureaucracy, Structural Violence, and Poverty in India*. Durham, NC: Duke University Press.

Gupta, Akhil, and James Ferguson. 1997. *Culture, Power, Place: Explorations in Critical Anthropology*. Durham, NC: Duke University Press.

Gupta, Charu. 2002. *Sexuality, Obscenity, and Community*. New York: Palgrave Macmillan.

Gupta, Charu S., and Subhadra Mitra Channa. 1996. "'Caste' among the Muslim Zardoz of Delhi: A Study of Occupational Culture and Sub-Group Identity." *Man in India* 76 (2): 103–13.

Gupta, Narayani. 1981. *Delhi between Two Empires 1803–1931: Society, Government, and Urban Growth*. New Delhi: Oxford University Press.

Haberman, David L. 2006. *River of Love in an Age of Pollution: The Yamuna River of Northern India*. Berkeley: University of California Press.

Haniffa, Farzana. 2013. "Piety as Politics amongst Muslim Women in Contemporary Sri Lanka." In *Islamic Reform in South Asia*, edited by Filippo Osella and Caroline Osella, 171–201. Cambridge: Cambridge University Press.

Hansen, Thomas Blom. 1999. *The Saffron Wave: Democracy and Hindu Nationalism in Modern India*. New Delhi: Oxford University Press.

——. 2001. *Wages of Violence: Naming and Identity in Postcolonial Bombay*. Princeton, NJ: Princeton University Press.

——. 2007. "The India That Does Not Shine." *ISIM Review* 19:50–51.

——. 2017. "On Law, Violence, and Jouissance in India: Dialogues." *Cultural Anthropology, Fieldsites*, November 1, 2017.
——. 2018. "Whose Public, Whose Authority? Reflections on the Moral Force of Violence." *Modern Asian Studies* 52 (3): 1076–87.
Harding, Susan Friend. 2001. *The Book of Jerry Falwell: Fundamentalist Language and Politics*. Princeton, NJ: Princeton University Press.
Hasan, Mushirul. 2008. *Moderate or Militant: Images of India's Muslims*. New Delhi: Oxford University Press.
Hasan, Mushirul, and Asim Roy. 2005. *Living Together Separately: Cultural India in History and Politics*. New Delhi: Oxford University Press.
Hasan, Zoya. 2012. *Congress after Indira: Policy, Power, Political Change (1984–2009)*. New Delhi: Oxford University Press.
Hefner, Robert W. 1993. "Introduction: World Building and the Rationality of Conversion." In *Conversion to Christianity: Historical and Anthropological Perspectives on a Great Transformation*, edited by R. W. Hefner, 3–46. Berkeley: University of California Press.
Hegland, Mary Elaine. 1998. "Flagellation and Fundamentalism: (Trans)forming Meaning, Identity, and Gender through Pakistani Women's Rituals of Mourning." *American Ethnologist* 25 (2): 240–66.
Hirschkind, Charles. 2006. *The Ethical Soundscape: Cassette Sermons and Islamic Counterpublics*. New York: Columbia University Press.
Hirst, Jacqueline S., and John Zavos. 2005. "Riding a Tiger? South Asia and the Problem of 'Religion.'" *Contemporary South Asia* 14 (1): 3–20.
Hyder, Syed Akbar. 2006. *Reliving Karbala: Martyrdom in South Asian Memory*. Oxford: Oxford University Press.
Islam, Maidul. 2012. "Rethinking the Muslim Question in Post-Colonial India." *Social Scientist* 40 (7–8): 61–84.
——. 2019. *Indian Muslim(s) after Liberalization*. New Delhi: Oxford University Press.
Jaffrelot, Christophe. 1999. *Hindu Nationalist Movement and Indian Politics, 1925 to the 1990s*. New Delhi: Penguin Books India.
——. 2007. "The 2002 Pogrom in Gujarat: The Post-9/11 Face of Hindu Nationalist Anti-Muslim Violence." In *Religion and Violence in South Asia: Theory and Practice*, edited by John R. Hinnells and Richard King, 173–92. London: Routledge.
——. 2017. "India's Democracy at 70: Toward a Hindu State?" *Journal of Democracy*, 28 (3): 52–63.
——. 2019. "A De Facto Ethnic Democracy? Obliterating and Targeting the Other, Hindu Vigilantes, and the Ethno-State." In *Majoritarian State: How Hindu Nationalism Is Changing India*, edited by Angana Chatterji, Thomas Blom Hansen, and Chris Jaffrelot, 41–67. New Delhi: HarperCollins.
Jairath, Vinod K. 2011. "Introduction: Towards a Framework." In *Frontiers of Embedded Muslim Communities in India*, edited by V. K. Jairath, 1–25. New Delhi: Routledge.
Jamil, Ghazala. 2017. *Accumulation by Segregation: Muslim Localities in Delhi*. New Delhi: Oxford University Press.
——. 2018. *Muslim Women Speak: Of Dreams and Shackles*. New Delhi: Sage.
Jeffery, Patricia. 1981. "Creating a Scene: The Disruption of Ceremonial in a Sufi Shrine." In *Ritual and Religion among Muslims in India*, edited by Imtiaz Ahmad, 163–94. New Delhi: Manohar.
——. 2000. *Frogs in a Well: Indian Women in Purdah*. 2nd ed. New Delhi: Manohar.
Jeffery, Patricia, and Roger Jeffery. 2006. *Confronting Saffron Demography: Religion, Fertility, and Women's Status in India*. Gurgaon, India: Three Essays Collective.

——. 2018. *Don't Marry Me to a Plowman! Women's Everyday Lives in Rural North India*. New York: Routledge.

Jha, D. N. 2009. *The Myth of the Holy Cow*. New Delhi: Navayana Publishing.

Jones, Justin. 2009. "The Local Experiences of Reformist Islam in a 'Muslim' Town in Colonial India: The Case of Amroha." *Modern Asian Studies* 43 (4): 871–908.

——. 2012. *Shi'a Islam in Colonial India*. Cambridge: Cambridge University Press.

——. 2014. "Shiism, Humanity, and Revolution in Twentieth Century India." *Journal of the Royal Asiatic Society* 24 (2): 415–34.

JTSA (Jamia Teacher's Solidarity Association). 2012. *Framed, Damned, Acquitted: Dossiers of a "Very" Special Cell*. New Delhi: Jamia Teacher's Solidarity Association. http://document.teacherssolidarity.org/JTSA_Report.pdf.

Juergensmeyer, Mark. 2000. *Terror in the Mind of God: The Global Rise of Religious Violence*. New Delhi: Oxford University Press.

Kakar, Sudhir. 1996. *The Colors of Violence*. New Delhi: Penguin Books.

Kapur, Ratna. 2012. "Hecklers to Power? The Waning of Liberal Rights and Challenges to Feminism." In *South Asian Feminisms*, edited by Ania Loomba and Ritty A. Lukose, 333–55. Durham, NC: Duke University Press.

Katz, Cindi. 2001. "Vagabond Capitalism and the Necessity of Social Reproduction." *Antipode* 33 (4): 709–28.

Kent, Eliza F. 2013. Introduction to *Lines in Water: Religious Boundaries in South Asia*, edited by Eliza F. Kent and Tazim R. Kassam, 1–36. Syracuse, NY: Syracuse University Press.

Kent, Eliza, and Tazim R. Kassam. 2013. *Lines in the Water: Religious Boundaries in South Asia*. Syracuse, NY: Syracuse University Press.

Khan, Muhammad Amir Ahmad. 2014. "Local Nodes of a Transnational Network." *Journal of the Royal Asiatic Society* 24 (3): 397–413.

Khan, Naveeda. 2012. *Muslim Becoming: Aspiration and Skepticism in Pakistan*. New Delhi: Orient Blackswan.

Khan, Sameera. 2007. "Negotiating the Mohalla: Exclusion, Identity, and Muslim Women in Mumbai." *Economic and Political Weekly* 42 (17): 1527–33.

Khan, Tabassum Ruhi. 2015. *Beyond Hybridity and Fundamentalism: Emerging Muslim Identity in Globalized India*. New Delhi: Oxford University Press.

Khan, Yasmin. 2007. *The Great Partition: The Making of India and Pakistan*. New Haven, CT: Yale University Press.

Khandelwal, Meena. 2004. *Women in Ochre Robes: Gendering Hindu Renunciation*. NY: SUNY Press.

——. 2016. "Cooking with Firewood: Deep Meaning and Environmental Materialities in a Globalized World." In *Mapping Feminist Anthropology in the Twenty First Century*, edited by Ellen Lewin and Leni M. Silverstein, 211–33. New Brunswick, NJ: Rutgers University Press.

Kirmani, Nida. 2013. *Questioning the Muslim Woman: Identity and Insecurity in an Urban Indian Locality*. New Delhi: Routledge.

Knight, Lisa I. 2011. *Contradictory Lives: Baul Women in India and Bangladesh*. Oxford: Oxford University Press.

Kotiswaran, Prabha. 2011. *Dangerous Sex, Invisible Labor: Sex Work and the Law in India*. Princeton, NJ: Princeton University Press.

Lamb, Sarah. 2018. "Being Single in India: Gendered Identities, Class Mobilities, and Personhoods in Flux." *Ethos* 46 (1): 49–69.

Lamphere, Louise. 1986. "From Working Daughters to Working Mothers." *American Ethnologist* 13 (1): 118–30.

Lelyveld, David. 1978. *Aligarh's First Generation: Muslim Solidarity in British India*. Princeton, NJ: Princeton University Press.

——. 2013. "Sir Sayyid, Maulana Azad, and the Uses of Urdu." NMML Occasional Paper, History and Society, New Series, 35. New Delhi: Nehru Memorial Museum and Library.

Lewis, Bernard. 2003. *The Crisis of Islam: Holy War and Unholy Terror*. New York: Random House.

Low, Setha M., and Denise Lawrence-Zuniga. 2003. "Locating Culture." In *The Anthropology of Space and Place: Locating Culture*, edited by Setha M. Low and Denise Lawrence-Zuniga, 1–47. Malden, MA: Blackwell Publishing.

Mahmood, Cynthia Keppley. 1993. "Rethinking Indian Communalism: Culture and Counter-Culture." *Asian Survey* 33 (7): 722–37.

——. 1996. *Fighting for Faith and Nation: Dialogues with Sikh Militants*. Philadelphia: University of Pennsylvania Press.

Mahmood, Saba. 2005. *The Politics of Piety: The Islamic Revival and the Feminist Subject*. Princeton, NJ: Princeton University Press.

——. 2009. "Religious Reason and Secular Affect: An Incommensurable Divide?" In *Is Critique Secular? Blasphemy, Injury, and Free Speech*, edited by T. Asad, W. Brown, J. Butler, and S. Mahmood, 64–100. Berkeley, CA: Townsend Center for the Humanities.

Maira, Sunaina Marr. 2009. *Missing: Youth, Citizenship, and Empire after 9/11*. Durham, NC: Duke University Press.

Malik, Jamal. 2003. "Islamic Institutions and Infrastructure in Shahjahanabad." In *Shahjahanabad/Old Delhi: Tradition and Colonial Change*, edited by Eckart Ehlers and Thomas Krafft, 71–92. Delhi: Manohar.

Mallampalli, Chandra. 2017. *A Muslim Conspiracy in British India? Politics and Paranoia in the Early Nineteenth-Century Deccan*. Cambridge: Cambridge University Press.

Mamdani, Mahmood. 2002. "Good Muslim, Bad Muslim: A Political Perspective on Culture and Terrorism." *American Anthropologist* 104 (3): 766–75.

Mander, Harsh. 2019. *Partitions of the Heart: Unmaking the Idea of India*. New Delhi: Penguin Viking.

Mankekar, Purnima. 2015. *Unsettling India: Affect, Temporality, Transnationality*. Durham, NC: Duke University Press.

Maqsood, Ammara. 2017. *The New Pakistani Middle Class*. Cambridge, MA: Harvard University Press.

Marsden, Magnus. 2005. *Living Islam: Muslim Religious Experience in Pakistan's Northwest Frontier*. Cambridge: Cambridge University Press.

Massey, Doreen B. 1991. "A Global Sense of Place." *Marxism Today* 38:24–29.

——. 2005. *For Space*. London: Sage Publications.

Mayaram, Shail. 2004. "Beyond Ethnicity? Being Hindu and Muslim in South Asia." In *Lived Islam in South Asia: Adaptation, Accommodation, and Conflict*, edited by I. Ahmad and H. Reifield, 18–39. New Delhi: Social Science Press.

——. 2005. "Living Together: Ajmer as a Paradigm for the (South) Asian City." In *Living Together Separately: Cultural India in History and Politics*, edited by Mushirul Hasan and Asim Roy, 145–71. New Delhi: Oxford University Press.

——. 2008. "Introduction: Rereading Global Cities: Topographics of an Alternative Cosmopolitanism in Asia." In *The Other Global City*, edited by Shail Mayaram, 1–32. New York: Routledge.

Menon, Gayatri A. 2018. "People out of Place: Pavement Dwelling in Mumbai." *Economic and Political Weekly* 53, (12): 85–91.

Menon, Gayatri A., and Aparna Sundar. 2019. "Uncovering a Politics of Livelihoods: Analyzing Displacement and Contention in Contemporary India." *Globalizations* 16 (2): 186–200. DOI:10.1080/14747731.2018.1479017.

Menon, Kalyani Devaki. 2010. *Everyday Nationalism: Women of the Hindu Right in India*. Ethnography of Political Violence Series. Philadelphia: University of Pennsylvania Press.

——. 2013. "Prayer and Power in the Sangh Parivar." NMML Occasional Paper Series, 20. New Delhi: Nehru Memorial Museum and Library.

——. 2018. "Ruminations on Beef." *Shuddhashar*, no. 10. September.

Metcalf, Barbara D. 1990. *Perfecting Women: Maulana Ashraf 'Ali Thanawi's Bihishti Zewar.* Berkeley: University of California Press.

——. 2006. *Islamic Contestations: Essays on Muslims in India and Pakistan*. New Delhi: Oxford University Press.

——. 2009. *Islam in South Asia in Practice*. New Delhi: Permanent Black.

Mohammad, Afsar. 2013. *The Festival of Pirs: Popular Islam and Shared Devotion in South India*. Oxford: Oxford University Press.

Mohanty, Chandra T. 1988. "Under Western Eyes: Feminist Scholarship and Colonial Discourses." *Feminist Review* 30:61–88.

Moin, A. Afzar. 2018. "Obeying God, Obeying Men: The Feminist Discourse of Dr. Farhat Hashmi." In *Hidden Histories: Religion and Reform in South Asia*, edited by Manu Bhagavan and Syed Akbar Hyder, 69–89. Delhi: Primus Books.

Mondal, Bidisha, Jayati Ghosh, Shiney Chakraborty, and Sona Mitra. 2018. "Women Workers in India." CSE Working Paper, 2018–3. Bangalore: Centre for Sustainable Employment, Azim Premji University.

Moore, Donald S. 1998. "Subaltern Struggles and the Politics of Place: Remapping Resistance in Zimbabwe's Eastern Highlands." *Cultural Anthropology* 13 (3): 344–81.

Murphy, Christopher P. H. 1986. "Piety and Honor: The Meaning of Muslim Feasts in Old Delhi." In *Aspects in South Asian Food Systems: Food, Society, and Culture,* edited by R.S. Khare and M. S. A. Rao, 85–119. Durham, NC: Carolina Academic Press.

Mustafa, Seema. 2020. *Shaheen Bagh and the Idea of India: Writings on a Movement*. Kindle ed. New Delhi: Speaking Tiger.

Naber, Nadene. 2006. "The Rules of Forced Engagement: Race, Gender, and the Culture of Fear among Arab Immigrants in San Francisco post 9/11." *Cultural Dynamics* 18 (3): 235–67.

Naidu, Sirisha C. 2016. "Domestic Labour and Female Labour Force Participation." *Economic and Political Weekly* 51, (44–45): 101–8.

Naik, Zakir. 2010a. *Focus on Islam*. New Delhi: Adam Publishers and Distributors.

——. 2010b. *The Quran and the Bible: In the Light of Science*. New Delhi: Adam Publishers and Distributors.

——. 2011. *Rights of Women in Islam: Modern or Outdated?* New Delhi: Madhur Sandesh Sangham.

Nandy, Ashis. 2000. "Time Travel to a Possible Self: Searching for the Alternative Cosmopolitanism of Cochin." *Japanese Journal of Political Science* 1 (2): 295–327.

Natrajan, Balmurli. 2018. "Cultural Identity and Beef Festivals: Toward a 'Multiculturalism Against Caste.'" *Contemporary South Asia* 26 (3): 287–304. DOI: 10.1080/09584935.2018.1504000.

Natrajan, Balmurli, and Suraj Jacob. 2018. "'Provincialising' Vegetarianism: Putting Indian Food Habits in Their Place." In *Economic and Political Weekly* 53 (9): 54–64.

Neyazi, Tabrez Ahmed. 2019. "The Politics of the Social Media." In *Re-Forming India: The Nation Today*, edited by Niraja Gopal Jayal, 524–36. Gurgaon: Penguin, Viking India.

Noorani, A. G. 2003. *The Muslims of India: A Documentary Record*. New Delhi: Oxford University Press.

Oberoi, Harjot Singh. 1994. *Construction of Religious Boundaries: Culture, Identity, and Diversity in the Sikh Tradition*. Chicago: University of Chicago Press.

Olsen, Keri. 2005. "Disrupting an Almost Seamless Discourse: Working-Class Muslim Women's Accounts of a Communal Clash and Curfew in the City of Ajmer." In *The Diversity of Muslim Women's Lives in India*, edited by Zoya Hasan and Ritu Menon, 323–53. New Brunswick, NJ: Rutgers University Press.

Ong, Aihwa. 1999. *Flexible Citizenship: The Cultural Logics of Transnationality*. Durham, NC: Duke University Press.

——. 2006. *Neoliberalism as Exception: Mutations in Citizenship and Sovereignty*. Durham, NC: Duke University Press.

Osella, Filippo, and Caroline Osella. 2013. "Islamism and Social Reform in Kerala, South India." In *Islamic Reform in South Asia*, edited by Filippo Osella and Caroline Osella, 139–70. Cambridge: Cambridge University Press.

Pandey, Gyan. 1990. *The Construction of Communalism in Colonial North India*. New Delhi: Oxford University Press.

Pasha, Mustapha Kamal. 2010. "In the Shadows of Globalization: Civilizational Crisis, the 'Global Modern' and 'Islamic Nihilism.'" *Globalizations* 7 (1–2): 173–85.

Pennington, Brian K. 2016. "The Unseen Hand of an Underappreciated Law: The Doniger Affair and Its Aftermath. Roundtable on Outrage, Scholarship, and the Law in India." *Journal of the American Academy of Religion* 84 (2): 323–36.

Pernau, Margrit. 2013. *Ashraf into Middle Classes: Muslims in Nineteenth-Century Delhi*. New Delhi: Oxford University Press.

Pinault, David. 2001. *Horse of Karbala: Muslim Devotional Life in India*. New York: Palgrave Macmillan.

Privratsky, Bruce G. 2001. *Muslim Turkistan: Kazak Religion and Collective Memory*. Richmond, UK: Curzon Press.

Puar, Jasbir K. 2012. "'I Would Rather Be a Cyborg than a Goddess': Becoming-Intersectional in Assemblage Theory." *PhiloSOPHIA: A Journal of Feminist Philosophy* 2 (1): 49–66.

Qureshi, Regula B. 1996. "Transcending Space: Recitation and Community among South Asian Muslims in Canada." In *Making Muslim Space in North America and Europe*, edited by Barbara D. Metcalf, 46–54. Berkeley: University of California Press.

Raheja, Gloria Goodwin, and Ann Grodzins Gold. 1994. *Listen to the Heron's Words: Reimagining Gender and Kinship in North India*. Berkeley: University of California Press.

Rahman, Abdur. 2019. *Denial and Deprivation: Indian Muslims after the Sachar Committee and the Ranganath Mishra Commission Reports*. New Delhi: Manohar.

Ramamurthy, Priti. 2004. "Why Is Buying a 'Madras' Cotton Shirt a Political Act? A Feminist Commodity Chain Analysis." *Feminist Studies* 30 (3): 734–69.

——. 2014. "Feminist Commodity Chain Analysis: A Framework to Conceptualize Value and Interpret Perplexity." In *Gendered Commodity Chains: Seeing Women's Work and Households in Global Production*, edited by Wilma Dunaway, 38–52. Stanford, CA: Stanford University Press.

Ramani, Priya. 2018. "Nobody Killed Pehlu Khan." In *Reconciliation: Karwan E Mohabbat's Journey of Solidarity through a Wounded India*, edited by Harsh Mander, Natasha Badhwar, and John Dayal, 53–56. Chennai: Context.

Rana, Junaid. 2011. *Terrifying Muslims: Race and Labor in the South Asian Diaspora*. Durham, NC: Duke University Press.

Ray, Raka. 2019. "'The Middle Class' and the Middle Classes." In *Critical Themes in Indian Sociology*, edited by Sanjay Srivastava, Yasmeen Arif, and Janaki Abraham, 209–24. New Delhi: Sage Publications.

Reddy, C. Rammanohar. 2019. *Demonetisation and Black Money*. 2nd ed. Hyderabad: Orient BlackSwan.

Ring, Laura A. 2006. *Zenana: Everyday Peace in a Karachi Apartment Building*. Bloomington: Indiana University Press.

Robinson, Francis. 2013. "Islamic Reform and Modernities in South Asia." In *Islamic Reform in South Asia*, edited by Filippo Osella and Caroline Osella, 26–50. Cambridge: Cambridge University Press.

——. 2014. "Introduction: The Shi'a in South Asia." *Journal of the Royal Asiatic Society* 24 (3): 353–61.

Robinson, Rowena. 2011. "Naata, Nyaya: Friendship and/or Justice on the Border." In *Frontiers of Embedded Muslim Communities in India*, edited by V. K. Jairath, 242–61. New Delhi: Routledge.

——. 2013. *Boundaries of Religion: Essays on Christianity, Ethnic Conflict, and Violence*. New Delhi: Oxford University Press.

Rosa, Jonathan, and Yarimar Bonilla. 2017. "Deprovincializing Trump, Decolonizing Diversity, and Unsettling Anthropology." *American Ethnologist* 44 (2): 201–8.

Ruffle, Karen G. 2011. *Gender, Sainthood, and Everyday Practice in South Asian Shi'ism*. Chapel Hill: University of North Carolina Press.

Sachar, Justice Rajinder. 2006. *Social, Economic, and Educational Status of the Muslim Community of India: A Report*. New Delhi: Government of India.

Said, Edward. 1979. *Orientalism*. New York: Vintage Books.

Salam, Ziya Us. 2019. *Lynch Files: The Forgotten Saga of Victims of Hate Crime*. New Delhi: Sage.

Sarkar, Tanika. 2002. "Semiotics of Terror: Muslim Children and Women in Hindu Rashtra." *Economic and Political Weekly* 37 (28): 2872–76.

Scott, James. 1990. *Domination and the Arts of Resistance: Hidden Transcripts*. New Haven, CT: Yale University Press.

Scott, Joan W. 1991. "The Evidence of Experience." *Critical Inquiry* 17:773–97.

——. 2007. *Politics of the Veil*. Princeton, NJ: Princeton University Press.

Sen, Atreyee. 2007. *Shiv Sena Women: Violence and Communalism in a Bombay Slum*. Bloomington: Indiana University Press.

Sethi, Manisha. 2014. *Kafkaland: Prejudice, Law, and Counterterrorism in India*. Gurgaon, India: Three Essays Collective.

Shah, Svati P. 2014. *Street Corner Secrets: Sex, Work, and Migration in the City of Mumbai*. Durham, NC: Duke University Press.

Sikand, Yoginder. 2004. *Sacred Spaces: Exploring Traditions of Shared Faith in India*. New Delhi: Penguin Books.

Singh, Nalini. 2006. "Two Shia Shrines of Delhi: History, Legends and the Rituals." In *Facets of Indian History*, edited by A. K. Sinha, 280–99. New Delhi: Anamika Publishers and Distributors.

Smith, Jane Idleman, and Yvonne Haddad. 2002. *The Islamic Understanding of Death and Resurrection*. Oxford: Oxford University Press.

Smith, Jonathan Z. 2004. *Relating Religion: Essays in the Study of Religion*. Chicago: University of Chicago Press.

Srinivas, Smriti. 2001. *Landscapes of Urban Memory: The Sacred and the Civic in India's High-Tech City*. Minneapolis: University of Minnesota Press.

Sriraman, Tarangini. 2018. *In Pursuit of Proof: A History of Identification Documents in India*. New Delhi: Oxford University Press.

Sunder Rajan, Rajeswari. 2003. *The Scandal of the State: Women, Law, and Citizenship in Postcolonial India*. Durham, NC: Duke University Press.

Taneja, Anand Vivek. 2012. "Saintly Visions: Other Histories and History's Others in the Medieval Ruins of Delhi." *Indian Economic and Social History Review* 49 (4): 557–90.

——. 2018. *Jinnealogy: Time, Islam, and Ecological Thought in the Medieval Ruins of Delhi*. Stanford, CA: Stanford University Press.

Tareen, SherAli. 2020. *Defending Muhammad in Modernity*. Notre Dame, IN: University of Notre Dame Press.

Tarlo, Emma. 2003. *Unsettling Memories: Narratives of the Emergency in Delhi*. Berkley: University of California Press.

Thapar, Romila. 2004. *Early India: From the Origins to AD 1300*. Berkeley: University of California Press.

Toor, Saadia. 2011. *The State of Islam: Culture and Cold War Politics in Pakistan*. London: Pluto Press.

Turner, Victor. 1969. *The Ritual Process: Structure and Anti-Structure*. Chicago: Aldine Publishers.

Uddin, Sufia. 2011. "Beyond National Borders and Religious Boundaries." In *Engaging South Asian Religions: Boundaries, Appropriations, and Resistances*, edited by Mathew Schmalz and Peter Gottschalk, 61–81. Albany, NY: SUNY Press.

van der Veer, Peter. 1988. *Gods on Earth: The Management of Religious Experience and Identity in a North Indian Pilgrimage Center*. London: Athlone Press.

——. 1992. "Ayodhya and Somnath: Eternal Shrines, Contested Histories." *Social Research* 59 (1): 85–109.

——. 1994. *Religious Nationalism: Hindus and Muslims in India*. Berkeley: University of California Press.

Vatuk, Sylvia. 2015. "What Can Divorce Stories Tell Us about Muslim Marriage in India?" In *Conjugality Unbound: Sexual Economies, State Regulation, and the Marital Form in India*, edited by Srimati Basu and Lucinda Ramberg, 190–216. New Delhi: Women Unlimited.

Venhorst, Claudia. 2012. *Muslims Ritualising Death in the Netherlands: Death Rites in a Small Town Context*. Zurich: LIT Verlag.

Vijayakumar, Gowri. 2018. "Is Sex Work Sex or Work? Forming Collective Identity in Bangalore." *Qualitative Sociology* 41 (3): 337–60.

Viswanath. Rupa. 2016. "Economies of Offence: Hatred, Speech, and Violence in India: Roundtable on Outrage, Scholarship, and the Law in India." *Journal of the American Academy of Religion* 84 (2): 352–63.

Visweswaran, Kamala. 2010. *Uncommon Cultures: Racism and the Rearticulation of Cultural Difference*. Durham, NC: Duke University Press.

Wadley, Susan S. 1994. *Struggling with Destiny in Karimpur, 1925–1984*. Berkeley: University of California Press.

Werbner, Pnina. 1996. "Stamping the Earth with the Name of Allah: Zikr and the Sacralizing of Space among British Muslims." *Cultural Anthropology* 11 (3): 309–38.

Willford, Andrew C. 2018. *The Future of Bangalore's Cosmopolitan Pasts: Civility and Difference in a Global City*. Honolulu: University of Hawaii Press.

Williams, Philippa. 2015. *Everyday Peace: Politics, Citizenship, and Muslim Lives in India*. West Sussex, UK: Wiley Blackwell.

Williams, Raymond. 1977. *Marxism and Literature*. Oxford: Oxford University Press.

Yeatman, Anna. 2010. "State, Security, and Subject Formation: An Introduction." In *State, Security, and Subject Formation*, edited by Anna Yeatman and Magdalena Zolkos, 1–15. New York: Continuum.

Yuval-Davis, Nira. 2011. *The Politics of Belonging: Intersectional Contestations*. London: Sage.

Zaman, Muhammad Qasim. 2002. *The Ulama in Contemporary Islam: Custodians of Change*. Princeton, NJ: Princeton University Press.

——. 2009. "Studying Hadith in a Madrasa in the Early Twentieth Century." In *Islam in South Asia in Practice*, edited by Barbara D. Metcalf, 225–39. New Delhi: Permanent Black.

Zamindar, Vazira Fazila-Yacoobali. 2007. *The Long Partition and the Making of South Asia: Refugees, Boundaries, Histories*. New York: Columbia University Press.

NEWS SOURCES

Al Jazeera
The Economic Times (India)
The Express Tribune (Pakistan)
The Hindu
The Hindustan Times
The Indian Express
Kafila (blog)
Quartz India
The Wire (India)

REPORTS

Delhi Minorities Commission. 2020. Report of the Fact-Finding Committee on North-East Delhi Riots of February 2020.

Graf, Violette, and Juliette Galonnier. 2013. *Hindu-Muslim Communal Riots II (1986–2011): Mass Violence and Resistance-Research Network*. Sciences Po.

Manufacturing Evidence: How the Police Is Framing and Arresting Constitutional Rights Defenders in India. 2020. The Polis Project. August 13, 2020.

The Status of Policing in India Report 2018: A Study of Performance and Perceptions. 2018. Published by Common Cause and the Center for the Study of Developing Societies (Lokniti, Delhi).

Index

Note: Page numbers in italics indicate figures.

About the Author

Kalyani Devaki Menon is an Associate Professor in the Department of Religious Studies at DePaul University, USA. She is the author of *Everyday Nationalism*.